Ashraf's Advice

DEATH
of a
MUSLIM©

Covers: *Photographs of Jannatul Baqee in Madeenah Munnawwarah wherein lie as many as 10,000 great Companions of Prophet Muhammad ﷺ of whom the grave of 'Uthmān ؓ (centre back cover) is the most famous.*

Ashraf's Advice Upon The
DEATH
of a Muslim©

ISBN-1-9026-2702-4

Based Upon the Teachings of

Shaykh Ashraf 'Ali Thānwi, Imām Al-Ghazzāli,
Shaykh Maseehullah Khān, Shaykh-ul-Hadeeth Zakariyyā,
Shaykh Mufti Muhammad Shafee, Shaykh Manzoor Nu'maani,
Khwajah 'Azeez-ul-Hasan Majzoob,
Shaykh Dr. 'Abdul 'Hai 'Ārifee, Shaykh Abrārul Haqq,
Shaykh-ul-Hadeeth Mufti Sahbān Mahmood,
Shaykh Mufti 'Ashiq Ellahi Madanee,
Shaykh Mufti Rafee 'Uthmāni, Shaykh Mufti Taqee 'Uthmāni,
Shaykh Ahmad Sādeeq Desai, Shaykh 'Abdur-Raheem Lajpoori,
Shaykh Mufti 'Abdur Rauf Sakhrawee,
Shaykh Mufti Ismā'eel Kacholvi,
Shaykh Tāreeq Jameel, Shaykh Hāfiz Dr. Sulayman Kaflethvi

Patron

Shaykh Muhammad Saleem Dhorat

Prepared & Published

by

Maulāna Yousuf, Hāfiz Maseehullah,
Hāfiz Muhammad 'Abdullah, & Hāfiz Aslam Patel

BA (Hons) Arch. Studies, Dip. Arch.

Ashraf's Amānat©

PO Box 12, Dewsbury, W. Yorkshire, UK, WF12 9YX

Tel: (01924) 488929

www.ashrafsamanat.org

ಔಟ

Dedication

During the preparation of the first edition of this kitab, two of our well-wishers passed-away:

Shaykh Hāfiz Dr. Sulaymān Kaflethvi ❀ &
Muhammad Muneer Vance of Perfect Print

This Kitab is Dedicated to them and all Muslims (living, deceased & arriving unto Qiyamah). May Allah ﷻ Perpetually Shower His Limitless Treasures, Mercies and Grant all Muslims the highest Rank in Jannah.

Ashraf's Advice Upon The Death of a Muslim© ~ ISBN-1-9026-2702-4
ISSN 1465-9271 ~ First Edition: Muharram 1422 AH (March 2001 CE)
This Enlarged Second Edition published: Rajab 1425 AH (September 2004 CE)
Prepared & Published by M. Aslam Patel of Ashraf's Amānat©, PO Box 12, Dewsbury, West Yorkshire, U.K., WF12 9YX
Copyright ©2004/1425 M. Aslam Patel of Ashraf's Amānat©
The right of M. Aslam Patel to be identified as author of this work, pursuant to s.77 of the Copyright, Designs & Patents Act 1988, is hereby inserted. All rights reserved. No part of this work may be reproduced in any material form (including photocopying or storing it in any medium by electronic means) without the WRITTEN permissions of the copyright owner and publisher, except in accordance with the provisions of the Copyright, Designs and Patents Act 1988. Any unauthorised act in this respect may lead to legal proceedings.

A catalogue record for this book is available from the British Library

United Kingdom
British Library Cataloguing-in-Publication Data. A catalogue record for this book is available from the British Library. Copies of this publication have been deposited with The Agent for the Copyright Libraries, London.

United States of America
This book has been registered with The Copyright Office, Library of Congress, 101 Independence Avenue, S.E., Washington, D.C. 20559-6000, U.S.A.

South Africa
A Copy of this book has been deposited with The Legal Deposit Office, National Library of South Africa

India
A Copy of this book has been deposited with the Director, Government of India National Library Belverdere, Calcutta 700027, India

Australia
Under the Australian Copyright Act 1968, a copy of this publication has been deposited with the Copyright Advisor at the Australian Library and the Australian Copyright Council

Canada
A Copy of this book has been deposited with The Legal Deposit Office, National Library of Canada, 395 Wellington Street, Ottawa, Ontario

France
A Copy of this book has been deposited at the Bibliothèque Nationale de France, France

Pakistan
A Copy of this book has been deposited with the National Library of Pakistan

New Zealand
A Copy of this book has been deposited with The Legal Deposit Office, National Library of New Zealand, PO Box 12-340, Wellington

Malaysia
A Copy of this book has been deposited with the Director, National Library of Malaysia

Ashraf's Amānat & Copyright

Shaykh Mufti 'Abdur Raheem Lajpoori writes in *Fatāwā Raheemeeyah (Vol. 3)... 'Any book comes into existence after the toil and labour of the writer, accordingly the foremost right of publishing it belongs to him alone. Moreover, besides the intention of propagating Knowledge of Deen, the author has the right to derive profit from his writings. Accordingly, until the author's interest is connected with the book, nobody else has the right to publish it. Other people who publish a popular book without (written permission from the author) do so only out of selfish commercial interest. Their argument of propagating the Knowledge of Deen (and being of benefit to Muslims) is baseless because if this was a true intention of theirs then what prevents them from buying the Kitāb in large quantities from the author and distributing it for the purpose of thawāb? Similarly, although everybody has the right to adopt a particular title for his (Jamā'at), nevertheless when a certain person has adopted a title for his activity and his finances are bound with the said title...then no one else has the right to use this very title for his business...'*

Ashraf's Amānat© is a non-profit philanthropic body of Huffāz. Through Tawfeeq from Allah ﷻ, we attempt to present authentic Teachings of Pious Scholars in the Light of the Glorious Qur'ān and Hadeeth for the benefit of western educated Muslims. Our work is ongoing, new titles are under preparation and would be assisted by your support & du'aa. If you wish to order our books or support our work please write or send Lillah donations to:

Ashraf's Amānat©
PO Box 12,
Dewsbury,
W. Yorkshire, UK,
WF12 9YX
Tel: (01924) 488929
email:info@ashrafsamanat.org

Or

Bank Sort Code: 40-19-17
Account Number: 91367765
Account Name: Ashraf's Amanat
Bank: HSBC
Branch: Market Place,
Dewsbury,
W. Yorkshire,
UK. WF13 1DH

Contents

Ashraf's Amãnat & Copyright iv

Introduction & Views of Senior Scholars & Mashã-ikh viii

* Chapter One
Statements of our Pious 9

* Chapter Two
What to do upon Approach of a Death 21
Shaykh Mufti 'Ashiq Ellahi & Dr. 'Abdul Hay 'Ãrifee ❀

* Chapter Three (Revised)
Legal Procedures in England & Wales:
Ghusl (Bathing), Kafn (Shroud) 29

* Chapter Four
Janãzah Salãh & Etiquette's of the
Cemetery 49
Shaykh Dr. 'Abdul Hay 'Ãrifee ❀

* Chapter Five (New)
Tajhees, Takhfeen & Tadfeen 63
Shaykh Muhammad Saleem Dhorat

* Chapter Six
Abode of Prosperity 91
Shaykh Ashraf 'Ali Thãnwi ❀

* Chapter Seven
Darse 'Ibrat (A Lesson to Heed) 109
Shaykh Maseehullah Khãn ❀

* Chapter Eight
The Method of Acquiring Success 119
Shaykh Muhammad Saleem Dhorat

* *Chapter Nine*
Episodes of Death & the Grave *131*
Shaykh-ul-Hadeeth Zakariyyā ﷺ *et al*

* *Chapter Ten*
A View of Jannah *145*
Shaykh Mufti Taqee 'Uthmāni

* *Chapter Eleven*
How Should Inheritance be Distributed? 163
Shaykh Muhammad Saleem Dhorat

* *Chapter Twelve*
Esāl-al-Thawāb & Qur'ān Ceremonies *185*
Shaykh Mufti 'Abdur Ra'oof Sakhrawee

* *Chapter Thirteen*
Fikr (Meditation) of Death *201*
Imām Al-Ghazzāli ﷺ *et al*

* *Chapter Fourteen*
Death of an Alim is Death of Alam *217*

* *Chapter Fifteen*
Delaying Janāzah, Overseas Burials *223*

* *Chapter Sixteen (New)*
The Importance of Wills in Islām *231*
1) Fill-in Copy of Health Care Proxy & Living Will..... *238*
2) Fill-in Copy of Last Will & Testament *245*
3) What is Probate? *265*
4) What is Inheritance Tax? *270*
5) How to Legally Avoid Inheritance Tax? *272*
6) The Four Stages in Acquiring a Probate *274*
Ashraf's Amānat's Other Books *277*

Salāt & Salāms upon our Beloved Nabee ﷺ

Introduction

Shaykh Muhammad Saleem Dhorat

Principal & Senior Lecturer in Hadeeth, Jāmeah Riyādul-Uloom, Islāmic Da'wah Academy, Leicester

Islām is a code of life which encompasses every aspect of human existence. Allah ﷻ mentions in the Glorious Qur'ān,

'Say (to them): 'Indeed, the death from which you flee will surely meet you, then you will return back to (Allah), the All-Knower of Unseen and the Seen, and He will inform you of what you used to do.' (8:62)

The intention for producing this Kitab, purely through Tawfeeq from Allah ﷻ, is to alert us Muslims to the everlasting life to come after death. Shaykh Ashraf 'Ali Thānwi ﷫ commented,

'Having abandoned the Sunnah, not only have we forgotten how to live but also how to die.'

It is truly heartbreaking to observe the behaviour of Muslims on occasions of death wherein we commence our journey back home to Jannah from where we originated.

We are delighted to be part of this *Kitab* published by Ashraf's Amānat©. It is yet another bouquet prepared with great care for Muslims living in western society. May Allah ﷻ accept the efforts of author Aslam Patel, my Jamā'at at Ashraf's Amānat©, the cover designer and all those associated with this publication. Āmeen, Was-salām,

pp. Hāfiz Maseehullah

What other Senior Scholars & Mashā-ikh have said about Ashraf's Amānat©...

Shaykh 'Abdullah Kapodrawi of Canada...
'These publications contain the works of our pious predecessors & elders upon which we have full confidence. May Allah ﷻ grant greater barakat.'

Shaykh Mufti Taqee 'Uthmānee...
'May Allah ﷻ approve your efforts and make them beneficial for the Ummah.'

Shaykh 'Abdul Hameed Isaac of South Africa...
'I am sure and, it is my du'aa, that by this great work Muslims living in western countries or whose mother tongue has become English, will be able to appreciate the great treasures of Islāmic Knowledge...'

Shaykh Mufti Rafee 'Uthmānee...
'Mashā'Allah! Excellent set of publications...'

Shaykh Mufti Zubayr Bhayat of South Africa...
'Mashā'Allah! The work being undertaken is very good & much needed.'

Shaykh Yusuf Darwan of UK...
'Through the infinite Mercy of Allah ﷻ, Ashraf's Amānat© have published a series of beneficial Islāmic books...'

Shaykh Ahmad Sadeeq Desai of South Africa...
'May Allah ﷻ accept your service & increase your Deeni activities.'

Shaykh Dr. Ismā'eel Mangera of South Africa...
'May Allah ﷻ fulfil your wishes to serve the Ummah. May your publications be a means of spreading the teachings of our akābir to others, young and old.'

Shaykh Dr. Muhammad Sābir...
'Shaykh Ashraf 'Ali Thānwi ﷺ narrated, 'After 50 years, my works will be translated and published on a large scale.' We are today witnessing this event...Mashā'Allah...the heart is pleased...this work is undoubtedly due to the sincerity of our cherished predecessors...'

Shaykh 'Abdur Rahmān Mangera of USA...
'Bringing into English the spirit of the work of our pious predecessors is a very noble deed. May Allah ﷻ accept it.'

References

- **Ma'āriful Qur'ān** (Original)
  Shaykh Muhammad Shafee' ﷺ .... Darul Ishā'at
- **The Noble Qur'ān** (Arabic with English translation)
  Shaykh Dr. M. Taqi-ud-Din & Dr. M. Muhsin Khan .... Maktaba Dar-us-Salām
- **Mazāhir Haqq** (Original)
  Shaykh Muhammad Qutbuddeen Khān Dehlwi ﷺ .... Darul Ishā'at
- **Ma'āriful Hadeeth** (Original)
  Shaykh Manzoor Nu'maani ﷺ .... Darul Ishā'at
- **Ahqām Mayyit** (Original)
  Shaykh Dr. 'Abdul Hayy 'Ārifee ﷺ .... Idārah Taleefāt Ashrafeeyah
- **Riyadus Sāliheen** (Original)
  Shaykh Muhyuddeen Abee Zakariyya ﷺ .... Darul Ishā'at
- **Al-Hidāyah** (Arabic)
  Shaykh-ul-Islām Burhanuddeen ﷺ .... Makatab Shirkatul 'Ilm
- **Fatāwā Raheemeeyah** (Original)
  Shaykh Mufti 'Abdur-Raheem Lajpoori ﷺ .... Maktab Rahmāneeyah
- **Heavenly Ornaments** (Original)
  Shaykh Ashraf 'Ali Thānwi ﷺ .... Darul Ishā'at
- **Arbaeen (Tableeh Deen)**
  Imām Al-Ghazāli ﷺ .... Idārah Taleefāt Ashrafeeyah
- **Lectures of Hakeemul Ummah** (Original)
  Shaykh Ashraf 'Ali Thānwi ﷺ .... Idārah Taleefāt Ashrafeeyah
- **Riyādul Jannah** (English)
  Shaykh Muhammad Saleem Dhorat .... Islāmic Da'wah Academy
- **Virtues of Sadaqāh** (Original)
  Shaykh-ul-Hadeeth Zakariyyā ﷺ .... Idārah Taleefāt Ashrafeeyah
- **What Happens After Death** (Original)
  Shaykh Mufti 'Ashiq Ellahi ﷺ .... Idārah Ma'ārif
- **Kashkool Majzoob** (Original)
  Shaykh Khwājah 'Azeez-ul-Hasan ﷺ .... Idārah Taleefāt Ashrafeeyah
- **Sawtul Haqq** (Original ~ Audio/CD)
  Shaykh Muhammad Saleem Dhorat .... Da'wah Book Centre
- **Majālis** (Original ~ Book & Audio)
  Shaykh Maseehullah Khān ﷺ .... Jāmea Miftāhul Uloom
- **Islāhi Discourses** (Original 13 Vols.)
  Shaykh Mufti Taqee Uthmānee .... Mayman Islāmic Publishers
- **Islāhi Lectures** (Original 4 vols.)
  Shaykh Mufti 'Abdur Ra'oof Sakhrawee .... Mayman Islāmic Publishers
- **Uswa Rasool Akram** ﷺ (Original)
  Shaykh Dr. 'Abdul Hayy 'Ārifee ﷺ .... Darul Ishā'at
- **Statements of Pious Elders** ﷺ (Original)
  Shaykh Mufti Taqee Uthmānee .... Idārah Tāleefat Ashrafeeyah
- **Why, Are You Ready for Your Death?** (Original)
  Nisaar Ahmad Khan .... Idāratul Qur'ān
- **Munājat Maqbool** (Original)
  Shaykh Ashraf 'Ali Thānwi ﷺ .... Darul Ishā'at
- **Virtues of Du'aa** (Original)
  Shaykh Mufti 'Ashiq Ellahi ﷺ .... Idārah Ishā'at Deeniyat
- **Al Hisnul Haseen** (Original)
  Allamah Muhammad Al-Jazri ﷺ .... Darul Ishā'at
- **What To Do After a Death in England & Wales**
  Booklet No D49 .... Department of Work & Pensions
- **How To Obtain A Probate**
  Booklet PA2 — w3 .... Court Service
- **Inheritance Tax**
  Capital Taxes ~ Various Leaflets .... Inland Revenue Capital Taxes
- **Law on the Web**
  Martin Davies, solicitor .... LAW on the WEB UK Ltd

Certain advises are those heard directly from the lectures and company of Scholars, Mashā-ikh, Huffaz and Professionals. May Allah ﷻ grant all of them the best of rewards.

The Reality of Life

Shaykh-ul-Hadeeth Zakariyyā ﷺ relates, 'Once Prophet Muhammad ﷺ sketched a diagram to illustrate the reality of this worldly existence:

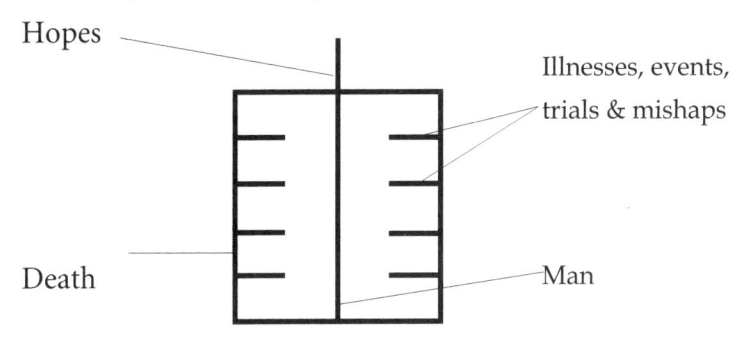

Hopes

Illnesses, events, trials & mishaps

Death

Man

Thereafter, Nabee ﷺ explained,

'The middle-line is man; the four surrounding lines (the square) is death which encapsulates him and from which there is no escape; the protruding line is his hopes which extend far beyond his life. The small cross-lines on both sides are illnesses and events which transpire around him.

Each short line is a trial...should he escape from one; another awaits...moreover, death surrounds him from all four sides, however his hopes (the protruding line) still extend even beyond death!'

(p393, Fadhā'eel Sadaqāt)

Prelude

Shaykh Tāreeq Jameel *dāmat barakātuhum* narrated, 'All actions of Muslims are connected to Allah ﷻ; not only salāh, saum, recitation of the Glorious Qur'ān. Praiseworthy qualities such as *sidq* (truthfulness), *wafā* (faithfulness), *deeyānat* (honesty), *amānah* (trustworthiness), *sadāqat* (sincerity), *sakhāwat* (generosity), *inābat* (repentance and turning towards Allah ﷻ), *ibaadah* (worship), *riyādhat* (abstinence), *teejārat* (trade), all are deeds. Even *hukoomat* (leadership - at whatever level of society) is a deed.

'Umar bin 'Abdul-Azeez ؓ (63-101AH/686-724 CE) was the leader of a vast Empire which stretched over three continents from the Atlantic to the Pamirs. His command from Damascus would reach Kashmir in the east to southern France and Portugal in the west; the gates of Istanbul in the north; to the vast deserts and plains of Africa towards the south!

Since he had acquired noble qualities and thereby the Pleasure of his Creator, Allah ﷻ displayed his acceptance in this world. When his death was imminent, 'Umar bin 'Abdul-Azeez ؓ summoned Rajā ibn Haiwat ؓ, the very person who had advised he be appointed *Ameerul Mu'mineen* and suggested:

> 'Look I have buried (my predecessor, uncle and father-in-law) the handsome 'Abdul-Maleek in his grave, but when I opened his shroud, his face had turned black and was

facing away from the qiblāh. Thereafter, I buried Waleed ('Abdul-Maleek's son, successor, my cousin and brother-in-law). When I opened his shroud, his face too had darkened and was facing away from the qiblāh. Lastly, I buried Sulaymān (my immediate predecessor): when I opened his shroud, his face too had turned black and was facing away from the qiblāh. Now the time for my departure has arrived...pray, open my shroud and see how I fare.'

However, even before his burial, Allah ﷻ displayed His Acceptance of 'Umar bin 'Abdul-Azeez ؓ. When his mayyit (bier) was brought to the cemetery, a sudden gust of wind brought down a piece of paper which gently landed upon the chest of 'Umar bin 'Abdul-Azeez ؓ. Herein was written:

'With the Name of Allah ﷻ, Most Merciful. From Allah ﷻ, a notification of freedom from Hell Fire for His servant 'Umar bin 'Abdul-Azeez.'

Rajā ibn Haiwat ؓ thereafter entered the grave to bury. When he opened the shroud, it appeared as if the face of 'Umar bin 'Abdul-Azeez ؓ was as bright as the moon of the fourteenth night!'

All actions and deeds of a Muslim are *ibaadah* if they confirm to the Commands of Allah ﷻ and the Sunnah of His Rasool ﷺ.

Majālis-e-Abrār

Shaykh Abrār-ul-Haqq *dāmat barakātuhum* narrates, 'It is of course a certainty that whomsoever arrives in this world has one day to depart: at a time appointed by our Creator. This knowledge is not known to anyone and is why a person, perfectly healthy, suddenly departs at his predestined time. Nowadays, this is assumed the result of a heart attack, but as Khwajah Majzoob ﷺ relates:

> *'Life, like a piece of ice is melting away,*
>
> *Silently, gradually, slowly, and perpetually,*
>
> *One's breath is a wayfarer to an unknown location,*
>
> *Suddenly, one day it will perish (thum)…oblivion,*
>
> *One day we have to die, death is ultimate,*
>
> *Do whatever you wish, Maut is ultimate.'*

Now when death is certain, either partner of every relationship must, of a surety, experience the sorrow of separation from the other. The wife upon her husbands death, children from their parents, brother upon sisters and vice-versa. It is also obvious, had anybody been given the choice, they would not choose to experience this sorrow. Be that as it may, only Allah ﷻ has full control in this matter ~

> *'It is He (Allah ﷻ) Who gives life and causes death. Moreover, when He decides upon a thing He says to it only, 'Be!' and it is.'* (Glorious Qur'ān, 40:68)

One further point to ponder upon is that the separation and loneliness caused by death is temporary, as if one's beloved had travelled to another country and was unable to return because of some reason. We, of course, are able and will go to meet him there, reflecting on this reality will lessen the grief and pain of our separation. This is the concept behind the Qur'ānic Ayah ~

> 'And certainly, We shall test you with something of fear, hunger, loss of wealth, lives and fruits, but give glad tidings to As-Sābireen (the Patient). Whom, when afflicted with calamity, say: 'Indeed to Allah we belong and truly, to Him we shall return.' (2:155-6)

We, all of us, are the creation and servants of Allah ﷻ. It is His right to manage and transfer His Creation, as He deems fit and appropriate. Therefore, ponder when this transfer causes us grief, that we all of us are going to be transferred to the place where our beloved has gone to.

Nowadays, people have a revulsion about hearing of death, whereas we should be saying the deceased has returned to his original home...and the graveyard is a station for this onward return journey home. My young grandson, often comes up to me when I do not take him to the cemetery and implores, 'When will you be taking me to the station of Jannah?'

This return journey to the Ākhirah is one of respect and dignity (for the Mu'min), when even a pauper is carried upon the shoulder's of great Mashā-ikh, Ulamā and nobility to the graveyard. He, who was a *muqtadee* (follower in Salāh), is now carried by the *Imām*. A retinue accompanies the deceased with great etiquette: do not walk in-front of the Janāzah; do not sit before the Janāzah is placed upon the floor, etc. Whilst royalty normally only travel in cars and carriages, upon death, their funeral is carried on the shoulders of *Ashraful Makhlooqāt* (best of creation)...the servants Janāzah is upon the shoulders of his master. Now ponder, whichever journey has such a beginning, what will be the condition and states of its other *manzils* (stages)?

'Your mayyit will enter the grave, of a surety,
Whatever you do, its reward you will receive, of a surety,
You were created for worship, remember,
To bow humbly unto Allah, remember,
Otherwise, there will be disgrace, remember,
For life is but a few days, remember!

Shaykh Ashraf 'Ali Thānwi ﷺ relates, 'The teenage son of my tutor Shaykh Muhammad Yāqûb ﷺ passed-away at the time of 'Eed Salāh. The pangs of death had started, Salāh time was fast approaching when Shaykh Muhammad Yāqûb ﷺ placed his fatherly hand of affection upon his son's forehead and softly spoke, 'Darling, we trust you unto Allah ﷻ, we have to go now as we have to pray Salāh. Inshā'Allah, we shall meet come the Day of Qiyāmah.'

So saying, he prepared for 'Eed Salāh, tears were flowing from his eyes but not one word of complaint or impatience emerged from his lips. He was contented with the *Hukm* (choice) of Allah ﷻ.' Another example is the death of the young son of Shaykh Rasheed Ahmad Ganghoi ﷺ. People were arriving for *taaziyah* (condolence) but were forced to maintain silence. Why? Because the Awliyā (Friends of Allah ﷻ) have a unique *ru'abb* (awe-inspiring dignity), which prevents anybody from speaking, moreover what to say anyway? If they were to comment, 'it is a great loss' or 'be patient,' Shaykh was aware of this and sitting quietly. Amongst this silence, one person mustered up courage and spoke, 'Shaykh, it is a tremendous sorrow.' Immediately, Shaykh Rasheed Ahmad ؒ replied, 'Yes, I am aware, what need is there to mention it?' Total silence. Despite such grief and sorrow, there was not an iota of difference in his *m'amool* (acts of worship), *ishrāq, tahajjud* and *awwābeen* (all optional Salāh's) were maintained. He even ate when meals were served...as if nothing had happened, yet he once confided to me, 'Severe sorrow has overwhelmed my heart and mind.'

Shaykh Mufti Taqee Uthmāni *dāmat barakātuhum* relates, 'When my late father Shaykh Mufti Muhammad Shafee' ؒ passed-away, I was overtaken by such sorrow never experienced before and was unable to even cry to lessen this grief. I notified my Shaykh, Dr. 'Abdul 'Hayy 'Ārifee ؒ of my condition to which he replied,

> 'Undoubtedly sorrow has its position, however to experience such extreme worry and grief on something beyond one's control is worthy of islāh (reformation).'

Although there should be sorrow and grief, because death is inevitable one should also act upon *radhā-bil-qadhā* (contentment will the Choice of Allah ﷻ).'

Prophet Muhammad ﷺ

Letter of Condolence upon death of the young son of his Companion Muʿāz bin Jabal ؓ

﷽

With the name of Allah, who is the Most Merciful, Very Merciful.

*F*rom Allah's Rasool Muhammad (ﷺ) to Muʿāz bin Jabal (ؓ). Salām upon you.

Firstly, (we) praise and glorify Allah besides whom there is no Creator. After praises, (I pray unto) Allah to grant you a beautiful reward and the tawfeeq to make sabr (patience), moreover (may He bestow us both) the ability to make shukr (gratefulness). Undoubtedly, our lives, wealth and family, (all) are the fortunate bounties borrowed unto us as amānat (trust). (Similarly, your son too was an amānat) from Allah Who had allowed you to enjoy and enliven your heart with his (company).

Now, in return for a tremendous reward, He has recalled him from you. Glad tidings of Allah's special Favours, Rahmat (Mercies) and Hidāyat (guidance) if you make sabr with intention of thawāb. Therefore, live with sabr and beware that your (undue) crying and (grief) do not wash away your reward, whereby you end up regretting. Also remember! Crying and wailing never brings back any deceased, neither does it lessen sorrow. Whatever is due to happen will take place and what was due has happened.

Was-salām.

(p 466, Maʾariful Hadeeth)

Chapter One

Statements of our Aslāf
(Pious Predecessors)

Shaykh Ashraf 'Ali Thānwi ۝,
Shaykh Maseehullah Khān ۝,
Shaykh-ul-Hadeeth Zakariyyā ۝,
Shaykh Mufti Muhammad Shafee ۝,
Khwajah 'Azeez-ul-Hasan Majzoob ۝,
Shaykh Dr 'Abdul-Hayy 'Ārifee ۝,
Shaykh Mufti Taqee Uthmāni
dāmat barakātuhum

Advance Notice

Shaykh Mufti Taqee Uthmāni *dāmat barakātuhum* relates from his father Shaykh Mufti Muhammad Shafee', 'Once a person met Malikul Maut (the Angel of Death) and complained,

> 'You behave very differently! Whenever anybody is summoned by a worldly authority, some form of notice is always served. This allows one to prepare for the meeting. However your behaviour is very strange, whenever you wish, without any prior notification, you arrive to capture the rûh (soul)...what kind of behaviour is this?'

> Malikul Maut replied, 'O brother, I forward so many notices that nobody in dunya sends such a large number... but what to do? You pay no heed to my notices! Listen, when you get a fever, this is one of my notices! Whenever you suffer some illness, this is one of my notices! When your hair begin to turn grey, this is one of my notices! When your grandchildren are born, this is one of my notices! I send so many notices, yet you fail to take lesson.'

This is precisely what Nabee ﷺ implied,

> 'Prior to occasion of regret, for Allah's Sake rectify and save oneself by making good usage of this opportunity and health...for Allah alone knows what may happen tomorrow?'

(p 109, Statements of our Akābir)

Meditation upon Death

Based upon the epic *Darse 'Ibrat*
by
Khwajah 'Azeez-ul-Hasan Majzoob 🌺

In the universe are lessons of death aplenty,
However, you are blinded by worldly hue & dainty,
Have you ever pondered and observed deeply?
How inhabitation's are reduced to heaps eventually!
As a place of attachment, this world is rot.
An abode to heed lesson; mere amusement not.
Many are entombed in soil, sigh!
Rulers, nobles, lord's' et al, why?
Will display your pomp for a while, fie.
Death will subdue men of might, nigh!
As a place of attachment, this world is rot.
An abode to heed lesson; mere amusement not.
Death did not spare either Kisrā or Dārius,
It was this that defeated Alexandrius,
Each departed with painful regret,
with all hopes of glory abject,
As a place of attachment, this world is rot.
An abode to heed lesson; mere amusement not.
Herein all happiness is transformed into sorrow,
Wherein weddings produce widows of tomorrow,
These are transformations in a sojourn narrow,
Changes take place with each breath in your marrow!

As a place of attachment, this world is rot.
An abode to heed lesson; mere amusement not.
Initially, infancy toyed you into years of play,
Thereafter adolescence turned you mad with fray,
Old-age arrived with thousands array,
Death will appear and annihilate your say!
As a place of attachment, this world is rot.
An abode to heed lesson; mere amusement not.
Your goal is to become the almighty,
In beauty and fashion the most lofty,
Why, has any person remained until eternity?
External facades have duped you in entirety!
As a place of attachment, this world is rot.
An abode to heed lesson; mere amusement not.
Could it be a home of play and joy?
Wherein every second death hovers ahoy,
Escape now from this ignorance, O toy,
Change this lifestyle of yours, O boy!
As a place of attachment, this world is rot.
An abode to heed lesson; mere amusement not.
This finite world is so beloved to view,
What has made it so enchanting to you?
Lacking in correct intelligence Aslam are you,
For men of wisdom have understood: unlike you!
As a place of attachment, this world is rot.
An abode to heed lesson; mere amusement not.
The famous are enjoined with dust, how?
Even town dwellers become homeless now,

The glamorous are disappearing now,
Earth has swallowed the sky, how?
As a place of attachment, this world is rot.
An abode to heed lesson; mere amusement not.

Old age and still dreading news of death?
Threatened, yet neither worried or alert of death,
Is there any limit to your negligence O beast?
Emerge from your insanity now at least!
As a place of attachment, this world is rot.
An abode to heed lesson; mere amusement not.

Neither will lovers of poetry remain,
nor the hankerer of fame and domain,
Non has remained or will remain,
only acts of piety will forever domain!
As a place of attachment, this world is rot.
An abode to heed lesson; mere amusement not.

Friends and associates depart in procession,
as they leave one after the other in quick succession,
When this scenario is often occurring,
why is your heart still submerged in worldly hoarding?
As a place of attachment, this world is rot.
An abode to heed lesson; mere amusement not.

Forever in this world is the wail of mourning,
somewhere the cry of starvation and wanting,
Yonder hails the complaint of theft and fraudulence,
in reality, only sounds of sadness, sorrow and sufferance!
As a place of attachment, this world is rot.
An abode to heed lesson; mere amusement not.

Wisdom of Allah ﷻ

Shaykh Ashraf 'Ali Thānwi ؒ relates, 'In a certain country, two people were on their deathbeds: one a Muslim, the other a non-muslim. The desire arose in the non-muslim's heart to eat fish...and despite having a pond in his garden; there were no fish present. A thought also arose in the Muslim's heart...to eat fresh ripe olives that were hanging upon a tree in his garden. Allah ﷻ commanded one of his angels,

> 'In so-and-so town, a non-muslim is about to die and his heart desires to eat fish. Go and place a fish in his pond so that his wish is fulfilled.'

To another angel, He commanded,

> 'In so-and-so town a Muslim is about to die and his heart desires to eat ripe olives which are in his garden. Go and destroy these olives thereby preventing fulfilment of his wish.'

Accordingly, both angels enacted their respected missions. Upon returning, they began to question each other's task; puzzled they began to fathom a reason. Unable to understand they asked Allah ﷻ,

> 'O Allah! Whilst we have carried out Your Command, we fail to comprehend why a Muslim, who obeys Your ahqāms and who had olives in his ownership was deprived from eating them? Moreover that non-muslim, who disobeys and disbelieves in You and who did not even have a fish, his wish is fulfilled, why?

Allah ﷻ replied,

> 'You are unaware of the Hikmat (Wisdom) behind Our Commands, the reality is Our attitude towards the kuffar and Muslims is very different. Since the kuffar too perform good deeds in this world, for example, they give Sadaqāh to some needy cause, but, because these amals are not acceptable to Us in the Ākhirah, therefore we reward them fully in dunya. Now when he appears before Us in the Ākhirah, any good deeds will already have been rewarded; We will owe him nothing. Our behaviour towards the Muslim is different. We desire that any penalization for sins he had committed takes place in dunya; thereby when he arrives to meet Us, he is pure and clean from sins!
>
> Accordingly, whatever good this kāfir had performed, We had rewarded him in dunya...except for one deed. Now, he was about to return to us, and when this desire arose in his heart to eat fish, We decided to fulfil his wish thereby settling his 'account.' With regards to the Muslim, during the time of his illness all his sins were forgiven... except one! Had he left dunya in this state, that one sin would have remained in his Book of Deeds. This is why We decided to destroy his olives and place a sorrow upon his heart by preventing him from eating...thus forgiving him his sin. He now returns to us pure and clean!'

None from creation is able to fully understand the *Hikmat* of Allah ﷻ, our small finite intellect is unable to comprehend reasons behind the *modus operandi* of this universe.

Advice to Caliph

Shaykh Mufti Taqee Uthmāni *dāmat barakātuhum* relates, 'There was once a very pious Saint, Shaykh Behlol ؓ and because he was submerged in the Love of Allah ﷻ, his state was a cause of others ridiculing him. Despite this mockery, the Caliph of that era, Haroon Rasheed ؓ (766-809 AH) had ordered the staff of his Royal Court to allow Shaykh Behlol ؓ entry whenever he wished. One day when he entered, Haroon Rasheed ؓ had a staff in his hand. Finding his presence amusing, he told Behlol ؓ:

Haroon Rasheed: '*Behlol, I have a request to make?*'

Behlol: '*Yes, what is it?*'

Haroon Rasheed: '*I give you this staff as an trust, should you find anybody more stupid than you, give it to him as a gift on my behalf.*'

Behlol: '*Very well.*'

The reason behind this act was for Haroon Rasheed to show that he considered Behlol to be a very foolish person. Some considerable years after this incident, the Caliph fell seriously ill and his death was imminent when Shaykh Behlol ؓ came for *iyaadat* (visiting the sick) and asked...

Behlol: '*O Ameerul Mumineen! How is your health?*'

Haroon Rasheed: '*What to say, I am about to depart on an unprecedented journey.*'

Behlol: '*After how many days will you return?*'

Haroon Rasheed: '*Brother, this is a journey towards the*

Ākhirah, from where none returns!'

Behlol: 'Well, if nobody returns, tell me what preparations have been made for your comfort and needs on this journey, how many troops and servants have you arranged?'

Haroon Rasheed: 'You still speaking nonsense? In the journey towards Ākhirah, nobody accompanies one; no body-guards, no servants and no troops. Man is all by himself.'

Behlol: 'Such a long journey and no preparations! Whereas I have observed all along, whenever you undertook even a small journey, months before preparations were made: cooks, tents, bodyguards, troops, etc., therefore why have you not planned for this journey from where there is no return?'

Haroon Rasheed: 'Undoubtedly it is not possible to take a retinue on this journey.'

Behlol: 'Salām upon you O Caliph! For many years I have kept an amānat of yours; a staff, which you had instructed me to hand over to a more foolish person than me. I have searched long and hard...but have failed to meet a more stupid person than you. Even in carrying out trivial acts, great preparations were made in the Royal Court and, now such a long journey and no preplanning? I consider you to be the most foolish person on earth, therefore here take back your amānat (staff)!'

Hearing this reply, Haroon Rasheed began to cry and spoke,

> 'Behlol! You have indeed spoken the truth; all along we had considered you to be stupid, yet your words are full of wisdom. Undoubtedly, I have wasted my life by not preparing for the Ākhirah.'

A Dream

Shaykh Maseehullah Khān ﷺ relates, 'Once a king had a dream wherein he observed a very large tray containing many varieties, shapes and sizes of flowers. Suddenly a knife appeared from above and cut these flowers, it would cut both large and small flowers. At this point the king awoke and began to ponder upon the meaning of this strange dream. He related it to his Court *mu'abbirs* (interpreters) but they all dismissed it as a product of the mind's imagination. Unconvinced and agitated, the king ordered that no cooking would take place in the kingdom until this dream is interpreted!

Coincidentally, a soldier returned home on leave...and asked for food. His mother replied, 'Dear, there has been no food cooked for three days, it's the king's command. Police patrols are going around, any sign of cooking smoke and instant arrest!' Her son replied, 'Well I don't care what great dream the king is supposed to have seen, I'm starving, please cook a meal for me; if the smoke gets noticed and the king summons me we shall take it from there.' Accordingly, the mother lit her stove and began cooking. Noticing smoke arising from a chimney, the Royal spies arrived and arrested the soldier and took him into the kings presence who asked, 'Why this disobedience?' The soldier replied, 'I am hungry, anyway please relate your dream.' The king described his dream. 'Allow me to eat and three days grace...if by then I do not bring an interpretation you may kill me,' commented the soldier. The king agreed. After having eaten, the soldier mounted his horse and roamed from city to city, town to town in trying to find an interpretation...but to no avail. Fatigued, he stopped at a small hamlet to request a drink of water from a young maiden spinning cloth in her porch way. The pious lady brought a pitcher of water and left it by the gateway. Puzzled, the soldier dismounted and drank the water. Then he asked, 'Madam you appear to be alone, where is your mother?' The young lady answered from inside her porch way, 'My mother has gone to deliver two from one!' Dumbfounded, the soldier thought, 'O heck! As if one dream to interpret was not bad enough...what does she mean by delivering two from one?' Thereafter he asked, 'Well, where is your father?' The young lady replied, 'My father has gone to enjoin clay with clay.' Just then the father appeared and the soldier commented, 'Your daughter is amazing, I asked her two simple questions and she gave such strange replies!' The father inquired, 'What did she say?'

Soldier: 'Well, first I asked her for a drink of water and she left some at the gateway.'

Father: 'My daughter is in purdah; shy and very modest. How could she possibly hand something to a non-mahram?'

Soldier: 'Secondly, I asked her, 'Where is your mother?' She replied, 'she has gone to deliver two from one!'

Father: 'Yes, my wife is a midwife, she was called to deliver a baby, this is what she meant by delivering two from one!'

At this point, the soldier thinking, 'hold on, we appear to have something very special here' asked, 'Thereafter, I asked her about you and she replied, 'My father has gone to enjoin clay with clay.'

Father: 'A local has passed-away and I attended his funeral, anyhow, who are you and where have you come from?'

The soldier related his whole predicament of interpreting the king's dream within 3 days or face the death penalty; and the kings command forbidding any cooking in the kingdom. Addressing his daughter, the father asked, 'Dear, did you hear the dream?' 'Yes father I heard.' 'Well, what do you say?' 'It's the king's dream, I wish to hear it directly from him before giving the interpretation.' Accordingly, all three left for the king's palace...

Soldier: 'Your Majesty, the girl who is to interpret your dream has arrived, please give a command allowing all your subjects to cook...should you find the meaning not to your liking, your majesty is king and may do as he wishes!'

A Royal Proclamation was given allowing people to cook again. Thereafter, the young lady, arrived and from behind a screen listened to the king's dream and then commented...

> 'The interpretation of this dream is as follows. The tray refers to earth, whilst its covering is the Heavens, the flowers therein are people and the knife represents death... which travels upon earth; 'cutting' some people in young age whilst others in later life. Some die in childhood, others in their teens, middle and old age. This knife keeps appearing and taking the souls of creation. Herein Allah ﷻ is warning you that it is not prudent for man to remain neglectful of death: because it may appear at any time in life. These are the meanings of the tray, flowers and knife!'

Overjoyed on hearing this interpretation, the king showered gifts as a sign of his appreciation.

Chapter Two

What to do Upon the Approach of a Muslim's Death

From the Teachings of

Shaykh Ashraf 'Ali Thãnwi ❀,
Shaykh Dr 'Abdul-Hayy 'Ãrifee ❀,
Shaykh Mufti 'Ãshiq Ellahi Madanee ❀

Upon Approach of Death

Shaykh Dr 'Abdul-Hayy 'Ārifee ﷺ relates, 'When signs of death appear upon a Muslim, lie him upon his back so that his right-side faces the *qiblah*. By use of pillows raise his head slightly towards or let his feet face the *qiblah*. Should this act be painful for the dying let him lie in whatever state he be in.

Recitation of Kaleemah-e-Shahādat

When the dying person's breath weakens and becomes erratic; when the legs loosen and drop; when the nose loses its straightness and the forehead subsides, then understand death to be imminent. Our beloved Nabee ﷺ suggested to encourage the dying one to recite the *Kaleemah Shahādat* by oneself reciting loudly:

اَشْهَدُ اَنْ لَآ اِلٰهَ اِلَّا اللّٰهُ وَحْدَهُ لَا شَرِيْكَ لَهُ
وَ اَشْهَدُ اَنَّ مُحَمَّدًا عَبْدُهُ وَ رَسُوْلُهُ

'I bear witness there is none worthy of worship besides Allah Ta'ālā. He is alone. He has no partners and, I bear witness; Muhammad ﷺ is His Servant and Messenger.'

- Remember, never to order or constrain the dying to recite the Kaleemah because this is a very delicate moment, nobody knows what they might utter.
- Once the dying has recited the Kaleemah, everybody should maintain silence. It is not at all necessary for the dying to be constantly reciting the Kaleemah until their last breath, because the intention is for this Kaleemah to be the last

verbal statement. Should they make any worldly talk, again loudly recite the Kaleemah, now when they have finished reciting, once again maintain silence.

Recitation of Soorah Yā-Seen (Juz 21-22)

- Aboo Zarr ؓ narrates that should a person be in the state of *naza'* (throes of death) and Soorah Yā-Seen be recited in his presence, then his death will be made easy. (Mazhari 9:574)

- One should remember never to divert the dying person's attention by naively ushering in children, wife and family members into his presence. This is the moment wherein a Muslim departs from this world to meet Allah ﷻ.

- Allah ﷻ forbid, but should any word of *kufr* (disbelieve) emerge from the dying person's tongue, do not pay attention or advertise it. Death is a strenuous occasion wherein the intelligence sometimes fails to operate correctly, such lapses are overlooked by Allah ﷻ, therefore make du'aa of forgiveness.

Upon Death

- When death takes place, relatives and those present should recite:

$$\text{اِنَّا لِلّٰهِ وَ اِنَّا اِلَيْهِ رٰجِعُوْنَ}$$

'Verily, we belong to Allah and unto Him is our return.'

$$\text{اَللّٰهُمَّ اَجْرِنِيْ فِيْ مُصِيْبَتِيْ وَ اخْلُفْ لِيْ خَيْرًا مِّنْها}$$

'O Allah! Reward me in my affliction and grant me better in return.'

Straightening Body Limbs

- Taking a wide strip of cloth enwrap it around the chin, ears, forehead and whilst softly closing the eyes recite:

$$\text{بِسْمِ اللهِ وَ عَلَى مِلَّةِ رَسُوْلِ اللهِ}$$
$$\text{اَللّٰهُمَّ يَسِّرْ عَلَيْهِ أَمْرَهُ}$$
$$\text{وَ سَهِّلْ عَلَيْهِ مَا بَعْدَهُ وَ أَسْعِدْهُ بِلِقَائِكَ}$$
$$\text{وَ اجْعَلْ مَا خَرَجَ اِلَيْهِ خَيْرًا مِمَّا خَرَجَ عَنْهُ}$$

'Beginning in the name of Allah and upon the Religion of Rasoolullah ﷺ. O Allah, ease upon this mayyit its trial and the forthcoming events to transpire. Bless him/her with the vision of Your Sight. Also make the place where he has gone to (i.e. Ãkhirah) better than the one which he has left (the dunya).'

- Thereafter straighten the mayyits hands, and feet by tying a cloth around the large toes of both feet and then placing the body on a bed or raised platform cover the whole body with a cloth. Do not leave body on the floor. Place a heavy item upon the stomach to prevent it from bloating.

- Anybody in the state of *janābat, haidh or nifaas* should not appear in the presence of the mayyit.

- If possible, place some halāl perfume (e.g. scented wood sticks) near the mayyit.

- Remember, one should not recite the Glorious Qur'ān near the mayyit until it has been bathed.

- One should hasten in arranging the ghusl, shrouding and burial of the mayyit. Even if it be Friday, do not wait until after Jumu'ah Salāh in expectation of a large congregation.

Common Shortcomings at Time of Death

Shaykh Ashraf 'Ali Thānwi ﷺ relates, 'Our condition nowadays has so deteriorated that we do not even know how to die! Whilst not all the Sahābah ؓ could read or write, nevertheless they were intelligent and understanding. This is the beauty and blessings of the Islāmic Sharee'ah wherein principles of dying have also been outlined. It would be wise to relate some of these:

1) Whenever a Muslim is ill, it is of course commendable to visit him. However, never utter such talk (no matter what the illness) which may depress or sadden him, rather adopt a tone whereby hope of speedy recovery is created. Some people have a habit of blurting inappropriate and depressing remarks thereby creating thought in the patient that his death is imminent. Our Nabee ﷺ even instructed mercy when slaughtering animals, that another animal should not be present to suffer heartache and fear in witnessing this act.

2) To please and refrain from saddening a Muslim is a big *ibaadah*. Always bear this in mind and a golden prescription for this is to understand that all Muslims are the *Walee* (Friends) of Allah, the only difference is in rank. Even those who are very advanced do not have it written upon their forehead, therefore consider every Muslim as a possible high ranking *Walee*...either now or sometime in the future and to honour him is compulsory,

> 'A Muslim is he from whose tongue and hands other Muslims are safe.' (Maut & Hayāt, p364)

3) When death is imminent and even the patient is certain

and aware of this, then do not relate any worldly or such talk which would divert him from Allah ﷻ. Nowadays wives will stand to one side of their husband and wail, 'to whom are you leaving us,' whilst children are made to cluster around the deathbed. These final moments should not be squandered in emotionalism, however should the person insist on seeing his wife or children, quickly allow them to meet him, very briefly, whereby his thoughts are freed.

4) Recite the Kaleemah, Allah's Name, Sûrah Yā-Seen, Taubah and Istighfar without actually instructing him. If necessary, recite in English or any other language understood by the dying: words like, 'O Allah forgive me my sins,' thereby encouraging him to do the same.

5) Describe the bounties of Paradise to him and refrain from mentioning Hell. Whilst at other times, one should maintain a balance between hope and fear thereby inclining towards *Āmal-e-Sālihāh* (good deeds) and refraining from sins, understand this is a delicate stage whereby hope of forgiveness and Jannah should be dominant so as to leave dunya in the state of *Imān*. Subhannallah! What a perfect Sharee'ah...full of wisdom. Our Nabee ﷺ commented,

> *'Allah Says, I am with My servant whom harbours good thoughts about Me.'* (Ihya-ul-Uloom, Vol 4, p 478)

6) At approach of death, try to face him towards the Qiblah and do not pay attention to any unbefitting statement of the dying person, because when a person is excused in state of severe illness, he is all the more exempted at such a traumatic time; for who knows what his soul is experiencing?

Accordingly, our Hajji Imdādullah Makki ﷺ related the final moments of a Saint in Lûharee who turned his face-away when people tried to persuade him to recite the Kaleemah. Shocked and aghast, those present began to think, 'what doubt is there now in his dying in the state of disbelief.' Lo and behold, Shaykh Noor Muhammad ﷺ arrived and inquired, 'Brother! How are you?' The dying person replied, 'Shaykh! Prohibit them from diverting my attention away from the Being and Vision of Allah ﷻ towards speech (Kaleemah).' Only now did those present realize the high status and rank of this dying Saint.

7) If the dying person appears to be suffering from severe pangs of death, do not misconstrue, because it is related that when Allah ﷻ wishes to elevate a person's rank who has many sins to his account, He inflicts death pangs which act as *Kaffarah* (expiation) for his sins. Thus this person leaves dunya pure from sin.

8) One silly custom in vogue nowadays is the habit of announcing the death to those in far-away places in expectation of them quickly arriving for the Janāzah Salāh... which is undoubtedly delayed on their behalf. All this achieves is to burden the bereaved with the worry, inconvenience and expense (usually from inheritance of the widow and orphaned children) of feeding and hosting a multitude of visitors. Therefore, when informing distant relatives, stress upon them not to undertake long journies... rather donate the expense of such trips for the *Esāl-al-thawāb* of the deceased.

Rasoolullah ﷺ commented,

'Allah ﷻ says, 'There is nothing but Jannah for the one who is patient and hopes for thawāb (reward) when I take away someone beloved to him."

(Hayātul Muslimeen, p202)

'Insān (man) considers life as beloved, whereas death is better for him.'

'When Malikul Maut appears to the pious servants of Allah, they make Salām and say;

'Salāms upon you O Friend of Allah! Arise and leave this abode which you had annihilated (by sacrificing your carnal desires) and come towards the home (Jannah) which you have furnished (by way of Ibaadah)."

(Both Hadeeth Quoted from States of Barzakh, p 27)

Shaykh Ashraf 'Ali Thānwi ﷺ relates, 'When the young son of 'Abdullah bin Mubārak ؓ passed-away, a person came and consoled him,

'Intelligent is he who puts into practice today what even a naive ignoramus will undoubtedly have to do after five days.'

Even an ignorant person will make *sabr* (be patient)...but when? After the opportunity and occasion to make sabr has passed.'

Chapter Three

Legal Procedures, Ghusl (Bathing) & Kafn (Shrouding)

Based upon the Teachings of
Shaykh Ashraf 'Ali Thānwi,
Shaykh Dr 'Abdul-Hayy 'Ārifee,
Shaykh Manzoor Nu'maani
Shaykh Ahmad Sādeeq Desai
dāmat barakātuhum

Legal Requirements in England & Wales

When a person dies in England & Wales, there are certain legal requirements which need to be observed:

1) Medical Certificate & Formal Notice

One needs to obtain a Medical Certificate from a doctor (normally the one who attended the deceased) which shows the cause of death (this will be in a sealed envelope addressed to the registrar). This is accompanied by a small form which states that the doctor has signed the Medical Certificate and gives basic details about registering the death.

Summary of Documents For REGISTRATION		
When Registering a death	The informant will usually get a	From/to
If the death is not referred to a coroner	*Medical Certificate* Stating cause of death.	The doctor addressed to the registrar
In all cases	*Formal Notice* Showing how to register the death	the doctor
If a baby is stillborn	*Medical Certificate of Stillbirth*	the doctor or midwife
If the death is referred to a coroner but there is no inquest	*Notification by the Coroner* (the Pink Form/form 100)	the coroner to the registrar (direct or via a relative)
If there is an inquest and the body is to be buried	*Order for Burial* (form 101 - giving all details required)	the coroner (direct) to the registrar

(© Crown Copyright ~ Original Copyright Holder)

2 How to Register a Death

The death must be registered (within 5 days) by the Registrar of Births, Marriages and Deaths for the sub-district in which it occurred.

This is a simple question-and-answer process, and to save time, worry and confusion, it is best to write down clearly all the details *before* you meet the registrar. The Department of Work & Pensions excellent Booklet (D 49) suggests one takes along the following:

* the Medical Certificate of the cause of death
* the deceased's medical card, if possible
* the deceased's birth and marriage certificates, if available.

You should tell the registrar:

* the date and place of death
* the deceased's last (usual) address
* the deceased's first names and surname (and the maiden name where appropriate)
* the deceased's date and place of birth (town and county if born in the UK, and country if born abroad)
* the deceased's occupation and the name and occupation of their spouse
* whether the deceased was getting a pension or allowance from public funds
* if the deceased was married, the date of birth of the surviving widow or widower.
* Fee. It is best to ask for several copies of the Death Certificate as the price increases later.

(What to do after a death in England & Wales)

Listed below is a summary of the forms and certificates the informant may receive from the registrar.

Summary of Documents From REGISTRAR		
WHEN REGISTERING A DEATH	**THE INFORMANT WILL USUALLY GET A**	**FROM**
If no coroner has issued a Certificate E for Burial Order	**Certificate for Burial** (also known as the Green Form) This Certificate from the registrar gives permission for the body to be buried.	the registrar
If Social Security needs to know about the death	**Certificate of Registration of Death** (form BD 8) This is for Social Security purposes only	the registrar
If you need evidence for obtaining probate, pensions claims, saving certificates and premium bonds.	**Death Certificate(s)** This is a certified copy of the entry in the death register	the registrar
If a baby is stillborn (born dead after the 24th week of pregnancy)	**Certificate of Registration of Stillborn**	the registrar
If a baby is stillborn. For burial	**Certificate for Burial** (the White Form)	the registrar

(© Crown Copyright ~ Original Copyright Holder)

Ghusl & Kafn
(Bathing & Shrouding the Deceased)

Rasoolullah ﷺ commented,

'Whomsoever bathes the mayyit becomes as pure from sins as if just born from his mother's womb, moreover whomsoever shrouds the mayyit...Allah Ta'ālā will don him with clothes of Paradise.' (p 41, Ahqāme Mayyit)

'Abdullah bin 'Umar ؓ relates Nabee ﷺ commented,

'Whenever one of your people passes-away, then do not keep him for long (in the house). Rather adopt haste in taking him unto his grave and cemetery.' (Ma'āriful Hadeeth)

Shaykh Manzoor Nu'maani ؒ comments, 'Whenever a servant of Allah ﷻ takes leave from this world for the Hereafter, the Islāmic Sharee'ah has defined a special way for his departure; one which is imbued with honour, dignity and grace. We are ordered to bathe the mayyit in a manner wherein a living person would acquire purity; such scents as camphor are used in water which achieve cleanliness and fragrance. Thereafter, without resorting to waste, the deceased is shrouded in good, clean and neat clothes. This is followed by a collective *Salāh-e-Maghfirat*, wherein supplication is made for his forgiveness and *Rahmat* with intense feeling and sincerity. Thereafter with great respect is the mayyit lowered into the grave and left unto the Mercy of Allah ﷻ.' (ibid.)

Who Should Bathe the Mayyit?

The foremost *haqq* (right) of bathing the mayyit belongs to his/her closest relatives, because this is their final act of *khidmat* (assistance) for their beloved. An adult male should be bathed by his father, son or brother. An adult female by her mother, daughter or sister. Any other person (of the same gender) may also bathe the mayyit, however it is best if the most pious person available be requested to perform this rite. If a very young non *baaligh* boy dies (the observance of whom would not arise any passion), then it is also permissible for ladies to bathe him.

Necessary Advice For Those Performing Ghusl

1) It is *makruh* (detestable) for any person in the state of *janaabah, haidh or nifaas* (classes of greater impurity) to bathe the deceased.
2) It is best that one be in the state of *wudhu* (ablution).
3) Ensure the place where ghusl is to be performed offers complete privacy (Sharee' Purdah).
4) It is totally forbidden to mention to other's any signs of physical deformity, face distortion (Allah Forbid) which may be visible on the mayyit's body. However, should signs of piety be visible, e.g. *nûr* (spiritual light) or happiness emanating from the face or areas of *wudhu* or *sujood*, etc. then it is *mustahab* to mention it to others.
5) Just as it impermissible to touch or view the *satr* of another during his life, similar is the case after a person's death. Therefore, don gloves or mittens to wash the private areas.

(Ahqām Mayyit)

Items Required for Ghusl

Shaykh Dr 'Abdul-Hayy 'Ārifee ﷺ suggests the following in his book *Ahqāme Mayyit*, 'All the required items for ghusl and kafn should be gathered beforehand:

1) Supply of clean lukewarm water.
2) A broad bench, stand or platform.
3) Two large buckets for warm water, one small bucket for mixing water with a little camphor for use at the end of ghusl.
4) Two pouring jugs (neither these or the buckets have to be new, merely clean and pure).
5) Kitchen Towels.
6) Leaves of Beer Tree (Zizyphus Jujuba) *if available*.
7) Lobaan (frankincense) or any other halāl incense - this is used to for smoking the bench.
8) 'Itr (halāl perfume) for men.
9) Camphor (Kafur) - about 100 grams.
10) A bar of soap.
11) Cotton Wool - approximately 250 grams.
12) Two Teh'bands (pieces of cloth 1.25m x 1.25m to cover the *satr*).
13) Two pairs of latex gloves or bag like mittens (for cleaning private parts).
14) Scissors (for removing the dead persons clothes).
15) One clean bath towel and one clean bed-sheet.

The Masnûn (Preferable) Method of Ghusl

1) Wherever possible, lukewarm water should be used in which leaves of the *bir* tree have been fermented.
2) The bench, stand or platform upon which the ghusl is to be performed should be washed, cleaned and fumigated with *lobaan* (or any other halāl aromatic) 3, 5 or 7 times.
3) If possible, place the body whereby the *qiblah* is towards its right-hand side.
4) Do not comb, cut or trim the mayyit's hair or nails but remove all jewellery, any dentures, etc.
5) Cover the *satr* (for males between navel to below knees and for females from above the breasts to the ankles) with one of the Teh'bands (which should be thick enough not to allow a view of the body even when wet). Remove all clothing there under (by cutting). Block nostrils, ears and mouth with cotton wool to prevent water entering during ghusl.
6) Wearing gloves but without viewing, massage the stomach gently and wash both places of *Istinja*.
7) Now, perform *wudhu* without pouring water into the mayyits nostrils or mouth. The proper sequence is to wash: i) The face. ii) Arms to the elbows. iii) Make Masah of the head. iv) Feet up to the ankles.
8) Should the mayyit have passed-away in the state of *Janaabat* (impurity including haidh or nifaas) whereby ghusl is *wājib,* then the mouth needs to be gargled and nostrils wetted by making use of pieces of wet cotton wool. Again cover these area's with wool to prevent entry

of water during ghusl.

9) After wudhu, the head (and for men the beard also) should be washed with soap and water.

10) Now, tilt the body unto its left side and starting from the head, pour water and scrub with soap all along the body in such a way as to ensure water reaches the left-hand underside. Repeat this process with water only; two more times.

11) Thereafter, tilt the body unto its right-hand side and wash the left side in a similar manner.

12) During performance of the ghusl constantly recite:

$$\text{غُفْرَانَكَ يَا رَحْمٰنُ}$$

13) Now raise the top-half of the body (into an almost sitting position) and massage slowly the stomach once again, starting from the top. If any waste emerges, wipe and wash it away. There is no need to repeat the wudhu or ghusl, because this najaasat does not affect the bath in any way.

14) Once again, turn the body unto its left side and pour camphor water from head to toe 3 times.

15) Now dry the body with a clean towel, changing the wet Teh'band for a dry one. Ensure you keep the *satr* covered at all times.

16) The *kafn* (shroud) should have been prepared beforehand to now receive the mayyit.

17) Cover the body with a sheet and carry carefully unto *kafn*. Remove all cotton wool from facial openings.

Kafn

Aboo Hurairah relates that Nabee advised, *'Whomsoever gives ghusl to the mayyit, he too should perform ghusl.'* (p. 47, Ahqām Mayyit)

Those people who participate in performing ghusl should also take a ghusl themselves.

Abdullah Ibn Abbass relates Nabee advised, *'You people should wear white clothing; such clothing is good for you, and (in this type of clothing) should you bury your dead.'*

Jābir and 'Ali relate, *'Whenever any of you shroud a deceased brother of yours, ensure (the kafn) is (of good quality).*

'Rasoolullah advised, 'Do not employ very expensive kafn because it (too) perishes very quickly." (p. 472-3, Ma'āriful Hadeeth)

Shaykh Manzoor Nu'maani comments, 'The purpose behind these ahadeeth is to emphasise the reverence of the mayyit, neither should there be (stinginess) nor (wastage) in employing a correct grade of kafn, which should be appropriate to the dignity of a Mu'min.'

Shaykh Dr 'Abdul-Hayy 'Ārifee relates: Just as it is *Fardh-e-Kifāyah* (collectively compulsory) to give ghusl, similar is the case with kafn.

- There is no harm in employing cloth already available at home as long as it is clean.

- The quality of the cloth should be appropriate to the mayyit's status, though this is no excuse for extravagance.
- The best kafn is white; whether new or used.
- Silk and cloth of yellow-orange colour are totally inappropriate and makruh for male, however these are permissible for ladies.
- It is indeed a cause of blessing to use kafn previously washed in Zam-Zam water. Similarly, it is also good to employ the worn cloth of an Awliyaa (Saint).
- It is forbidden to place any Qur'ānic Ayahs, du'aa's, or write the Kaleemah upon the kafn or Sina'band.
- The 3 pieces of kafn for males and 5 for females are *masnun* (see table). This method should also be used for children nearing buloogh as well as those younger.

	MALE & FEMALE KAFN			
	NAME OF GARMENT	LENGTH	WIDTH	DESCRIPTION
1	Izaar	180 cm	150cm/180cm	To cover from head
2	Lifafah Chadar	225 cm (2½ yards)	150cm/180cm (60"/72")	15 cm longer than Izaar
3	Qamees Kafni	180cm to 250cm	90 cm (36")	From shoulder to below the knees
ADDITIONAL ITEMS FOR FEMALES ONLY				
4	Khimaar Orni	140 cm (1½ yards)	90 cm (36")	to cover head & hair over breasts
5	Sina'band	180cm to 250cm (60"/72")	90 cm (36")	From under the armpits to the thighs

The Masnûn (Preferable) Method of Kafn

Shaykh Dr 'Abdul-Hayy 'Ārifee ﷺ relates, 'Lay out the kafn and fumigate it 3, 5 or 7 times, thereafter place the bathed mayyit and remove the cotton pieces which had covered facial openings.

The methods of putting on kafn differ for males and women and are described below:

For Males

1) First spread the *Lifafah*, thereafter the *Izaar* and upon it the underside of the *Qamees*. The top portion of the *Qamees* should be folded and rolled back towards the head side.

Order of Male Kafn

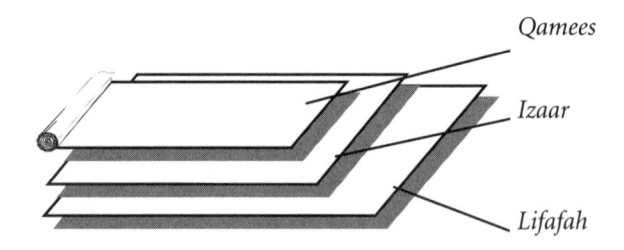

Qamees
Izaar
Lifafah

2) Slowly lower the mayyit unto the laid out kafn, and cover body upto the calf's with the rolled-up portion of the *Qamees*.

3) Remove the *Teh'band* and sheet used for covering the satr.

4) Rub *Itr* (or any other halāl fragrance except saffron) unto the beard and head.

How Qamees should be cut and folded

5) Then rub camphor mixture paste upon the places of *sujood* (those parts of the body which touch the ground in Salāh: forehead, nose, palms, knees and feet).

6) Now fold the left flap and on it the right flap of the *Izaar* over *qamees*.

7) Thereafter fold the *lifafah* in the same manner. Remember the right flap must always be on top.

8) Finally, fasten the ends of the *lifafah* at the headside, middle and feet-end with strips of cloth to prevent the kafn from opening during movement. (p 59, Ahqām Mayyit)

For Ladies

1) For females, first lay the *lifafah*, thereupon the *Sina'band* and then the *izaar*. On top of these 3 pieces lay the underside of the *qamees* with the top side pre cut and rolled-up towards the head side.

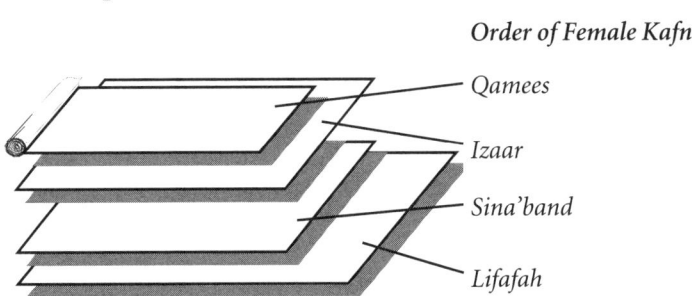

Order of Female Kafn

- Qamees
- Izaar
- Sina'band
- Lifafah

2) Gently lower the mayyit from the ghusl board unto the kafn, and cover with the rolled up portion of the *qamees* from the head side down towards the feet.
3) Remove the *tehnaband* (the covering cloth employed during ghusl).
4) Rub camphor mixture paste upon the places of *sujood* (those parts of the body which touch the ground in Salāh: forehead, nose, palms, knees and feet).
5) Thereafter divide hair of the head into two and place upon the chest on the *qamees* on either side.
6) Now cover the hair (without plaiting or tying them) with the *khimaar/orni* (scarf).
7) Finally, fold the *izar* over the mayyit in such a way whereby the left edge comes to rest under the right side (the scarf thus ends up inside the fold).
8) Now bring the *sina'band* (chest-wrap) from under the arm-pits over to the chest and unto the knees and tie together the right and left ends.
9) Repeat this method with the *lifafah*, whereby the right edge stays on top of the left.
10) Finally, taking strips of cloth, tie together the *kafn* at head, feet and middle (here with a longer strip), thereby preventing the danger of opening when the mayyit is being transported.

Some Necessary Advice

Mas'alah: Follow the Sunnah method of preparing the Janāzah and with *sabr* and grace bid the *musāfir* farewell towards its *Janāzah Salāh*.

Mas'alah: Whichever *mahram* you wish to allow to view the face, do so, however ensure ladies do not wail, congregate or follow the mayyit outside the house in total conflict with the teachings of purdah.

Mas'alah: It is necessary to cover the Janāzah of a female with a cloth (of any colour - this is not part of the kafn but ensures privacy).

Mas'alah: Some people apply *it'r* to the kafn and place scented cotton into the ears. Similarly, it is not permissible to comb the hair, apply surmah to the eyes or cut the nails and hair of the mayyit. All these are acts of pure ignorance, only follow the practices stipulated by the Sharee'ah.

Mas'alah: Whatever items are left over after ghusl, kafn and burial should not just be handed over to anybody. If they have been purchased or acquired from the estate of the deceased, to return it to the estate is *Wājib* (compulsory) in order to ensure correct distribution. If any individual had contributed these items they should be returned to him.

Relatives who are Non-Muslim

Shaykh Ahmad Sadeeq Desai *dāmat barakātuhum* states, 'When a non-muslim relative, e.g. mother or father dies and there is only a Muslim relative to organize the burial, the mayyit should be handed over to the non-muslims. If for some reason the non-muslims refuse, then the Muslim relative should attend to the burial. Masnûn kafn and burial are not permissible for non-muslims. However, the body should be washed in the same way as impure cloth is washed, wrapped in any cloth and (buried in a cemetery) without observing the Islāmic way of burial.'

Stillborn & Miscarriage

- In the case of a stillbirth (where no signs of life were present), although the baby will be given ghusl, the kafn should not be as formal: merely wrap it in a piece of clean cloth; give the child a name and bury it without Janāzah Salāh.
- Should there be a miscarriage and signs of limb formations are visible; hands, legs, feet, nose, mouth, etc. then the above rule applies: perform ghusl, choose a name and wrap in a piece of cloth and bury.
- However, should no limbs be visible, do not perform ghusl or kafn, merely wrap in cloth and bury it.
- At the time of birth, should only the head emerge and signs of life were noticeable before death, the same ruling applies as for stillborn. However, if more than half the body emerges and the child lives before dying, then it will be considered as if born alive. Half the body implies emergence of the top torso up to chest (if a head-first delivery) and up to navel (if feet-first delivery).

Legal Registration of Stillborn Babies

If a baby is stillborn (born dead after the 24th week of pregnancy), in the UK a signed **Medical Certificate of Stillbirth** is issued by the midwife or doctor, which should be given to the registrar. If no doctor or midwife was present and no doctor or midwife has examined the body, you must sign **form 35** which the registrar will give you. The registrar will give you a **Certificate for Burial** and a **Certificate of Registration of Stillbirth.**   (What to do after a death in England & Wales)

Disasters, Accidents & Tragedies

Shaykh Dr 'Abdul-Hayy 'Ārifee ﷺ relates: 'Nowadays, because of the evil deeds of mankind, horrendous tragedies and disasters occur on a regular basis. Frequently, we hear and read of earthquakes, flooding, accidents, sinking, bombings, genocide, etc., in which thousands of people die...amongst whom are many innocent Muslims. Allah ﷻ protect all Muslims from such disasters.

Often as an outcome of these mishaps, Muslim bodies become so entangled and injured, it becomes difficult to perform ghusl, shroud and pray Janāzah Salāh. On such occasions it is not always possible to consult pious 'Ulamā, therefore the following guidelines are presented.

Drowning &/or A Bloated Body

If a person drowns (Allah Forbid), then it is still necessary (fardh) to perform ghusl. The fact that he has drowned in water does not negate the need for ghusl, because it is compulsory for the living to bathe the dead, and in drowning the living play no part. Nevertheless, if at the time of removing body from the water an intention for ghusl is made and the mayyit be agitated inside the water, ghusl will become complete. Thereafter, it is still necessary to enact normal kafn, Janāzah Salāt and burial.

If a body becomes bloated, whether in water or because of (any delay) and becomes so precarious as not fit to be touched, i.e. if normal ghusl was to be performed, the body would disintegrate, then under such circumstances only pass water over the mayyit. There is no need to rub it. Thereafter, perform kafn and Janāzah Salāt, however, if the body 'ruptures' before Janāzah Salāt, it should be buried without performance of Janāzah Salāt.

A Body Which Smells

Janāzah Salāh will be performed for a body which has started to 'smell' yet has not 'ruptured.'

A Decomposed or Ruptured Body

Janāzah Salāh is not performed for a body which has ruptured and decomposed.

Mere Bones

Neither is ghusl or Janāzah Salāh performed on a body whose meat and flesh, etc., have disintegrated whereby only bones survive. Any remains should be wrapped in a clean cloth and buried.

Burnt Body

Ghusl, kafn, Janāzah Salāh and Sunnah burial should be performed upon a person who dies by burning as long as the body has not bloated or burst.

Body which becomes Charred

There is no Ghusl, kafn, Janāzah Salāh or Sunnah burial for a body which is totally charred. Such a body should be wrapped in a clean cloth and buried. However, should a greater portion of the body be free from burns (or only slightly burnt), even though the head be decapitated or at least half the body (including the head) be sound (i.e. the flesh, meat and bones) then Ghusl, kafn, Janāzah Salāh and Sunnah burial needs to be performed.

Crushed or Fallen Body - Transport Accidents

When somebody perishes in a building or rock collapse or falls from a height or in a plane accident and, the majority of the body is intact, then ghusl, kafn, Janāzah Salāh and Sunnah burial needs to be performed. However, if the accident was the result of kuffar, bandit or rebel hostility, the rules of *Shaheed* will apply.

Motor, rail and transport accidents also come under one of the above categories.

Inaccessible Body

A body which is present but inaccessible...for example, buried in a building or water-well and irremovable, then as a last resort, its ghusl and kafn are waived. The place of 'burial' will be considered its grave and Janāzah Salāh will be prayed at this site (only).

Body Missing - Drowned or Death at Sea, etc

A person who drowns and is lost at sea and similarly when a body is missing, then neither is ghusl, kafn or Janāzah Salāh possible: because for Janāzah Salāh to be valid the body must be present.

However, should a person die on board a ship, the mayyit will be given ghusl, kafan and Janāzah Salāh will be performed.

If land is nearby and there is no fear of the body decomposing, burial should be delayed until the ship docks. If land is far away and there is fear of decomposition, the body should be lowered into the sea. (p16, Kitabul Janā-iz)

Overseas & Distant Burials

Shaykh Ashraf 'Ali Thānwi ﷺ commented upon this practice of sending the mayyit to distant places for burial, 'Why? Do they think they will be drinking their mother's milk in the grave also?' Shaykh Muhammad Saleem Dhorat *dāmat barakātuhum* writes, 'There seems to be a growing culture amongst the Muslims of UK of sending their deceased overseas...so they be near to the graves of their loved ones...Before a body is sent abroad, a process known as 'embalming' has to take place to preserve and sanitise the body. The body needs to be certified as 'embalmed' before any airline company would allow it to be flown. Random checking of the body takes place at the airport to assess whether it is adequately embalmed.' Embalming involves draining blood from the body and replacing it with formaldehyde (plus a pinkish dye) pumped in under pressure. This achieves a hardening and disinfecting effect. Organs of the body are pierced, treated with chemicals and consequently re-stitched and concocted to achieve a 'sleeping' look. It is quite obvious, that this desecration of a Muslim's body, merely in order to satisfy some tradition is incorrect. Shaykh-ul-Hadeeth Mufti Sahbān Mahmood ﷺ commented, 'It appears from Hadeeth, when the mayyit is placed upon a bier for taking to the graveyard, if the person was pious, he calls out (although we are unable to hear him), 'Take me quickly towards my *manzil* (station), do not delay!' This is because at the time of his death, he is informed of his final abode in *Jannah*, and he knows what bounties await.'

(See also Appendix A & C)

Chapter Four

Janāzah Salāh, Burial & Etiquette's of Visiting the Muslim Cemetery

𝒪nce Jibra'eel ﷺ appeared and advised Nabee ﷺ, *'Muhammad ﷺ! No matter how long you live, death must appear one day. And whatever action you do (whether good or bad), you will receive its recompense. And with whomsoever you maintain a bond (in dunya), one day you must separate from them (either through their or your death). Understand well, a humans' success is in tahajjud salāh and his honour is to remain aloof from creation.'*

(Fadhāil Sadaqāt. Vol. 2, p 403)

Accompanying the Janāzah

Aboo Hurayrah 🌸 relates our Nabee 🌸 commented,

'Whomsoever, in the state of Imān with intention of thawāb accompanies the Janāzah of any Muslim and stays until Salāh and burial, then he returns with two qirāt's. One of these qirāts is equal to Mount Uhud. Whomsoever returns after only performing Janāzah Salāh, i.e. he does not participate in burial, then he returns with one qirāt.'

'Make haste with transporting of the Janāzah, for if he is good, the qabr is better for him (as a stage) wherein you transport him to quickly. Moreover, if he is evil, then you are delivering a load off your shoulders. Walk quickly and discharge this burden off your shoulders.' (Ma'āriful Hadeeth)

'Whomsoever lifts all four corners of the coffin, then 40 major sins of his are forgiven.' (p 63, Ahqām-e-Mayyat)

Shaykh-ul-Hadeeth Zakariyyā 🌸 relates,

'Once Aboo Darda 🌸 was accompanying a Janāzah when a wayfarer asked, 'Whose janāzah is this?' Aboo Darda 🌸 replied, 'This is your Janāzah and if you dislike what I say then it is my Janāzah.'

The reason behind this rebuke is to bring to our attention the opportunity of reflecting upon our own death on such occasions. Nowadays, people talk nonsense and squander these moments by meeting and greeting friends whilst the burial is still taking place!

Mas'alah: The preferred method of lifting the janāzah is to carry the left front of the coffin on one's right-shoulder for 10 steps. Thereafter, carry the rear left side for 10 steps. Then carry the right front side on one's left shoulder for 10 steps and finally the right rear for 10 steps. Much reward is reported in Ahadeeth for carrying the janāzah for 40 steps. However, care should be taken and this method foregone if there is danger of inconveniencing others.

Mas'alah: Whilst it is *masnûn* to walk briskly with the janāzah, care should be taken not to jolt the body.

Mas'alah: It is best for those accompanying the janāzah to walk behind, not in front or at either sides.

Mas'alah: Those accompanying the janāzah should not recite any *zikr* or du'aa loudly.

Mas'alah: Those accompanying should not sit down before the janāzah is lowered from the shoulders.

Mas'alah: Those accompanying should not depart without first performing the janāzah salāh. However, after praying salāh one may depart after taking permission from those responsible for the mayyit.

Hadeeth:

> '*Whenever Nabee ﷺ accompanied any janāzah, he walked, commenting, 'I do not (ride) when Angels are walking.*'
>
> '*Whenever Nabee ﷺ accompanied any janāzah, he kept quiet pondering upon death in his heart.*'

(p64-6, Ahqām-e-Mayyat)

Janāzah Salāh

For a Muslim mayyit, Janāzah Salāh, which in reality is a du'aa (prayer), is Fardh Kifāyah. This salāh does not consist of any *ruku* or *sujood*, but has 4 Takbeers which take the place of 4 Rakāts.

Mas'alah: Jamā't (congregation) is not a condition for the validity of Janāzah Salāh. Hence, if even one person - man or woman - performs it, the Fardh obligation is discharged. However, the larger the Jamā't the better, because this is a du'aa wherein many Muslims gather to plea on behalf of the mayyit in the Court of Allah ﷻ. There is greater chance of Divine Acceptance and the showering of *Rahmat*.

Mas'alah: Two things are Fardh in Janāzah Salāh:

1) To recite *'Allahu Akbar'* four times.
2) Qiyām - to perform the Janāzah Salāh standing (unless one has a valid Sharee' reason for sitting).

Mas'alah: Three things are Sunnat in Janāzah Salāh:

1) *Hamd* - to recite Praises of Allah ﷻ.
2) *Durood* upon Nabee ﷺ.
3) *Du'aa* for the mayyit.

Mas'alah: Should any Muslim die on Jumu'ah (Friday) and it is possible to perform ghusl, kafn and janāzah salāh before Jumu'ah Salāh then one should do so. To wait merely in order to achieve a larger congregation after Jumu'ah Salāh is *makrûh* (reprehensible).

Mas'alah: Should the janāzah arrive at a time when any congregational Salāh is about to commence, then one should perform the Fardh and Sunan first and thereafter pray janāzah salāh.

Mas'alah: Should the janāzah arrive at time of 'Eed Salāh, first perform this salāh and then Janāzah Salāh.

Mas'alah: Unlike the 5 daily Fardh Salāhs, Janāzah Salāh is not governed by conditions of time. It could be performed at any time. While there are three Makrooh times wherein one should not perform any Nafl or Sunan Salāh, viz:

1) Sunrise 2) Zawwāl (mid-day) 3) Sunset

However, it is permissible to pray Janāzah Salāh even during these times according to the following rules:

1) If the Janāzah arrives or is ready for the Salāh precisely at the Makrooh time, the Janāzah Salāh should be performed immediately.

2) If the Janāzah arrives or is ready for the Salāt before the setting in of the Makrooh time, then it is Makrooh to delay the Janāzah Salāh for the Makrooh time. In this case, performance of the Janāzah Salāh in the Makrooh time is Makrooh Tahrimi.

3) Janāzah Salāh is permissible after the Asr Salāh.

(p 35, Kitabul Janā-iz)

Wearing Shoes in Janāzah Salāh

Nowadays, some people perform Janāzah Salāh wearing shoes. It is important to note that both their place of standing and their shoes should be *tāhir* (pure) otherwise their Salāh will not be valid. However, should anybody remove their shoes and thereafter stand upon them...only the top portion (which touch the feet) need to be *tāhir*, even if the soles of the shoes or the ground is impure. (p 63, Ahqām-e-Mayyat)

Validity of Janāzah Salāh

There are two types of conditions for the validity of Janāzah Salāh: firstly, those relating to the performer and secondly to the mayyit.

Performer of Salāh	Mayyit
1) Tahārat (purity)	1) Mayyit must be a Muslim (therefore it is not permissible to perform Janāzah Salāh for shiahs & qadianis)
2) Satr Awrat (covering of necessary portions of body)	2) The body & kafan of the mayyit must be tāhir (pure). Emergence of any najāsat after ghusl does not matter
3) Facing Qiblah	3) Covering of Wājib portions
4) Niyyat	4) Mayyit to be present in-front of those praying.
5) To recite Allahu Akbar four times	5) The mayyit should be upon the ground
6) Qiyām - unless there be a valid reason	6) Physical presence of the mayyit.

Mālik bin Hurayrah ؓ relates that Nabee ﷺ commented,

'Whichever Muslim servant passes away and 3 rows of Muslims perform Janāzah Salāh (asking du'aa for Maghfirat and Jannah) for him, then of a surety Allah Ta'ālā makes Maghfirat and Jannah compulsory for him.'

The Method of Janāzah Salāh

Ā'ishah ؓ relates that Nabee ﷺ commented:

'Upon whichever Muslim mayyit a large Jamāt totalling one hundred perform Salāh, and they all plea for (Forgiveness and Rahmat for) the mayyit in the Court of Allah, then of a surety this plea and du'aa of theirs is accepted.' (p85, Ahqām-e-Mayyit)

The Masnoon method of performing Janāzah Salāh is to place the mayyit in front with the Imām standing in line with the mayyit's chest. It is Mustahab to form 3 rows behind the Imām.

1) Niyyat (Intention)

The following Niyyat should be recited (or an intention, in whichever language, should be made in one's heart):

نَوَيْتُ اَنْ اُصَلِّىَ صَلٰوةَ الْجَنَازَةِ لِلّٰهِ تَعَالٰى وَ دُعَاءً لِّلْمَيِّتِ

'I make Niyyat of performing Salātul Janāzāh for Allah Ta'ālā and as a du'aa for the deceased.'

2) Takbeer & Thanā

As soon as the Imām calls out Takbeer, recite softly *'Allahu Akbar'* and raising one's hands to the ear-lobes, fold both hands as usual for other Salāhs. Now recite the *Thanā*,

سُبْحَانَكَ اللّٰهُمَّ وَ بِحَمْدِكَ وَ تَبَارَكَ اسْمُكَ وَتَعَالٰى جَدُّكَ وَ جَلَّ ثَنَاؤُكَ وَ لَآ اِلٰهَ غَيْرُكَ

3) Durood Ibrāheem

After Thanā, recite *'Allahu Akbar'* (without raising the

hands) and thereafter recite *Durood Ibrāheem,*

اَللّٰهُمَّ صَلِّ عَلٰى مُحَمَّدٍ وَّ عَلٰىٓ اٰلِ مُحَمَّدٍ كَمَا صَلَّيْتَ عَلٰىٓ اِبْرَاهِيْمَ وَ عَلٰىٓ اٰلِ اِبْرَاهِيْمَ اِنَّكَ حَمِيْدٌ مَّجِيْدٌ اَللّٰهُمَّ بَارِكْ عَلٰى مُحَمَّدٍ وَّ عَلٰىٓ اٰلِ مُحَمَّدٍ كَمَا بَارَكْتَ عَلٰىٓ اِبْرَاهِيْمَ وَ عَلٰىٓ اٰلِ اِبْرَاهِيْمَ اِنَّكَ حَمِيْدٌ مَّجِيْدٌ

'O Allah! Send Your Mercy upon Muhammad ﷺ and upon His progeny as You have sent Your Mercy on Ibrāheem and his progeny. No doubt, You are Great and Praiseworthy!

'O Allah! Send Your Blessings upon Muhammad ﷺ and upon His progeny as You have sent Your Blessings on Ibrāheem and his progeny. No doubt, You are Great and Praiseworthy!'

4) Du'aa

After Durood Ibrāheem, recite *'Allahu Akbar'* (without raising the hands) and thereafter recite a du'aa for the mayyit. If the mayyit is a bāligh (of age) male or female recite the following du'aa:

اَللّٰهُمَّ اغْفِرْ لِحَيِّنَا وَ مَيِّتِنَا وَ شَاهِدِنَا وَ غَائِبِنَا وَ صَغِيْرِنَا وَ كَبِيْرِنَا وَ ذَكَرِنَا وَ اُنْثَانَا اَللّٰهُمَّ مَنْ اَحْيَيْتَهٗ مِنَّا فَاَحْيِهٖ عَلَى الْاِسْلَامِ ۽ وَمَنْ تَوَفَّيْتَهٗ مِنَّا فَتَوَفَّهٗ عَلَى الْاِيْمَانِ

If the mayyit is a non-bāligh boy, recite:

اَللّٰهُمَّ اجْعَلْهُ لَنَا فَرَطًا وَّ اجْعَلْهُ لَنَا اَجْرًا وَّ ذُخْرًا وَّ اجْعَلْهُ لَنَا شَافِعًا وَّ مُشَفَّعًا

If the mayyit is a non-bāligh girl, recite:

$$\text{اَللّٰهُمَّ اجْعَلْهَا لَنَا فَرَطًا وَّ اجْعَلْهَا لَنَا اَجْرًا وَّ ذُخْرًا وَّ اجْعَلْهَا لَنَا شَافِعَةً وَّ مُشَفَّعَةً}$$

Mas'alah: If one cannot remember the du'aa for Janāzah Salāh, then recite the following:

$$\text{اَللّٰهُمَّ اغْفِرْ لِلْمُؤْمِنِيْنَ وَ الْمُؤْمِنَاتِ}$$

If this too is not possible, merely reciting the 4 Takbeers, *'Allahu Akbar'* will suffice because neither is *Durood* or du'aa Fardh but Masnoon.

Mas'alah: One should not raise the hands after Janāzah Salāh and make du'aa as it is makrooh and not an established Sunnah; the Janāzah Salāh itself is a du'aa.

Mas'alah: Janāzah Salāh is the same for both the Imām and Muqtadee (follower); the only difference is that the Imām will recite the Takbeers and Salām loudly. However, both will recite Thanā, Durood and du'aa softly.

Mas'alah: It is Mustahab in Janāzah Salāh to have 3 rows: to the extent that even if there be only 7 people; 1 will be the Imām; 3 will form the first row; 2 will be in the second row and only 1 person will form the third row.

Makruh to Perform Janāzah Salāh in Masjid

Mas'alah: It is Makrooh Tahrimi (reprehensible and not permissible) to pray Janāzah Salāh inside a Masjid wherein the 5 daily Salāhs, Jumu'ah or 'Eedain are performed irrespective of whether the mayyit is inside or outside.

Janāzah Salāt will be valid only if the body is present. Janāzah Salāt for a mayyit in another city/country is not valid.

Common Shortcomings

Question: When accompanying the janāzah, it is usually observed how people walk ahead of the janāzah and make zikr (especially of *Kaleemah Shahādah*) in a loud voice...please inform whether such practices are allowed in the Sharee'ah.

Shaykh Mufti 'Abdur Raheem Lajpoori replies, *'When accompanying the janāzah, one is allowed to make zikr silently (but not loudly). The making of loud zikr ahead or behind the janāzah is contrary to the teachings of Hadeeth and makroohe-tahreemi. Qays Ibne 'Ubaadah says that the Companions of the Prophet disliked the raising of voices upon three occasions; (at the times of) janāzah, war and zikr. It is mentioned in Fatāwā Sirājiyyah that (when accompanying the janāzah) to raise voices in zikr, recitation of the Qur'ān or in making any other remarks regarding death (wailing) is bid'ah (innovation). Other (authentic) books of jurisprudence are also unanimous on this issue (however to recite silently is permissible).*

What should be remembered is that janāzah salāh itself is a form of du'aa, in fact the best possible form of du'aa, for the deceased, and therefore to make a collective du'aa other than this is against the Sunnah. However, to make du'aa of forgiveness for the deceased following the burial, and to recite the Glorious Qur'ān and remit the reward thereof to the deceased is a practice consistent with the Sunnah and therefore preferable...'

(Fatāwā Raheemeeyah)

Burial

You have to depart from here one day,
Will be laid out in your grave one day,
Will show unto Allah your face, one day,
Now no longer waste in folly even one day,
One day we have to die, Death is ultimate,
Do whatever you wish, Maut is ultimate.

Mas'alah: Just as it is Fardh-e-Kifāyah to bathe and shroud a mayyit, similarly it is incumbent to bury the mayyit. If no one executes this duty, the whole community is sinful.

Mas'alah: To transport the mayyit from one town to another for burial is reprehensible. Burial should take place immediately after the Janāzah Salāh has taken place. There should be no unnecessary delay.

Types of Qabr (grave)

Nabee ﷺ did not allow graves to be high nor be embellished or furnished with bricks, stones, etc: all these acts are makrooh. Muslim graves should be left in their simple natural state and may be of two types:

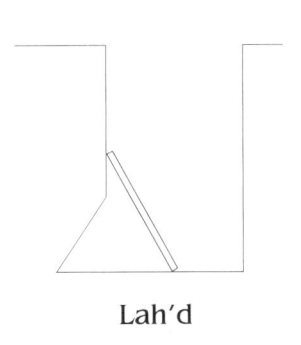

1) The Lah'd When the ground is firm, a shallow recess should be dug along the *qiblah* side of the grave at the bottom to allow the mayyit to be buried therein. The recess should then be closed with timber or unbaked bricks before soil is thrown into the grave.

Lah'd

2) The Shiq

This type of grave is recommended where the soft nature of the soil does not allow a Lah'd type recess.

A shallow trench is dug in the centre and the mayyit placed herein. Thereafter, this trench is covered with timber, before throwing of the soil.

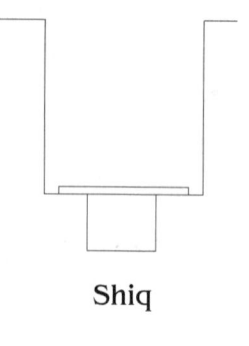

Shiq

Method of Lowering Mayyit into the Grave

1) The Janāzah should be brought and placed at the *qiblāh* side of the qabr whereby the *qiblāh* is towards the mayyit's right.

2) It is *mustahab* when burying a female to cover the burial with purdah...and should there be danger of exposure it is *wājib* to cover the mayyit.

3) A few people, say 3 or 4 (not necessarily an odd number) should descend into the grave, face the *Qiblāh* and receive the mayyit from several people outside. It is *mustahab* for all those handling the mayyit to recite:

بِسْمِ اللهِ وَ عَلَى مِلَّةِ رَسُوْلِ اللهِ

'In the Name of Allah and on the Deen of Rasoolullah (ﷺ).'

4) When the mayyit is laid to rest, it is *masnun* to turn the whole body unto its right side towards the *qiblāh* (**not merely the face**).

5) The outer strips of cloth (which had been tied to prevent the kafn from opening) should now be loosened.

6) After the mayyit is laid, the timber supports should be

laid. Any openings should be closed with sods of soil. Those inside should come out...and remember it is *makruh* to recite the Azān on these occasions.

7) Whilst throwing soil, it is *mustahab* to commence from the head side. Each person should try (without pushing or jostling others) to throw three handfuls of soil (with both hands). Whilst throwing, recite:

$$مِنْهَا خَلَقْنٰكُمْ وَفِيْهَا نُعِيْدُكُمْ وَمِنْهَا نُخْرِجُكُمْ تَارَةً اُخْرٰى$$

8) Only that amount of soil should be thrown into the grave which was initially extracted. To add extra is *makruh* when the grave becomes greater in height (off the ground) by 30 cm.

9) It is *mustahab* for the shape of the grave to be humped like a camel's back. After filling the grave it is *mustahab* to sprinkle water upon it.

After Tadfeen (Burial)

After burial, It is *mustahab* to recite the opening few verses of Surah Baqarah up to *Muflihoon* at the head side and the last ruku' of Surah Baqarah from *Aamanar Rasoolu* at the feet side. Whilst making du'aa at the graveside, the hands may only be raised towards *Qiblah* (not towards the grave).

After burying the mayyit, our beloved Nabee ﷺ and his Sahābāh ؓ used to pray for the success of the deceased in answering the question of *Munkir & Nakeer*. They also encouraged others to pray for their Muslim brother. It is *mustahab* to stay for a while at the graveside after burial and make du'aa for the mayyit; recite the Glorious Qur'ān and transfer *thawāb* to all Muslims.

How Should Du'aa be made in the Cemetery?

Question: *'What do our Respected Ulamā and Muftiyān-e-Kirām advise about the practice of lifting hands when making du'aa in the graveyard? Is it masnun or a bid'at? Should du'aa be made whilst standing or sitting and is it necessary to face the Qiblah? What is proven from Ahadeeth?'*

(Fatāwā-e-Raheemeeyah, no. 848, vol 3, p102)

Shaykh Mufti 'Abd'ur-Raheem Lajpoori ☙ replies, *'In the cemetery, to make du'aa with hands raised whilst standing and facing the Qiblah is amongst the etiquettes. Moreover, it is masnun and not bid'at, for it appears in Hadeeth, 'Nabee ☙ upon reaching the graveyard stood for a very long period of time after which he ☙ lifted his hands three times.'*

(Saheeh Muslim, p 313, Vol. 1)

Imām Nawawee ☙ comments, 'From this we may conclude that it is Mustahab to make a lengthy and recurring du'aa and, to lift the hands...also...to stand and make du'aa in the graveyard holds more excellence than to sit and make du'aa.'

(ibid.)

'When one intends to make du'aa, he should stand facing towards Qiblah.'

('Ālamgeer, p350, vol 5)

Hāfiz Badr-ud-Deen 'Ainee ☙ relates, 'It is amongst the etiquette's of visiting the grave to not sit down and, when making du'aa to face the Qiblah.' To sit facing another direction, and to make du'aa without raising the hands is also permissible. In brief, at the time of making du'aa in the graveyard, one should not adopt such measures whereby an onlooker may think this person is pleading from those entombed. Therefore, should one raise the hands at the time of du'aa, ensure one is facing the Qiblah.'

Chapter Five

Tajheez, Takhfeen & Tadfeen

An eye-opening analysis of the incorrect practices and customs enacted in our society on the occasions of bathing, shrouding, burial & condolence,

by

Shaykh Muhammad Saleem Dhorat

dāmat barakātuhum

Based upon a series of Jumu'ah Lectures delivered

at

Masjid-An-Noor, Leicester, UK

During Winter 1997 CE/ 1418 AH

﷽

$\mathcal{O}$ur beloved Rasoolullah ﷺ commented:

'The grave is either a garden from the Gardens of Paradise or a pit from the Pits of Hell.'

Respected 'Ulamā-e-kirām, elders and my young friends. Weddings and sorrows are two such occasions when Muslims generally transgress the limits prescribed by Allah ﷻ and His Rasool ﷺ. During times of happiness, the *aql* (intellect) becomes overpowered with joy, whilst on occasions of sorrow; the *aql* becomes overwhelmed with grief. Sometimes, being affected by happiness one is involved in disobeying Allah ﷻ, whilst at other times, being affected by sorrow one is involved in disobeying Allah ﷻ.

During these two occasions (of joy and grief), one should behave with resolution and instead of acting with emotion and fervour, one should act with farsightedness taking into cognition the rulings and decrees (*ahqāms*) of Allah ﷻ and His Rasool ﷺ. One should ponder upon these *ahqāms* and then with full attention and longing, act upon these directives of Allah ﷻ and His Rasool ﷺ ignoring any 'customary' rituals which may be in vogue.

Tajheez, Takhfeen & Tadfeen

On this occasion, I wish to draw attention towards the numerous malpractices that our society (*muaasharat*) enacts when somebody passes away: from before *tajheez* (bathing), *takhfeen* (shrouding) until well-after *tadfeen* (burial). There are no Qur'ānic *ahqāms* of Allah ﷻ, His Rasool ﷺ or examples from the lives of the Sahābāh ؓ or our Akābireen for these customs. Whenever somebody passes-away, we observe various rituals and customs that we have wrongly assumed to be acts connected to Deen…as if whatever is practiced constitutes Deen.

Accordingly it is necessary to ascertain, for whatever activity of life we undertake, whether the particular practise is in accordance with the Pleasure and Wishes of Allah ﷻ and His Rasool ﷺ. All modes of living that confirm should be practised and promoted, moreover all deeds which conflict with the *ahqāms* of Allah ﷻ and His Rasool ﷺ should not only be shunned but our family, friends and associates should also be discouraged and prohibited with polite and dignified advice (*mau'izat-e-hasanah*).

The Mahbub (Beloved) of Allah ﷻ

Allah ﷻ mentions in the Glorious Qur'ān:

> *'Say (O Muhammad ﷺ to mankind): 'If you (really) love Allah then follow me, Allah will love you and forgive you of your sins. And Allah is Forever Forgiving, Most Merciful." (3:31)*

If you are true in your claim of loving Allah ﷻ…and every claim has a proof, then the proof of this assertion is to make your entire life in accordance to the Seerah of Allah's Rasool ﷺ. One's appearance, dealings, character, social life, acts of worship all should confirm to those of Rasoolullah ﷺ. If you are able to do this, then not only will the love of Allah ﷻ become ingrained in your heart, but Allah ﷻ will also love you. 'Allamah Ibn Katheer ﷫ has related a couplet:

> 'It is no distinction if you should have somebody's muhabbat (affection), excellence is when you become somebody's mahbub (beloved).'

How should Muslims observe death?

At the time of death, when the *ruh* (soul) is about to depart, how should a Muslim observe this momentous event? Pangs and pains of regret upon *firāq* (separation) is a natural reaction, however, upon somebody's death, are sorrow and grief the only experiences? If we have true affection for the dying person, we should be more concerned about their welfare and well-being than ours. This is an extremely dangerous and precarious occasion; should a person depart without *Imān*, then he is doomed to everlasting failure. However, should the dying person depart proclaiming the *Kaleemah*, then it appears in a hadeeth:

> 'Whomsoever dies in the state whereby his heart testifies to 'There is no god but Allah and Muhammad is the Rasool of Allah,' then he will, of a surety, enter Jannah (with some narrations mentioning)… 'of a surety, Allah will forgive him.' (Virtues of Zikr, p105)

We are only concerned with ourselves: our sorrow; what will become of the children, the wife, relatives? etc. We fail to realise that by indulging and expressing in all these *khurafat* (futile baseless activities and talks) we are diverting the attention and heart of the dying person at a critical juncture, occasion and trial. Shaytān is launching his final, most intense and complete assault.

After burying the *mayyit*, Rasoolullah ﷺ and his Sahābāh ؓ would stand next to the grave and make du'aa for the *mayyit's* steadfastness in answering the questions posed by Munkar & Nakir. They encouraged others to do the same,

'Make du'aa of steadfastness for your brother.'

(Za'ad ul Mu'ad, p91, Ahqām Mayyit)

Sufyan Thawree ؒ has deduced from these du'aa's that after death, when the body is buried and the Angels pose questions, even here Shaytān is present attempting to mislead the Muslim. How is this proven? If the assault of Shaytān was only whilst alive, why did Rasoolullah ﷺ make the above du'aa? Some scholars have stated that even in the grave when the Angels are questioning, Shaytān tries to draw the servant towards him by saying, 'tell them I am your creator.'

The Effects of Suhbat (Companionship)

These are monumental trials, which is why a Muslim is willing to give up his life (in Jihād) to die in the state of Imān...yet we, out of naivety and emotionalism try to divert the dying person's attention away from the Creator towards creation. Relatives crying with a sorrowful posture...but is this true muhabbat? May Allah ﷻ protect us from such associates and environment at the time of death. What need is there for such people, who cajole the dying person to open his eyes and take a final look at his wife, children & mother? Whether the dying should recognise or speak to his relatives or associates is irrelevant; what is absolutely important is the fact that he should die with *kaleemah*. This will decide his future destiny: whether he goes to Paradise or Hell.

This is why our Ulamā have advised that when a person is dying, the character of those around him have an effect. Accordingly the *sulaha* (pious) should be summoned whereby their *suhbat* (companionship), piety and *barakah* have a beneficial effect and through their blessings the dying person departs with Imān. Moreover, the Ulamā have recommended that no such person should be present whose presence may divert the dying persons attention away from Allah ﷻ. Should the dying person insist on meeting his wife, children, brother, sister, etc, then our Ulamā suggest, that with affection explain to him his destination, 'you are going towards Jannah, you are going to meet Allah ﷻ, accordingly recite the *kaleemah, durood,* make *ruju* towards Allah ﷻ and you will meet all these associates in Jannah.' However, should the dying person be adamant and insist on meeting his children, wife etc., and an experienced person is able to conclude that the only way to incline this person towards Allah ﷻ is to allow him to meet them, then briefly usher them into his presence and thereafter quickly turn his *ruju* towards Allah ﷻ.

Our Custom

Nowadays, the thought of requesting a scholar or pious person to attend is not even envisaged. Every Tom, Dick and Harry is allowed to gather around: people of all gender with no regard for *purdah*. Whether the dying person departs with Imān or not appears to be irrelevant to us...we are only concerned with our wishes and customary practices. Whereas, Rasoolullah ﷺ advised:

> *'Remind your dying to recite the kaleemah,' (instead of instructing them, those around him should recite loudly 'Lā ilāha illallāh Muhammadur Rasoolullāh,' so that the dying person listens, then when he has recited, maintain silence).'*
>
> (Muslim quoted in Riyādhus Sāliheen, Vol. 2, p17)

Although we too make *talkeen* of the kaleemah, nevertheless the environment around our dying is quite another, hence how will the *kaleemah* register upon the dying person's tongue and mind? Mentally, his heart is still captivated with his wife and children...he begrudges their separation. The criterion for success in the Hereafter is recitation of the *kaleemah*...not whether his last act was the meeting with his loved one's.

We have to prepare the outlook of people, not only when a person is dying, but beforehand whereby such an environment is created which fosters enthusiasm in the heart of the *mayyit* to meet Allah ﷻ. Rasoolullah ﷺ commented,

> *'Whomsoever looks forward and is enthusiastic of meeting Allah, then Allah also looks forward to meeting him. Whomsoever dislikes meeting Allah, then Allah ﷻ also dislikes meeting him.'*
>
> (Narrated by 'Ubadah bin Thaamit ؓ, Muslim, p 139)

Observance of Purdah

At the time of death and thereafter, ensure full and complete observation of *purdah*. Only the mahrām of the deceased are allowed to view the body. Nowadays, our *muaasharat* has become so corrupted that the *janāzah* of men is placed in a ladies room where all class of females appear. Even after death, the *ahqāms* of *purdah* apply; ask the Ulamā as to who is allowed to view. However, our outlook is so retarded that when a person is informed of the Commands of Allah ﷻ and His Rasool ﷺ, for example, 'you are not allowed to view my mother or sister because you are not a mahram,' people are prepared to argue, dispute and break asunder close relationships!

The Need for Haste in Burial

After death, *tajheez* (bathing) and *takhfeen* (shrouding) should be performed as quickly as possible. If it is possible to bury the *mayyit* in the morning, one should not delay until late afternoon, for Rasoolullah ﷺ has emphasised:

> *'Make haste in burying the mayyit: because if it is the janāzah of a pious servant, then enjoin this goodness with its station quickly; and if it is the janāzah of an evil person then quickly dispose of such a load from your shoulders.'* (Bukhāri quoted in Riyādhus Sāliheen, Vol. 2, p28)

The Ulamā have stated, 'If a person dies on a Friday, it is better to make all arrangements and bury the deceased before the Jumu'ah congregational Salāh. Holding on to the prepared body with the thought that there will be more participants in the Janāzah Salāh after Jumu'ah is makrooh (detested).' Moreover, the blessings and *maghfirat* (forgiveness for the mayyit) that will be acquired in a few (even though it be a handful) praying Janāzah Salāh before Jumu'ah in accordance to the command of Rasoolullah ﷺ is not available in delaying the Janāzah Salāh for later, notwithstanding the greater number of participants.

Sometimes, on account of a certain relative being overseas and this person's inability to arrive quickly, for example because of unavailability of flight, *tadfeen* (burial) is delayed for up to two or even three days. The Sharee'ah has prohibited such a loathsome development.

The Responsibility & Benefit for Relatives

As far as the responsibility and duty of *tajheez, takhfeen & tadfeen* is concerned, close relatives should play a leading role. Many virtues and great importance for this has been related by Rasoolullah ﷺ in the ahadeeth. Our greatest benefit in undertaking these duties of bathing and shrouding the mayyit is awareness for one's own death; such consciousness that is not acquired by viewing either the Janāzah or grave. When one observes the mayyit: totally lifeless and helpless; unable to speak, indicate, rinse its mouth, alter sides, move its hands, urinate or obtain purity...totally dependent upon others. When this scenario beholds, a person's awareness (in his heart) of the fleeting and temporary nature of this world becomes complete, 'I too have to pass through this experience tomorrow.' This is why we should participate and be aware of the *mas'āeels* (rulings) related to these acts. Even if we are unaware, we should observe those who have knowledge and experience, especially on the occasions when our close one's are being bathed. This is our final act of *khidmat* (service) for our dear ones.

Death of a Relative - Best Opportunity for Taubah

Shaykh-ul-Hadeeth Zakariyyā ﷺ narrates, 'Consider the occasions when a relative passes away to be excellent opportunities to make *taubah* (repentance) and gain the Proximity of Allah ﷻ.' Why? Whenever we hear the death of a non-relative, we ponder for a few moments as if we have heard from one ear and then resume our worldly medley as if the news has disappeared through the other ear. However, when our father, wife, relative, shaykh, ustadh or other loved one dies, it affects our heart and mind continuously for months. For weeks, when we sit down to eat, food appears unpalatable...there is no relish. This is the very awareness of death which we have been told to remember in abundance in the hadeeth and which is experienced upon the death of a close one. On such occasions, to perform ibaadah, taubah and attain the Closeness of Allah ﷻ becomes very easy.

Taaziyah (Visiting to Console the Bereaved)

When one goes for *taaziyah* (consoling the bereaved), there should be no worldly nonsense; rather such talk and topics should be initiated whereby strength and encouragement are created in the hearts of the deceased. This is the entire purpose of *taaziyah*, which should permeate all facets of our behaviour, rapport, tone and attitude whereby the bereaves sorrow is lightened and his fortitude increases. However, our visits which start-off with the ubiquitous crying and wailing appear to serve the purpose of destroying whatever courage, steadfastness and resolution the bereaved have acquired. What need was there for you to cry so profusely? Seek a verdict from your heart and the answer will be *riya* – merely to show people. You were quite capable of controlling your emotions...yet that would have appeared uncaring and indifferent to the others present, so you unleashed a torrent of crocodile tears. Our Rasoolullah ﷺ sent a message of condolence to his beloved daughter Zaynab ؓ upon the death of her child,

> 'Undoubtedly, what Allah has taken belonged to Him, what He had given belonged to Him. Moreover, there is an appointed time by Him for everything (which may not be altered by lack of patience or scheming). Accordingly, be patient and have hope of reward.' *(Mishkhāt, Virtues of Du'aa, p323)*

If anybody were to lend us their car for a month and allow us to make usage of it freely and thereafter come after one month to reclaim the car, we do not experience any complaint in the heart. Rather we feel obliged and are grateful to the lender for kindly granting us the opportunity to drive his car...similarly, we need to firmly understand, that whatever we have is the Bestowal and Property of Allah ﷻ and, when we acknowledge this, we must also accept that He may recall his favour at any time He wishes. Just like the car owner...if he were to come after two weeks and request his car back, we would not object, it is his car and the free usage of it for even two weeks was a great favour. Similarly, our mother, father, children, wealth, business, whatever, all belong to Allah ﷻ. If He should allow us to make benefit and usage or reclaim it, in all circumstances Allah ﷻ is the owner.

> 'Undoubtedly, what Allah has taken belonged to Him, what He had given belonged to Him. Moreover, there is an appointed time by Him for everything (which may not be altered by lack of patience or scheming). Accordingly, be patient and have hope of reward.'

Whatever Allah ﷻ bestows is for a specified time…this life, children, wealth and business are not eternal or until Qiyāmah. Allah ﷻ Says in the Glorious Qur'ān:

> 'Who, when afflicted with calamity, say, 'Truly, to Allah we belong and truly, to Him we shall return.' 'They are those on whom are the Salawāt (blessings and forgiveness) from their Lord and, who receive His Mercy and, it is they who are the guided ones.' (2:156-7)

This small bountiful child of yours who has passed away, if not today, then either tomorrow, or the next day, month, year or decade, he would undoubtedly have left this world. In actual fact, it is a boon that he has left in the state of innocence because tomorrow on the Day of Qiyāmah he will arrive as a means of *shafā'at* (intercession) and take you into Paradise. This is the method of *taaziyah* (consoling the bereaved), however, we utter so much nonsense on such occasions as to perplex and aggravate the bereaved. To the widow, we say,

> 'O dear! How terrible, there is nobody to support you now, who will see to your needs now? What will become of your young children? O dear!'

What irresponsible behaviour! For the sake of *riya* we attempt to show the bereaved how grieved we are: this is the only reason we attend. Whereas what we should be saying is:

> 'Dear, do not fear…we are present, if you or your children need anything, we are at your service. Remember; to where your husband has departed we too have to go…either tomorrow or quite soon thereafter we

shall be meeting him there. He has died in the state of kaleemah and inshā'Allah gone straight to Paradise. He is now free from all worldly anxieties, pains, illnesses and inconveniences...he will be strolling and enjoying himself in Paradise at this moment. If you are undergoing pangs of separation, then you should maintain firmness, control and such effort over your nafs (self) and obedience to the Commands of Allah ﷻ that He raises you also with the kaleemah and grants you immediate entry into Paradise and meeting with the deceased. Understand well, should you fail to conduct your life properly on Seeratul Mustaqeem and disobey the Commands of Allah ﷻ then you will leave here without kaleemah...and such a person will enter Hell. Remember, if you enter Hell, you will not be able to meet the deceased.'

This is the type of sensible, intelligent, positive and affectionate talk which should be related: whereby greater courage and fortitude is created in the bereaves heart: whereupon their sorrow is transformed into happiness.

A New Form of Taaziyah ~ on 'Eed Days

Nowadays, a new form of *taaziyah* has appeared in our society...the custom of visiting the bereaved on 'Eed days. If there are the households of twenty relatives in our locality, it does not matter if we do not visit the houses of nineteen, but we must visit the home wherein there was a death within the past year. Moreover, we also have to transform their day of happiness into one of sorrow: 'alas, if the deceased had been present today it would be a very happy occasion.' The result of such drivel and folly is to bring tears to the widows eyes, witnessing which, her children too start crying. Remember well, nobody is forbidding visiting relatives whose close ones have passed away on 'Eed days...but this is an occasion of joy not another day of *taaziyah*. The entire purpose of visiting relatives on 'Eed days is to express happiness, therefore our purpose should be to change and lighten their sorrow with happiness.

The Ulamā have stated, '*taaziyah* for the bereaved is only *masnoon* for three days.' However, in our society, twenty or thirty people will gather for umpteen days, sitting well past midnight, drinking tea and talking about every topic possible. If anybody would boldly ask these people, 'why have you come?' All of them will reply, 'for *taaziyah*.'

Remember well, this world is the house of coming and going. Today, a Janāzah is coming out of this house, whilst tomorrow from that house...this is why our scholars advise us to quickly forget brooding over the event and engage ourselves in beneficial activities. After *tadfeen*, the bereaved should not sit around at home in expectation of welcoming those who arrive to pay their respects for more than three days. Accepted, there is leeway for people with valid reasons, e.g. they live far-off or overseas, to attend after three days to express their affection, but this is no licence to carry on the customary rituals for two or three weeks.

The New Custom of Mu'ānaqah in the Cemetery

Another new custom in vogue is the practice of making *mu'ānaqah* (embracing) and *musāfahah* (shaking hands) with the bereaved after *tadfeen* (burial) in the cemetery. A line of people awaits a short distance away from the grave to meet. Do such acts strengthen the bereaved or cause further sorrow and grief? Think rationally and intelligently, the poor soul is just climbing out of the grave having placed and thrown soil over his beloved's body grief stricken and, you wish to embrace, shake hands and unleash tears! We act in accordance with whatever appeals to our intellect. This is *riya*. We appear to have completely lost understanding of the Deen and its demands. I have observed many crying and hugging immediately after burial, yet just a few minutes later in the car park, the very same person is joking and smoking, totally care-free; what has happened to the mountain of sorrow that you displayed at the graveside, in front of everybody, a few seconds earlier? I have even observed such people, who chat and smile even as the *mayyit* is being buried, yet when meeting the bereaved, they show a mountain of sorrow thereby breaking the bereaves heart.

The Limits & Conditions of Feeding the Bereaved

Whenever there is a death in the household, the residents are naturally grieved. When news of the death of Sayyidina J'āfar ؓ arrived in Madeenah, our Nabee ﷺ, who was also his cousin commented,

> '*Prepare food for the household of J'āfar, for upon hearing this news they are in such a condition as not to able to concentrate on such matters as eating.*'
>
> (Tirmizee, Ma'āriful Hadeeth, Vol. 3, p464)

It is amongst the teachings of Deen for relatives to prepare and send food to the bereaved, however, like all matters limits and conditions apply here also. In our society, the prevailing custom in families is for each household to send food in order of rank. For example, if there are ten households in a clan, food will arrive firstly at midday from the residence of the eldest brother…not only for the immediate family of the bereaved, but for the whole ten families who will gather together to eat! Thereafter, in the evening, food for all ten families will arrive from the second brother's house and so on until food has arrived from every ten households! Is this a funeral or a wedding? Why are 50-100 people eating two meals together a day for up to a week?

We should indeed feed, but who has priority? Firstly, it is the responsibility of the closest relatives to feed those only in whose house the death has taken place. Secondly, a few members of the hosting household should join in and eat with the bereaved in order to encourage them to eat, otherwise if you just deliver the food and leave, they out of sorrow and grief may not eat. Thirdly, if the closest relative are unable to afford the expense of supplying food, any other person/s may undertake the expense…for in Islām there is no place for difficulties and pompous formality.

In our society, the ostensible reason why food is still being served after three days is the false notion that every household of the clan must supply a meal…with each family thinking, 'if we do not feed, what will people say?' Some families even aver, 'if we do not feed, then when such a tragedy hits our home, who will feed us?' This is the state of our *ikhlaas* and the colour of our *muhabbat* (love and affection). Every act is motivated by self-interest!

Collections & Eating at the Bereaved

In certain localities, a new trend is for each household (of a particular heraldry) to make a regular monetary contribution towards a fund, which caters for such occasions. Seek a verdict from the Mufti-e-kirām as to whether this is permissible. The Sharee'ah has taught us a simple method… what need is there then for a special collection and formality for this purpose? What great expense is involved in cooking a simple meal of rice and lentils for five to ten family members at the most?

Another incorrect and bad custom is for arriving visitors to the Janāzah from distant towns to eat only at the house of the bereaved despite there being numerous relatives and acquaintances in the locality. The Sharee'ah is advising us to feed the bereaved whereas we are eating from the bereaved!

Moreover, the food that is prepared by the 'leading' lights at the bereaves is from the inheritance of the mayyit. I have come to know that a fortnight after the funeral these prominent *khādims* present their bill of expenses to the bereaved to be paid from inheritance. Only the expenses of *tazheez, takhfeen & tadfeen* may be taken from inheritance, since when has it been possible to deduce the expense of feeding 300+ visitors? If there are non *baligh* (immature) children inheritors, then even their consent to this additional expense is not acceptable. Accordingly, in such a case, the 300-400 people who have dined have eaten *harām*.

Even if all the inheritors are *baligh* (mature), but permission has not been taken from every inheritor (and when is it ever taken? For the eldest brother assumes the 'seat' as head of the household); even then without permission from every inheritor to this additional expense, the food that has been eaten is *harām*. What are we doing in the name of Deen, affection and aid? There is absolutely no need for such expenses.

There are certain, quite commendable families living in the UK, who have the principle, that although it is okay to eat at weddings, we should never eat at the bereaves on occasions of death. They attend funerals, in distant towns with pre-packed lunches just like we arrange to take sandwiches for trips and journeys.

Death of the Daughter of Shaykh-ul-Hadeeth

When the respected daughter of Shaykh-ul-Hadeeth Zakarriyā passed-away, he was involved in teaching Hadeeth. Upon being informed of her death, he instructed, 'make preparations for *tajheez & takhfeen* and bring the *janāzah* outside the Madrasah so that I may lead the *janāzah salāh*.' Why, because he realised that the task he was undertaking would accrue *thawāb* for his daughter. Numerous akabireens, elders, friends, associates and well-wishers of Shaykh-ul-Hadeeth Zakarriyā were still alive and would wish to attend the funeral. However, he quickly wrote a few letters to these personalities with the instructions,

> 'Firstly, there is no need to undertake difficulty and inconvenience in making taaziyah...rather spend the time it would have taken you to visit me in recitation of

the Glorious Qur'ān and send its thawāb for the deceased.'

This is the demand of intelligence, to ascertain and enact what is beneficial for the Ākhirah.

'Secondly, the expenses you would have incurred in coming to-and-fro, donate this amount in the Path of Allah ﷻ and transfer thawāb for the deceased.'

The lesson from this episode is twofold: haste in burial and complete absence of formality. We need to act upon this example and encourage our loved ones and associates also. However, this is an era bereft of sincerity, moreover every person feels his presence should be noticeable…I must show my face to let it be known that, 'I attended.'

Delay in Commencing Janāzah Salāh

Another malpractice at funerals is the 'custom' of delaying the start of Janāzah Salāh, sometimes by up to 30 minutes! Acknowledged, the person who deliberately dallies and attends late should be penalised but why should the punctual attendee have to undertake the difficulty of waiting for such long periods huddled in the open in winter? Numerous people will arrive early and commendably form rows, amongst whom will be many who are ill, infirmed and aged. However, these poor souls end up waiting half an hour to accommodate the stragglers. Some of those waiting have difficulty maintaining their *wudhu*…I have personally witnessed a person, who after having waited patiently for 20 minutes, had to leave the row to make a fresh wudhu only to return and miss the Janāzah Salāh. I have witnessed another old-aged person, who after waiting for a lengthy period was reduced to tears at the discomfort and pain being experienced in the cold.

Accepted, Janāzah Salāh is *Fardh-e-kifayah* (a collective fardh), accordingly a wait of two to three minutes is understandable…however, this habit of always delaying the start has implanted the notion amongst the stragglers that even if we attend late, the Imām will wait for us, notwithstanding the inconvenience caused to the waiting 250 people. Not so is the case with the Imām who insists on starting upon time, when the public becomes aware of his punctuality, they too attend on time.

When the time of Janāzah Salāh is announced, numerous people take time-off from employment to attend, however they end-up returning late to work because of this unnecessary delay. This is a breach of promise by everybody involved…a very Indian and unintelligent practice of delaying the start of every activity.

This misconduct too needs to be addressed. How? When you are responsible for a Janāzah, make the announcement that Janāzah Salāh will commence *exactly* on time…without any delay for anybody. Moreover, encourage the Imām to commence on time, for many a time and place, the poor Imām is so under pressure that he is unable to commence until instructed from behind. Compare this delay with our behaviour in the masājid, when if the Imām should appear even two minutes late for Salāh, we begin to look around with disapproval.

Our Relationship with the Scholars

What does this attitude of ours confirm? It testifies to our misconception that the scholar should remain within our jurisdiction and control. When it is our desire and convenience that Janāzah Salāh should be delayed, then the Imām should appease and, when we desire Salāh in the masājid to be on time, again the Imām should pacify. This is precisely why when a particular Ālim, summons people towards the call of Haqq, whether it be sweet or bitter, people find it unpalatable and are antagonistic towards him, 'O this shaykh's a bit too strict!' However, the scholar who nods his head to whatever the laity wish: when they label something as halāl, he pronounces it halāl; when they label something as harām, he pronounces it harām; when they label something as permissible, he pronounces it permissible; when they say salāh should be performed at 1.00 pm, he consents, etc. As long as he appeases to our choice, then such a scholar is thought of as very civilised and of good character, whereas in reality, this is a crime and spiritual misappropriation.

May Allah ﷻ grant us correct Tawfeeq. The Ahl-e-Ilm (Ulamā, Aimma & Huffaz-e-kirām) are not advocating obeisance to themselves but to the *ahqāms* of the Sharee'ah. It is not a question of personal *hukumat*, for rulership belongs only to Allah ﷻ. Even if a scholar should advise you of anything which is against the principles of the Sharee'ah, then it is incumbent upon you to oppose him. An Ālim's standing and worth is only and until he speaks and conducts himself within the Light of the Sharee'ah: the Glorious Qur'ān and Hadeeth.

Walking Behind (not in-front) of the Janāzah

Immediately after the Janāzah Salāh, *tadfeen* (burial) should take place. It appears in a hadeeth of Bukharee wherein Baraa ibn Athib 🌸 narrates, 'Allah's Rasool 🌸 commanded us to walk behind the Janāzah.' Deducing from this hadeeth, our Ulamā have passed a decree that if in any locality, either all or the majority of people walk in front of the Janāzah, with none or very few people walking behind, then this practice is *makrooh*. Another common malpractice in our society, at this juncture, is for people to form long, long rows in front. Shaykh Mufti 'Abdur Raheem Lajpoori 🌸 has written in *Fatāwah-e-Raheemiyāh* that this practice is incorrect, because when rows are formed in front, consequently the majority of people proceed forward.

The correct method is for 5 to 6 people to proceed from behind the Janāzah and stand either side in front. Nevertheless, this malpractice of forming long rows is now so widespread that a cure seems incomprehensible. However, if the people reading were to make a firm intention to refrain from any deed or course of action which is against the Sunnah...and thereafter endeavour to pass on this knowledge to a few people, then slowly, slowly, such incorrect customs will be rectified. Our Ulamā have related *hikmats* of walking behind the Janāzah: firstly, constantly viewing it in front reminds us of our own death. Secondly, *ihtiraam*, whenever a person is respected, he is allowed to proceed in front. Therefore, we should make an effort to revive these Sunnahs.

Dr. 'Abdul Hayy 'Arifi ؒ relates, 'Another incorrect custom is that at the time of raising the *mayyit* onto the shoulders and during transport: those carrying recite the *Kaleemah Shahadat* loudly. Moreover, those accompanying also begin to recite the *kaleemah* loudly, whereas to do this or recite anything else loudly is not amongst the Sunnats of Rasool ﷺ. At this juncture, Rasoolullah ﷺ used to maintain silence.'

(p240, Ahqām-e-Mayyit)

Conducting Ourselves in the Cemetery

Another misfortune, quite prevalent, is our shocking behaviour whilst inside the cemetery...which does not appear to be too different to that outside: the same prattle and nonsensical talk. Scrutinise the behaviour of other cultures at their funerals. You will not find loud conversations or disrespect of the Janāzah...the very *taleem* advocated by our Sharee'ah. It appears we have totally forgotten and are indifferent to the stay in the grave and life in the Hereafter. It is related in Tirmizee Shareef, that when Sayyidina 'Uthmān ؓ visited or passed-by a grave, he would cry so profusely that his beard would become wet. Why, because he had understood and was convinced that he too would have to experience this *manzil*. Despite having knowledge, reading, listening, viewing and relating this reality, because we have not given it a place in the inner recesses of our hearts, such *naseehat* fail to make impact. Relates the poet ~

> 'When you observe being carried in the cemetery a Janāzah, do not think, 'it is somebody's Janāzah,' rather address yourself, 'after this will appear my Janāzah!''

This is a reality; our Janāzah will also be arriving after somebody else's Janāzah…none of us knows, for our *kafn* (shroud) or coffin may already have arrived in the shops.

The Purpose of Visiting the Cemetery

'Abdullah ibn Mas'ood ؓ narrates,

> *'Rasoolullah ﷺ commented, 'I had (previously) forbidden you from ziyaarat (visiting) the graves: now (I grant you permission) to visit the grave; because (the benefit is) it creates indifference to dunya and remembrance and concern for the Akhirah.'*
>
> (Sunnan Ibn Mājah, quoted in Ma'āriful Hadeeth, Vol. 3, p488)

The whole purpose of visiting the cemetery is to remember one's own death, however we go assuming our presence will be beneficial for the mayyit, increasing their rank and maghfirat. Moreover, these are the thoughts of the 'good' amongst us, because the only reason the 'not so good' attend is to ensure their names and presence is noted by the living bereaved. The proof for this claim? On a Sunday afternoon, when most people are free, an announcement is written on the Masājid notice board regarding Janāzah Salāh that very afternoon, but because the mayyit is not a relative or associate, we do not attend. However, when one of 'our' acquaintances passes-away, even in mid-week, we will take time off work to attend his funeral so that our presence is noted. Remember well, the rich and the poor; the king and the subject; the Imām and the follower; the famous and the unknown; all are sleeping together…no differences. Since the death of my Respected Father (Shaykh Hāfiz Ibrāheem ؒ) I have made it a practice every Jumuʻah to visit the cemetery, which is a barren field, with nobody else in sight. We should derive lesson from this spectacle. This is why the eminent scholar Shaykh Yazeed ar-Raqqasee ﷺ commented,

> 'Whomsoever passes a grave and fails to heed lesson, then this person is no human but an animal.'

Our tongues should be completely closed except for the recitation of the Glorious Qur'ān, thikrullah, istighfaar and duʻaa-e-maghfirat for oneself and the deceased.

Spectacle of the Grave

Rasoolullah ﷺ had observed Hell also, yet he says, 'I have not observed a more terrifying sight than the period of the grave.' In a hadeeth of Ibn Majah, Anas bin Malik ﷺ narrates from Baraa ibn Athib ﷺ,

> 'We accompanied Rasoolullah ﷺ in the burial of a janāzah. Rasoolullah ﷺ proceeded towards a grave and cried so profusely that the ground became wet and He advised, 'Brothers! Make preparations for this (i.e. to enter the grave).' *(Virtues of Sadaqah, p455)*

On another occasion,

> 'Rasoolullah ﷺ passed-by a gathering from where the boisterous noise of laughter emanated. Rasoolullah ﷺ commented, 'In your gatherings also mention the destroyer of delights.' The Sahābāh ﷺ inquired, 'O Rasoolullah ﷺ, what is the destroyer of delights?' Rasoolullah ﷺ replied, 'Death!' *(ibid., p458)*

Contrast this with our behaviour in the cemetery, wherein we talk worldly nonsense, some even resort to futile and immoral conversations whilst the *mayyit* is being lowered into the grave! How distant we have become from the Ākhirah; this laughter, this indifference, for how long? These smiling teeths will fall onto the chest and this face will lose its features within days. The eyes will fill with pus and nothing will remain except bones. Today we sit resplendently under lights and frills, tomorrow; we will be all alone in darkness and solitude. Aboo Hurayrah ؓ narrates,

> 'We accompanied Rasoolullah ﷺ in the burial of a janāzah. Rasoolullah ﷺ proceeded towards a grave and commented, 'Not a day passes wherein the grave eloquently and clearly makes an announcement, 'O son of Adam! You have forgotten me? I am the abode of loneliness; the abode of forlornness; the abode of terror; the abode of insects; the abode of extreme constriction except for the person for whom Allah ﷻ makes me spacious.' (Thereafter, Rasoolullah ﷺ commented), 'The grave is either a garden from the Gardens of Paradise or a pit from the Pits of Hell.' *(ibid., p454)*

Journey of the Ākhirah & Journeys of this World

When we visit the cemetery, how truly concerned are we about the mayyit? Do we show the same concern for their concern in the Hereafter as we do when a relative makes a journey to some distant land in this world? If their passport or visa are not in order or luggage is excessive, we do not feel contented until they have reached their destination and phoned to confirm their safe arrival. Such anxieties and worries for well over twenty-four hours for a worldly journey; compare this with our behaviour over the mayyit's departure to the first station of the Ākhirah. If he or she is successful in the grave, all forthcoming stages will be easy.

This is why the famous companion 'Amr ibn-al 'Aas ؓ bequeathed his sons,

> 'When you have buried me, then stay at my grave for so long as it takes to slaughter, skin, cut and distribute the meat of a camel...so that your presence (and recitation of the Glorious Qur'ān) encourages, strengthens and aids me in the trial of answering questions (of Munkir & Nakīr).' (Muslim, quoted in Riyādhus Sāliheen, Vol. 2, p31)

Contrast this with our behaviour at the graveside, whilst du'aa is taking place, some people will talk away, whilst others will only bother to make the du'aa that the Imam is making...nothing extra. Ask from Allah ﷻ; these occasions when our sister, brother, father, mother, other relatives and friends have been buried are times of strengthening our bond with Allah ﷻ. This is precisely why we have arrived here, to ask *maghfirat* for ourselves and for our Muslim brother and sister...

> 'O Allah! We are sinners and not worthy of asking for forgiveness, however O Allah, you accept the du'aa of the absent for the absent...therefore accept our plea on their behalf. O Allah! You are Gracious, ease all of their stages in the grave and the Ākhirah.'

If with sincerity we make du'aa for the mayyit out of brotherly affection and concern for the Ākhirah, then we may hold complete confidence in the Mercy of Allah ﷻ of having our plea accepted. May Allah ﷻ grant all of us correct understanding and Tawfeeq.

Āmeen

Shaykh Muhammad Saleem Dhorat
dāmat barakātuhum

These inspiring Lectures and many others are available on audio-tape & CD from

Da'wah Book Centre

Berners Street, Highfields, Leicester, UK, LE2 0FU
Tel: 0116 210 7949 ~ Fax: 0116 242 5016
www.idauk.org

ಸಾಡಾ

Riyādul Jannah

is a monthly journal which will appeal to Muslims from all walks of life. It promotes a greater understanding and awareness of the Qur'ān and Sunnah. For details visit:
www.riyaduljannah.com

ಸಾಡಾ

Shaykh Ihtishām-ul-Haqq Thānwi ﷺ relates, 'Friends of Allah ﷻ state that man arrives in this world crying, whilst all those around him rejoice. One should live such a noble and blessed existence according to the Sunnah of Nabee ﷺ, whereby at the time of your departure, you leave with joy whilst all around mourn your loss.'

Chapter Six

Abode of Prosperity

*An Abridged Lecture
of*
Shaykh Ashraf 'Ali Thãnwi ﷺ

Herein Bounties of the Ãkhirah are related in order to comfort the bereaved and alert us to the everlasting nature of the life to come.

*This lecture was delivered on
16th Sha'ban 1337 AH
(corresponding to 16-05-1919)
at Muzaffar Nagar, India,
and was originally transcribed in Urdu
by*
Shaykh Zafar Ahmad 'Uthmãni ﷺ

إِنَّ فِىْ ذٰلِكَ لَآيَةً لِّمَنْ خَافَ عَذَابَ الْآخِرَةِ ۚ ذٰلِكَ يَوْمٌ مَّجْمُوْعٌ ۙ لَّهُ النَّاسُ وَذٰلِكَ يَوْمٌ مَّشْهُوْدٌ ۝ وَمَا نُؤَخِّرُهٗۤ اِلَّا لِاَجَلٍ مَّعْدُوْدٍ ۝ يَوْمَ يَاْتِ لَا تَكَلَّمُ نَفْسٌ اِلَّا بِاِذْنِهٖ ۚ فَمِنْهُمْ شَقِىٌّ وَّسَعِيْدٌ ۝ فَاَمَّا الَّذِيْنَ شَقُوْا فَفِى النَّارِ لَهُمْ فِيْهَا زَفِيْرٌ وَّشَهِيْقٌ ۝ خٰلِدِيْنَ فِيْهَا مَا دَامَتِ السَّمٰوٰتُ وَالْاَرْضُ اِلَّا مَا شَآءَ رَبُّكَ ۚ اِنَّ رَبَّكَ فَعَّالٌ لِّمَا يُرِيْدُ ۝ وَاَمَّا الَّذِيْنَ سُعِدُوْا فَفِى الْجَنَّةِ خٰلِدِيْنَ فِيْهَا مَا دَامَتِ السَّمٰوٰتُ وَالْاَرْضُ اِلَّا مَا شَآءَ رَبُّكَ ۚ عَطَآءً غَيْرَ مَجْذُوْذٍ ۝

(103) Indeed in that (there) is a sure lesson for those who fear the torment of the Hereafter. That is a Day wherein mankind will be gathered together, and that is a Day when all (the dwellers of the Heavens and the earth) will be present. **(104)** And We delay it only for a term (already) fixed. **(105) On the Day when it comes, no person shall speak except by His (Allah's) Leave. Some among them will be wretched and (others) blessed. (106)** As for those who are wretched, they will be in the Fire, sighing in a high and low tone. **(107)** They will dwell therein for all the time that the heavens and the earth endure, except as your Lord wills. Verily, your Lord is the Doer of whatsoever He intends (or wills). **(108)** And those who are blessed, they will be in Paradise, abiding therein for all the time that the heavens and the earth endure, except as your Lord Wills: a gift without an end.'

(Ayah 103-8, Sûrah 11, Hûd, Juz 12)

Introduction

Allah ﷻ mentions in these Ayahs of the Glorious Qur'ān the Day of Qiyāmah (Judgement): wherein every person will be rewarded in accordance to his deeds. Therein will be two groups of people, *shaqee* (wretched) and *sa'eed* (blessed). The wretched will scream in *Jahannam* (Hell) until and unless Allah ﷻ decides otherwise, whilst the blessed will abide in *Jannat* (Paradise).

I wish to draw attention to the error of those people who consider all pleasure to exist only in *dunya* (world) and that the Ākhirah, especially the grave, is an empty abode and no more. Because people are unaware of the *nemats* (bounties) of the Hereafter, they only comprehend and understand the openness and extensiveness of *dunya* and fail to appreciate pleasures of the Ākhirah.

Even those who posses knowledge, due to lack of *istehzaar* (awareness), they fail to take heed. Admittedly people do contemplate upon *Jannah* after *Qiyāmah*, but between death and *Qiyāmah* they consider the confines of the grave as everything, whereas in reality it is only a home for the physical body. Although our *rûh* (souls) has a relationship with the grave, nevertheless, it is not confined here.

Remember, relationship is one concept and confinement is quite another. Ponder, this earth has a relationship with the sun whose light illuminates the whole planet, but is the sun confined by earth? Of course not, the sun is umpteen times the size of earth; similar is the similitude of our *rûh*. You will have observed the reflection of the sun in a tumbler of water, but is it possible to claim that the glass contains the sun? Another example is our image in a mirror, which although reflecting our body does not contain it. After death, similar is the relationship between the *rûh* and body wherein the latter is confined to the grave whilst the soul is not, and the importance for a human is his *rûh*. Should a person not be buried in a grave but be eaten-up by a flesh eating animal (Allah Forbid), one will say his body has been eaten not his soul. Therefore, to consider the grave as a confine for the human is incorrect, it is merely an imprisonment for the physical body. Should someone not be buried, why will his body escape this confinement? Therefore, fully understand, the soul is not imprisoned by the grave.

Generally, people only reflect upon this restriction of the grave and those who do posses *ilm* (knowledge) they too wrongly assume and allegorise the vastness of the Hereafter as that of some barren African plain. We never ponder upon the infinitely superior quality of fruits, palaces, gardens and delights which awaits the *Mu'min* in the Ākhirah. This failure to reflect upon these nemats is the general cause for our dislike of the Ākhirah, because the majority of people only incline towards pleasures. Very few people ponder upon the Hereafter solely as to gain the *Qurb* (closeness) of Allah ﷻ, this is why He mentions...

> '...*And for this let (all) those strive who want to strive (i.e. hasten earnestly to the obedience of Allah).*' (83:26)

Rasoolullah ﷺ advised,

> '*The world is the abode of a person who has no home; it is the wealth of the person who has no wealth. He who has no*

intelligence accumulates the wealth of the world (i.e. more than what is necessary).' (Hayātul Muslimeen, p 185)

Accordingly, Allah ﷻ says,

'And those who are blessed, they will be in Paradise...'

In everyday terminology, *Jannah* refers to Gardens, whilst in the preceding Ayah,

'As for those who are wretched, they will be in the Fire...'

This Glorious Qur'ān of Allah ﷻ is so perfect that in both cases, the mere usage of one word (Jannah and Fire) beautifully conveys the whole concept and teaching to us. By *Garden* is implied, trees, flowers, fruits, shade, cool breeze, stream...now adjoin the term to the Garden of Allah ﷻ, obviously it will be no ordinary garden. Even in dunya, stately and royal gardens contain numerous landscape features, ornaments and pavilions of delights. Obviously the Garden of Allah ﷻ will contain infinitely more, which the blessed will receive, therefore do not consider the Mu'min after death to be forlorn...they are enjoying unimaginable comforts. Previously, this concept was ingrained in the minds of Muslims, whilst nowadays our behaviour conveys the impression for which the *kuffar* are synonymous...

'O you who believe! Be not like those who disbelieve (hypocrites) and who say to their brethren when they travel through the earth or go out to fight: 'If they had stayed with you, they would not have died or been killed,' so that Allah may make it a cause of regret in their hearts...' (3:156)

Why? Because the *kuffar* regard this worldly life as

everything, they are totally oblivious of the Ākhirah and the life to come. Their similitude is like that of an insect, which lives beneath a rock and regards the heavens, earth and everything to be contained in this one rock.

Negligence

Jalaalud-Deen Rûmi ⚛ has beautifully highlighted this ignorance of ours by relating the story of a bedouin whose locality was struck with drought. His wife noticing his inactivity suggested in desperation, 'Why do you not go to the Caliph of Baghdad who is renown for his generosity? It is just possible that one favour of his could completely transform and cure our poverty.' The bedouin replied, 'Indeed you have made a good suggestion, however we should take along an appropriate gift.' His wife suggested, 'Well the whole country has been suffering from a drought for quite some time, however our local stream still has some famous mineral water, I am sure it will be well appreciated by the Caliph for when will he have ever tasted such water?'

Accordingly, his wife carefully sealed a water-container, which the bedouin balanced on his head all the way to Baghdad: across deserts and jungle. Eventually, he arrived at the palace gates and requested an audience with the Caliph in order to present a precious gift. The Caliph ordered he be permitted entry and in-walked our bedouin with the pot upon his head...

Caliph: 'O Respected Bedouin! What gift do you bring?'

Bedouin: 'Your Majesty! I bring water from Jannah!'

The Caliph opened the seal...the result of which was to fill the whole Royal Court with the foul smell of putrefied water. However, this Caliph had been blessed with such sagacity and magnanimity by Allah ﷻ, that not a flicker of disapproval was noticeable upon his face. And, therefore, none from the Court officials had the courage to raise their noses in disgust. The Caliph thanked the bedouin; 'Indeed you have brought a unique gift.' He then ordered the bedouin be housed and treated hospitably in the Royal Visitors Lounge, and his pot be filled with jewels as appreciation. Also at time of departure, the bedouin be taken along the Royal embankments on the River Tigris so he himself realizes that the Caliph was not in need of his gift...as he enjoyed much cleaner fresher water upon his own doorstep! Consequently, as the bedouin was escorted away from the palace carrying his pot of jewels...along the river, at every step his feet began to tremble and sink...

> *'Allahu Akbar! The Caliphs acceptance of my 'gift' was indeed his sagacity...and his filling of my pot with jewels is akin to the magnanimity of Allah ﷻ, 'Verily, Allah will change their evil for good deeds."*

Beloved, in the same way this bedouin was ashamed to call his gift 'water' upon observing the River Tigris, similarly by Allah ﷻ, when we observe *nemats* of the Ākhirah, we shall be ashamed to call pleasures of this world as nemats. We are unaware of the bounties of the Hereafter, this is why when we eat mangoes, watermelons, etc., we remember our deceased and say, 'O, he is not present to eat with us.' Wallah! Leave aside eating, our Mu'min brothers in the

Ākhirah do not wish to even look at worldly fruits. Many people, even those well-learned, have the habit of gifting (to charity) items which were the favourite of their deceased...on the assumption that because they are not here to enjoy them, at least by donating the same item its reward will reach them. As proof, they furnish the Ayah:

> 'You shall never attain righteousness unless you spend from what you love. And whatsoever you spend, Allah is fully aware of it.' (3: 92)

The Deceased Receive Thawāb

However, this Ayah actually implies spending of one's own treasured item not that of the deceased, as there is greater *ikhlaas* (sincerity) in this. Undoubtedly, by spending in charity, the deceased receive reward ~

> 'It is neither their meat nor their blood that reaches Allah, but it is piety from you that reaches Him...' (22:37)

Here Allah ﷻ has made clear, that it is not meat of the *Qurbani* (sacrificed) animal which reaches Him, rather your sincerity, and should you wish, its reward to the deceased.

Comparing Nemats

The reason why so many of us fail to appreciate the value of thawāb is that we are not aware of the nemats of Jannat and compare them to worldly items, whereas in reality they are similar in name only. For example, there will be goblets in Jannah,

> 'Crystal-clear, made of silver. They will determine the measure thereof (according to their wishes).' (76:16)

These have no resemblance to glassware here in dunya, for

when is it possible to look straight through worldly silver? Consequently, we wrongly desire that our deceased should still be here with us, whilst they desire we be with them! Allah ﷻ alone knows what there is here which so infatuates us? Heavenly nemats may be appreciated from ahadeeth, for example, one Hadeeth describes the head covering of *Hûrs* (Heavenly Damsels) to be so exquisite that should only one portion appear in this world, both the sun and moon would be eclipsed. These *hûrs* are so elegant their beauty radiates even under seventy layers of clothing. Similarly, the soil of Jannah is made of jewels and musk whilst *Hauth-e-Kauthar* (the Lake gifted to Prophet Muhammad ﷺ) has been described as ~

'Whomsoever takes a drink thereof will never again experience thirst.' (Dunya & Ākhirah, p 537)

A further joy will be inclination towards and pleasure in it even when not thirsty...this is impossible in any worldly drink. Imagine all nemats upon these few examples and understand the similarity between Heavenly and worldly bounties to be in name only. Therefore, to desire our beloved to be present today with us is nothing other than absurdity, in all probability if worldly nemats were to be placed in front of them now they would vomit in disgust.

Placing Flowers upon Graves

I mentioned this to a person, who although a student of Hajji Imdādullah Makki ﷺ, was involved in *simaa & urs* (incorrect customs). Upon arrival in Gangoh (India) he visited and placed some roses on the grave of Shaykh 'Abdul Quddus ﷺ.

Thereafter he visited me and hung a garland of flowers around my neck; 'I bring these from a garden because like Shaykh you too are beloved to me.' I replied, 'You have made a big mistake in placing flowers upon the grave because one of two conditions exists. His soul is either able to perceive or not. If not, then what benefit is there in placing flowers? Moreover, if it can discern, then tell me what comfort would it provide to a person who enjoys the fragrances and comforts of Jannah? Comparatively speaking, worldly flowers would only discomfort him.'

Once this principle is understood, all nemats of this world will appear insignificant in front of the luxuries of Jannah. Another difference to remember is that all worldly nemats eventually rot and emit such odour, which is nauseating, a feature unknown in Jannah. Therein whatever you desire, eat to your content...and with one pleasant burp or scented sweat all food and drink will be digested. There will be no urine or faeces; therein is no discomfort of any sort. This is why some Ulamā have written that Prophet Ādam ﷺ was forbidden from eating of that tree in Jannah which belonged to this world and had been placed as a trial, because eating fruit of this tree would produce stool...and there is no place in Jannah for impurity. Upon eating, the need arose for Ādam ﷺ to visit toilet. Therefore the Order was issued, 'Depart from Jannah for dunya wherein you may defecate!' Accordingly, his removal from Jannah was for this reason not as reproach, for when is a beloved ever reprimanded?

Consequently, our desire of wishing worldly nemats for our deceased is completely incorrect for they are enjoying such blessings, which we have never ever dreamt or thought. Yet, our limited imagination still desires quite ordinary items for ourselves and loved one's.

For example, once a chain-smoker asked Shaykh Muhammad Ya'qûb ﷺ, 'Will a match be available in Jannah to alight a pipe?' This is the curse of smoking, that even the blessed hours of early morning, which is a time of worship for the pious, is wasted by the smoker in scrounging for a light and puffing smoke into mouth, nostrils and stomach. In reality, these are features of a *Jahannamee* (person in Hell) which some naive people also wish to experience in Jannah!

Amazing Fruits of Jannah

The result of this ignorance is failure to reflect upon the nemats of Jannah, this is why we are so enamoured and captivated by worldly comforts. It is related in some Kitabs, that fruit will be presented to a *Jannatee*, he will peel the fruit, wherein a beautiful *hûr* will appear. Do not be surprised at this, even in dunya, certain chefs concoct exquisite and surprising dishes. Once a noblemen's chef served what appeared to be quite a frugal meal to two distinguished visitors, who upon eating the few pieces of bread and curry were requested to eat the plates and tablecloth. Insulted, the visitors retorted, 'What, how dare you tell us to eat such things!' Immediately, the cook pleaded, 'Sire! It is a special dish, do break and taste it.' Upon 'breaking' and tasting it was found to be a delicious dessert consisting of cream whilst the tablecloth turned out to be sweet *roti*. Whilst such fanfare is occasionally witnessed by the wealthy in dunya, it will be a daily experience in Jannah, therefore do not consider one's deceased to be deprived. Our Muslim brethren enjoy such comfort in the Ākhirah that they desire we too be with them. Accordingly, Allah ﷻ states in the Glorious Qur'ān:

> 'And never take those killed in the way of Allah as dead. Rather, they are alive, with their Lord, well-provided, happy with what Allah has given them of His grace; and they feel pleased with the good news, about those who, after them, could not join them, that there shall be no fear for them nor shall they grieve. They feel pleased with blessings from Allah, and grace, and with the fact that Allah would not let the reward of the believers be lost.' (3:169-171)

The Ākhirah is better than dunya

Now conclude, is our view better or those of Ahl-e-Jannah? Undoubtedly they are correct in saying we should join them. Allah ﷻ says:

> 'Nay, you prefer the life of this world. Although the Hereafter is better and more lasting.' (88:16-17)

We should desire to be with them and not wish they be with us, therefore forget worrying about the deceased and be concerned about meeting them. This concept was beautifully conveyed by a bedouin to 'Abdullah ibn 'Abbās ؓ upon the death of his father:

> 'O Ibn 'Abbās! Adopt sabr for observing you patient will enable us to be sābir, because the patience of followers is dependent upon the sabr of leaders. And why should one not be patient? For reality is that in the departure of

> *'Abbās, there is no loss for either of you. You will receive reward for his separation which is better for you than the presence of 'Abbās; and he has received Allah ﷻ in departing from you...which is undoubtedly infinitely better for him.'*

'Abdullah ibn 'Abbās ؓ relates that no body else had comforted him in such a manner, because the reason why we feel so much sorrow is we never really reflect upon the Ākhirah. The proof for this claim is that if we did, then undoubtedly we would not keep on remembering about our deceases daily rituals.

Natural sorrow and pangs of separation aside, we should be pondering upon their enjoyment and comfort in *Jannah* and desire that we join up with them. Ponder, if our child was made mayor of a capital city, would we desire that he should not have left us to go there or would we cherish to be present in the capital to physically observe him enjoying the splendour, glory and pomp of his office? Undoubtedly, we would wish to be present with him, then why do we desire our deceased to be still present with us and why do we not long to be in Jannah with them? The whole problem is we have understood dunya to be everything and this is why we do not yearn for the Ākhirah.

Jannat is Free from Distress

> *'...Therein you shall have (all) that your inner-self desires, and there you shall have (all) for which you ask. An entertainment from (Allah), the Oft-Forgiving, Most Merciful.'* (Glorious Qur'an, 41:31-2)

It appears in Hadeeth that some people will desire to farm in Jannah. Allah ﷻ will Reply, 'O Ibne Ādam, you are indeed greedy, what need is there for farming in Jannah?' The servant will reply, 'O Allah ﷻ, it is a heartfelt desire of mine.' Immediately, a plantation will blossom in front of him and the crop will be harvested and sorted right before his eyes.

Even before Qiyāmah, the Mumins *rûh* will reside in the form of green birds, which will nest within lanterns suspended under the *Arsh* (Throne) of Allah ﷻ. This will allow the Soul to fly to whatever place it wishes. These are the comforts of the Ākhirah for which the Close Friends of Allah ﷻ long. Accordingly, Nabee ﷺ commented,

> 'What relationship have I with this world? My similitude with the world is like a traveller with a tree under which he halts after a tiresome journey. He halts a while under the shade of the tree and then leaves it again to continue his journey.'

Now, is our condition not worthy of regret in that we are totally infatuated with this dunya although everybody is certain of his or her departure from dunya, yet we still inculcate its love in our heart.

The reason for this is nothing other than the thought and understanding amongst people that after death we are laid to rest all alone in a narrow confine. Thinking of this loneliness is abhorrent to us: whereas in reality this forlornness will be a means of comfort; wherein such pleasures will be experienced by Allah ﷻ, which are unattainable and unimaginable elsewhere. Ask those Friends of Allah ﷻ who have adopted aloofness, what pleasure there is in solitude... they have absolutely no interest in meetings, gatherings and association, therefore to consider loneliness in the grave as frightening is incorrect.

It appears in Hadeeth, when a Muslim dies, his *rûh* departs for *'Alame Arwāh* (Abode of Souls) wherein all the other Souls warmly receive him and inquire of their relatives which this *rûh* has just left behind. Thereafter, one of them comment, 'Let him rest, he has arrived fatigued from dunya.'

When my beloved grandmother was about to die, she observed our Nabee ﷺ who commented, 'Come with me, the road is clear, you have nothing to fear.' Therefore, from ahadeeth and occurrences it is obvious that loneliness ceases upon death and the Muslim's Soul is able to meet Nabee ﷺ and other relatives, friends and associates in *'Alame Arwāh*. Therein is such happiness unimaginable to us here in dunya. Allah ﷻ Says ~

> 'No laghw (dirty, false, evil vain talk) will they hear therein, nor any sinful speech (like backbiting). But only the saying of: Salām! Salām! (Greetings with peace)!' (56:25-6)

To feel sorrow, pain and grief upon the death of a beloved is beyond one's control and condoned. Therein is *Hikmat* (Divine Wisdom) that the Mu'min achieves *tawajju illallah* (inclines towards Allah) and thawāb. However, to constantly brood and tear out one's heart in grief is reprehensible.

Whenever, there is a bereavement (or sorrow), I always prescribe the following. Never, never keep on refreshing the calamity, for whilst both sorrow and grief have a beginning and are beyond one's control, their continuation are largely due to constant thinking and brooding over the misfortune.

Nowadays, when somebody passes away, all visitors will inquire separately, especially women, who upon arrival will embrace the bereaved lady. This poor soul is one and has already suffered and cried, now 100 females will hug her, cry once themselves but make her cry and hurt her heart another 100 times! This is totally ridiculous. Whenever, I go for Ta'aziyah, I advise,

> 'Brother! Whatever was destined to happen has happened. Crying and wailing will not bring back the deceased...therefore of what benefit is there in continuing this brooding?
>
> Practice those Āmal (good deeds) which will be of benefit to both you and them. Recite the Glorious Qur'ān and bless rewards to them. Pray Nafl Salāh, recite Allah, Allah (i.e. make Zikr) and bestow its rewards to them.
>
> Make du'aa for them and ponder, 'they have reached Jannah, wherein there is more comfort and rest than here. Now after some time, quite soon, we too are to depart for there and meet up with them."

This is precisely the method of positive approach shown in the Hadeeth and by our Fuqahā...that people of the locality should not visit for the purpose of bereavement after three days to avoid brooding, yes, outsiders are exempt.

Reality of Sa'ādat (Good Fortune)

Rasoolullah ﷺ commented:

'A Believer is to be marvelled because every condition of his is good. This is exclusive to the Believer, If he attains happiness he makes shukr (is thankful) and if calamity overtakes him, he adopts sabr.' (Sharee'ah &..., p 70)

By Allah ﷻ, your deceased is in a better condition, should you wish to learn of their comfort in detail, read *Shawq-e-Watan* (Desire for the Ākhirah). Placing trust upon Allah ﷻ, I may claim that after reading this kitab the living will desire and envy their deceased residing in Jannah. In reality, only those of good fortune will reside in Jannah forever...and this is dependent upon *Āmal-e-Sāleh* (good deeds), the Tawfeeq (ability) for which too comes only from Allah ﷻ.

Herein I wish to alert the *taalib-ul-ilm* (Students of Deen), an overwhelming majority of whom become negligent after acquiring Ilm and do not act upon what they have learnt. Even more surprising is their claim after graduating of being the Deputy of Nabee ﷺ. What is this Ilm without practice upon what you claim to be a deputy? In reality, real Ilm is that which enables one to acquire *Ma'arifat* (Knowledge) of Allah ﷻ and this just is not possible without *Amal* (practice). Remember, even slight punishment in the Ākhirah is intolerable, therefore we should all endeavour to acquire necessary Ilm and practice thereupon.

Should we continue to reflect on what has been mentioned, I have great hopes, Inshā'Allah, of the bereaved (upon whose death this lecture was delivered) achieving peace and contentment. One final point is not to keep reflecting and mentioning the last illness and death of the bereaved...for this rekindles the wound and pain.

Now I conclude by making du'aa that Allah ﷻ grants us perfect good fortune, correct understanding and guidance upon the Straight Path and enlightens the graves of all Muslims. Salāt and Salām upon Rasoolullah ﷺ and our final call and praise are to Allah ﷻ - the Creator of the Universe. Āmeen

Shaykh Ashraf 'Ali Thānwi ؒ

The New Enlarged, Revised & Comprehensive
ASHRAF'S BLESSINGS OF
Marriage

An Intimate Step-by-Step Guide to Nikah,
Marital Bliss, Adabs of Private Life,
Proven & Wholesome Cures to Marital Sexual Problems,
Pregnancy, Childbirth & Infant Care,
Correct Tarbiyyah (training) of Muslim Children

Shaykh Ashraf 'Ali Thānwi ؒ

'A Must for every Muslim Couple & Home. Essential Reading Before & After Nikah. An Ideal Wedding Present!'

Ashraf's Amānat©
PO Box 12, Dewsbury, W. Yorkshire, UK, WF12 9YX
Tel: (01924) 488929

Chapter Seven

Darse 'Ibrat
(A Lesson To Heed)

*An Abridged Lecture
delivered
upon the sudden death
of the Young son of
Hāfiz Muhammad Ilyas
by*
Shaykh Maseehullah Khãn ﷺ
at
Jalālābad, India,
on
18th. Jamadil Ãkhir AH,
(5th January, 1991 CE)

'Then take admonition, O you with eyes (to see).'

These (sudden deaths) are indeed lessons to heed as mentioned at numerous places in the Glorious Qur'ān. Such lessons have occurred in abundance since the time of Ādam ﷺ precisely in order to teach and enlighten us.

Experience Sorrow, Do Not Retain Sorrow

Al-Hakeem (The Wise) is a *Sifat* (Attribute) of Allah ﷻ, no Command of His is bereft of this quality! Always taking into account the benefit of His servants, whatever He enacts, He does. Therefore immediately maintain your gaze and thoughts upon Him. Accordingly, at times of sorrow, to experience grief is not at all wrong, for it is Allah ﷻ who created sorrow, a natural quality, however, to retain grief and constantly brood is incorrect. Had sorrow not been natural, how would there be mutual compassion and grief? How would anybody support and comfort another at times of loss? The whole purpose behind sorrow is that Allah ﷻ grants His servants the ability and lofty status of *Sabr* (patience). These are high concepts which are not understandable by mere study of books, this is why our Elders advise ~

> *'Neither from books nor from lectures nor from wealth is Deen brought alive. Deen is brought alive from the attention given by the Shaykh (Friend of Allah ﷻ).'*

Understand that sorrow will be felt. Why? did Nabee ﷺ not experience sorrow upon the death of His son Ibrāheem ﷺ? Moreover, did Fātimah ﷺ not cry out, 'O my dear father!' 'O my dear father!' at the time of her Fathers death?

Incidentally, when Shaykh-ul-Hadeeth Husayn Ahmad Madanee ﷺ delivered a lecture on this incident during his *dars* in Bukhāree, immediately tears welled from his eyes as he recited the concern of Fātimah ﷺ, 'O my dear father!' 'O my dear father!'

Two States; Sabr & Shukr

Therefore, sorrow is a natural quality which Allah ﷻ has created so that we incline towards Him and attain Sabr. By reciting, *'Verily, to Allah we belong and unto Him is our return.'* We herein are taking refuge and support from Allah ﷻ, because in reality, there are only two states for a Mu'min; *Sabr* (patience) and *Shukr* (gratefulness), a third condition just does not exist. Consequently, this sorrow (upon a beloved's death) too is a *Karam* (Favour) from Allah ﷻ, a *Rahm* (Mercy), therefore to experience grief and tears on such occasions is not reprehensible, however we have no mandate to maintain this sorrow. *Taaziyah* (condolence) of three days to relatives and friends has been encouraged, wherein the bereaved should be fed and supported, for where will they have time to cook? Allah ﷻ is *Kareem*, He is Knower of the Unseen, He is *Al-Hakeem* (The Wise), no act of His is devoid of wisdom and reason. Therefore, when being confronted with any event which is displeasing to one, immediately ponder that it is an act of Allah ﷻ wherein is some wisdom. Whatever has occurred is the most appropriate. Who knows what might have transpired had our beloved lived? Just as the incident is related in the Glorious Qur'ān of the travels of Moosā and Khidr عليهما السلام ~

'Then they both proceeded, till they met a boy, and he (Khidr) killed him. Moosā said: 'Have you killed an innocent person who has killed none? Indeed, you have committed a dreadfully evil thing!'

Eventually, Khidr ﷺ explained his action to Moosā ﷺ - the Rasool of his era ~

'And as for the boy, his parents were believers, and we feared lest he should oppress them by rebellion and disbelief. So we intended that their Lord should change him for them for one better in righteousness and nearer to mercy.' (18:74, 80-1)

To Reflect Upon Maut

Accordingly, by focusing our gaze on Allah ﷻ and His Infinite Wisdom, sorrow will either vanish or at the very least lessen: that yesterday's young healthy only recently wedded son, has left dunya for the everlasting life in Jannah - his young wife now a widow. Allah ﷻ is All-Knowing, who knows what might have transpired later on in life, herein is hikmat and a lesson. Ponder, when a child is born, Azān and Iqāmah are recited in his ears, thereby serving notice that we have arrived in preparation for Salāh... which Salāh? Janāzah Salāh!

'Whichever mortal arrives in dunya, death whispers in admonition, 'I too tread behind you, pay heed and be attentive!''

Allah ﷻ relates in the Glorious Qur'ān:

'Everything will perish save His Face. His is the Decision, and to Him you (all) shall be returned.' (28:88)

Nabee ﷺ advised ~

'Remember much the destroyer of all pleasures, Maut.'

This is why our Mashā-ikh prescribe *Muraqabah Maut* (contemplation upon death and the ensuing events in the grave and Hereafter). However, in view of the weakness within us, we should seek permission and guidance from a Shaykh to prevent harm before practicing.

Harms of Incorrect Reflection

Shaykh Ashraf 'Ali Thānwi ﷺ related the episode of a king who often visited some pious Saint living all alone in a jungle hut. In those days, even kings respected the Ulamā and Sulahā. Accordingly, when visiting, the king noticed this Saint taking a tablet every time. Puzzled, the king pondered, 'Why does Shaykh take these tablets?' Immediately, the Saint offered a tablet, which the king swallowed. Thereafter, his libido and desire to make love arose with uncontrollable urge. Returning to his palace, he slept with every one of his wives and maid girls on numerous occasions, but the urge remained. He began to ponder,

'I have only taken one tablet...and look at the force it created in me, none of my ladies could satisfy my lust, and there he is, supposedly all alone in the jungle, taking one of these pills every day. Oho! It appears, prostitutes must be visiting him daily.'

This *bad ghuman* was, of course unfounded, therefore incorrect and sinful. Nevertheless, the king did not stop visiting the Saint (such was the dedication, friendship and loyalty of previous times). Upon his next visit he related what had transpired after taking the one pill. However, the king did not reveal his suspicions and baseless conclusions...of which the Saint was inspired! In order to reform and educate the king, the Saint cried-out, 'Oho! It appears your death is imminent within the next 40 days, engross your self in the *Zikr* of Allah ﷻ. Abdicate and delegate the kingdom to your son.' Immediately upon mention of death, the king's face and shoulders drooped. Shaykh spoke, 'Do not worry, here take 40 of these pills, one a day, Inshā'Allah, they will maintain your strength and spirit.'

The king departed home, abdicated his throne and sat down to spend his time in zikr and nafl salāh. Forty days passed in this 'depressive' state. Surprised, on the 41st. day, he came running to the Saint and cried-out, 'Sire! My death did not come like you predicted, and I have gone and lost a kingdom!' The Saint spoke, 'The kingdom is not lost, you have merely transferred it to your son from whom you may reclaim it anytime. But, I ask you, did you take every one of those pills like I suggested? 'Yes, Shaykh, of course I did, heaven knows what would have happened had I not done so,' replied the king, still flustered. 'Well, taking one pill everyday, did the need not arose to visit your wives and maids?' asked the Saint. 'Why, Shaykh, how could the worry of death allow me to think of such things?' replied the embarrassed king. Upon this the Shaykh commented, 'Your Majesty, you were given a 'respite' of 40 days, whilst this servant does not even have any guarantee, that the air which is breathed-in will come out again before arrival of maut!' Jolted, the king apologised for his suspicions.

When is Firmness Established in Man?

This is the reality of understanding the hadeeth,

'Remember much the destroyer of all pleasures, Maut.'

Once Shaykh Ashraf 'Ali Thānwi ﷺ related the episode of the death of a person's father who was a squire. After kafn, salāh and burial the son arrived home. It was lunch time, when usually the servants would serve dinner, however in view of the calamity which had fallen upon the household, the chef had not cooked. The son called out, 'Butler, where is my meal?' 'Sir! What? Lunch today? Your father has just passed-away, there has been no cooking today!' The selfish son growled, 'He died of his own accord, why, do you wish to kill me from starvation? Bring me something to eat!'

Observe, such people exist in dunya, though in reality they are not worthy of being called human. Why? Because what do they know of *huqooqs* (rights)? These people neither fulfil *Huqooqullah* (Rights of Allah) nor *Huqooqul 'Ebād* (Rights of Creation), and the complete human is he who fulfils rights of both the Creator and creation.

Therefore, to experience and suffer grief on occasions of sorrow is but natural...otherwise why did the Prophets display tears upon death of their loved one's? Even Prophet Nûh ﷺ, knowing the kufr (disbelieve) of his son pleaded for his salvation (at time of the great flood), why? Because this is natural. Accordingly, when we read of the concern of Fātimah ﷺ upon observing death pangs of Nabee ﷺ, 'O my dear father!' Although we were not present, the cry is so vivid as to bring tears to our eyes. Similarly, the scenes of emotion experienced by the Sahābāh ﷺ on that occasion are well recorded.

To Obey Rasool ﷺ and to Worship Allah ﷻ

Aboo Bakr Siddeeq ؓ, the closest friend and companion throughout the Mission of Prophethood was absent on this occasion. Upon the death of Nabee ﷺ, 'Umar Farooq ؓ unsheathed his sword and declared, 'Should anybody say that Rasoolullah ﷺ has died, I shall strike his head off!' This was an indirect expression of his intense love and devotion.

Immediately, Aboo Bakr ؓ returned, walked over to the Janāzah, lifted the sheet and looking at the blessed face he recited loudly from the Glorious Qur'ān:

> 'And Muhammad is but a Messenger, there have been (Prophets) before him. Therefore, If he dies or is killed, will you turn back on your heels? And whoever turns back on his heels, not the least harm will he do to Allah; and Allah will soon reward those who are Shākireen (grateful).' (3:144)

Understand from this Ayah and incident that only Allah ﷻ is *Al-Haiyul Qayyum* (the Everlasting and Self-Existing Sustainer of Life). Accordingly only He is worthy of worship until the end of our time; and whilst we obey Rasoolullah ﷺ, we worship only Allah ﷻ. Therefore to experience sorrow is natural, and the person who does not feel this is either a Saint (in some spiritual state) or a lewd and immoral person. Whatever, this state is not in keeping with the Sunnah of Nabee ﷺ, whose behaviour is the touchstone.

One wisdom behind sorrow is mutual support and comfort,

both at times of grief and happiness - in accordance with the haqq (right) of creation. Understand well, this haqq (of creation) too is but a Right of the Creator...why? Because it is by His Command; and whatever is by His Command becomes an 'Ibādah. Therefore, both sorrow and happiness (of the Mu'min within limits of the Sharee'ah) are 'Ibādah. However, to cling onto sorrow is forbidden just as it wrong to become vain and arrogant on occasions of joy; because this would be against the Rights of Allah ﷻ. Yes, at time of bereavement when food is served at meal times, one has no appetite...we are unable to swallow, this is natural and precisely why Allah ﷻ states many a times in the Glorious Qur'ān:

'Then take admonition, O you with eyes (to see).'

Just as you make use of your faculty of *basārat* (eyesight), also employ your faculty of *baseerat* (insight or seeing with the 'eyes' of the heart). Derive lesson, ponder upon the Hikmat of Allah ﷻ because this is what shaytān failed to do and thereby became *murdood* (rejected). We Muslims should always keep our gaze when confronted with any event, no matter what the severity, upon the Wisdom of Allah ﷻ. Therefore, O young one's! Why wait for middle and old-age? Moreover, O middle-aged one's! Why wait for old-age?

'Living negligently in this world is not befitting humans,
it is imperative to remember maut at all times.'

It is also recommended that at times of sorrow and loss, do not just commence a lecture on *Sabr*, rather share his grief by adopting a woeful look. Now is not the time to convince the bereaved, because the condition or state of sabr is not immediate or constant, it will Inshā'Allah come of its own accord. You may assist by sharing with the bereaved their grief, otherwise the grave danger exists of such people being unable to both mentally and physically tolerate such *naseehat* and suffer harm (e.g. faint).

It appears in Ahadeeth, that when you recite the Glorious Qur'ān, one will come across both types of Āyah's, *tabsheer* (glad-tidings) and *anzaar* (warnings). These produce a barrier between oneself and sinful acts and a craving and longing for *āmāle sālihāh*. Friends! This is why our Mashāikh prescribe *zikr* (Remembrance of Allah ﷻ), to assist in understanding and comprehending the original acts of worship. For example, it is just not possible to make real *tilāwat* (recitation) of the Glorious Qur'ān until one has a habit of making *zikr* in abundance:

> 'O you who believe! Remember Allah with zikr in abundance.' (33:41)

Nowadays, although we do make zikr, nevertheless the throng and longing (to meet and obey Allah ﷻ) is lacking: hence the standing around upon street corners and meeting people unnecessarily; to waste away time in futile conversations. Therefore, these occasions of death should be used properly,

> 'Then take admonition, O you with eyes (to see).'

May Allah ﷻ grant us Tawfeeq and be our Protector, Āmeen,

Shaykh Maseehullah Khān ﷺ

Chapter Eight

The Method of Acquiring Success in Dunya & Ākhirah

*An Abridged Lecture
of*
Shaykh Muhammad Saleem Dhorat
damat barakaatuhum
at
*Masjid-An-Noor, Leicester, UK,
on
Jumu'ah, 4th. September 1998*

Respected Ulamā, brethren, elders and my beloved young friends! On this occasion, it would be prudent to remember and mention our final *manzil* (stage) *Maut*, which launches us into the Ākhirah. Our Nabee ﷺ advised that if one wishes to achieve success in the Hereafter, he should remember death in abundance. If you wish everlasting success, to be *muqarrab-e-Illahi* (a favourite of Allah ﷻ), to acquire the rank of *wilāyat* (friendship of Allah ﷻ) and *Taqwā*, then remember death in abundance. May Allah ﷻ grant all of us Tawfeeq (ability) to act upon this advise of our beloved Nabee ﷺ.

Most Intelligent Person

The eminent Sahābee 'Abdullah ibn 'Umar ؓ relates that once a group of us were fortunate to visit our beloved Nabee ﷺ and posed a question,

> 'O Rasool of Allah ﷺ, kindly inform us as to who is the most intelligent and careful person amongst people?'

Now a person of intelligence in our sight maybe someone who has a BA, MA, or PhD qualification, luxurious mansions, factories, owner of umpteen shops, the holder of worldly posts and rank. However, the real intelligent is he, whom Nabee ﷺ described in these words,

> 'Those people whom remember death the most and prepare for maut the most...these are the people who acquire Sharaafat (nobility) of dunya and I'zāz (honour) of the Ākhirah.' (Fadhāil Sadaqāh, Vol. 2, p 451)

Therefore, two prerequisites for being the most intelligent

person are to remember and prepare for death. Why? Because the person who is worried about only expanding his academic, industrial, commercial, financial empire, and any other worldly objective without any thought for the Ākhirah has placed his sight upon a finite item. However, he who reflects and prepares for death has achieved success for an unlimited life. Why? Because nobody is able to save himself from death!

Allah ﷻ relates in the Glorious Qur'ān regarding those *mushriks* (kuffar) of Makkah who would come to our Nabee ﷺ and taunt Him and the Muslims, 'Why will Muhammad not die? If not today then surely tomorrow: 10, 20, 30 years, and whenever He does die so will His religion! Allah ﷻ revealed the following Ayah in the Glorious Qur'ān ~

> '*And We granted not to any human being immortality before you (O Muhammad ﷺ): then if you die, would they live forever?*' (21:34)

Herein Allah ﷻ is consoling His beloved Rasool ﷺ, 'O My Messenger, there is no need to take their taunts to heart for we have made it a feature of this worldly life, that whomsoever arrives in dunya comes to die! Nobody before you was granted immortality: Ādam ؑ arrived to leave, Moosā ؑ also came to die, all the Prophets ؑ, all Awliya, Ulamā, Huffaz, Zāhid, faajir, faasiq, men, women and children all arrived to leave! These mushriks are merely chiding you, why? Do they think that after the death of Muhammad ﷺ they are to live forever? You will pass-away and they also will die! Everybody has to depart.'

Life consists of a series of Manzil's (stages)

Understand, that life consists of a series of *manzils* (stages), and none of us know how many of our *manzil's* have already been expended. Relates Khawajah Majzoob ~

> *'Initially, infancy toyed you into years of play,*
> *Thereafter adolescence turned you mad with fray,*
> *Old-age arrived with thousands array,*
> *Ajal (death) will appear and annihilate your say!'*

Childhood was spent in play and when appeared teens, you became completely insane. You began to believe that neither Divinity, any authority, parents, nor family could control you. No respect for elders: the intoxication, strength and courage of adolescence...those nemats which were bestowed on you by your Creator, you are employing in His disobedience! Whereas, our beloved Nabee who was *Rahmatullil-'Aalameen* (Mercy for the Universe) advised ~

> *'Consider (certain) five things as a treasure before (another) five things overtake you: 1) Youth before old age; 2) Health before illness; 3) Wealth before poverty; 4) Peace of mind before worry; 5) Life before death.'*

(Tirmizi, quoted in Hayaatul Muslimeen, p 106)

Appreciate Youth before Old Age

When old-age appears and man visualizes his death in front of him, he regrets the folly and time wasted in youth and his physical inability now to perform *Amāl-e-Sālihah*. He now dreads his descent into the grave, questioning by Angels, meeting with Allah, the *Pûl-Siraat* (Bridge over Hell) and having to answer for his time. This is why Nabee advised,

'(Appreciate) youth before old age...'

In another hadeeth it appears the youth who spends his night and day in obedience of Allah ﷻ, who utilizes his strength to awake for Tahajjud and Fajr Salāh, in regular recitation of the Glorious Qur'ān and Zikr, and physically strives in the Path of Allah ﷻ, helps the orphans, widows and needy, respects and is kind to elders. Such a youngster who is obedient to Allah ﷻ, when he reaches 50, 60, 70 years of age and tries to now awake for Tahajjud, help the needy, caress the orphans head, strive for *'Ella Kaleematullah*, but finds it difficult because of physical weakness, Nabee ﷺ related that Allah ﷻ upon observing His servant's frustration, addresses His Angels, 'O My Malaa'ikah! When this servant was young, he was punctual in My obedience, why is this slave no longer practicing these acts?' The Angels reply, 'O Lord! You have grown him old, if you would return his youth and strength, of a surety he would again practice these acts.' Allah ﷻ Commands, 'O My Malaa'ikah! From the time he has become old until he dies, bear witness that I shall continue to accrue thawāb to him even sitting in old-age for all those acts which he performed in his youth and would still undertake but is now unable to do so.'

Plea to Our Youth

Therefore, my beloved young friends, I plead you to recognize and acknowledge the Perfect Power of Allah ﷻ that this youth will not last forever. Those aged persons, whom you observe, whose hair have turned grey, whose back has become hunched, they too were young and like you had airs upon their strength and courage. Nobody's youth will remain forever, it is well possible that either death may appear in youth and clutch your neck or you will pass through youth into old age and having squandered such a golden opportunity, there will remain nothing but regret and remorse ~

'Initially, infancy toyed you into years of play,
Thereafter adolescence turned you mad with fray,
Old-age arrived with thousands array...'

Now such a person will ponder, 'Alas! I wasted my youth in zina, booze, drugs, stealing, disobeying my parents, vexing others and tyranny! Woe, what is to become of me for there is nobody to support me.' This grief is eating-away at him, the Tawfeeq to make Taubah and practice good deeds are absent,

'...Will arrive ajal (maut) and completely uproot you!
As a place of attachment, this world is rot.
An abode to heed lesson; mere amusement not.'

Ponder upon these words, appreciate this life before death, for our existence is akin to ice which slowly, slowly melts away. Only that person who employs ice before it disappears is fortunate ~

'Life, like a piece of ice is melting away,
Silently, gradually, slowly, and perpetually.'

Birthdays - Our Misconception

This life is seeping out of our hands, yet unable to appreciate we cling unto the misconception whereupon every birthday we rejoice with parties. We envisage progress, yet this is neither mine nor your advancement, everyday, every second...*tick, tick, tick,* we advance towards the Ākhirah. This passing of life in the disobedience of Allah ﷻ, whereby no salāh is performed throughout the year except for Jumu'ah and 'Eed; interest money is devoured; Zakāt is overlooked; eyes, tongue and ears are used in evil; harām enters the stomach...thousands of acts of disobedience with only a few moments of good. Ponder when the year passes in this state and birthday arrives, what is there to celebrate? The opportunity Allah ﷻ had bestowed to make our Ākhirah is being blatantly squandered.

If someone possesses a million pounds and from these a 100 thousand were lost, what grief and sorrow this person would feel. He will not feel contented upon the remaining 900 thousand but suffer anguish over the lost 100 thousand and scheme a method to try and reclaim this money. In complete contrast, after wasting a whole year we celebrate our birthdays by baking and decorating a cake with candles then blowing thereupon. O servant of Allah ﷻ! Reflect for a few seconds, what are we celebrating? The squandering of a whole year in disobedience! Relates the poet ~

> *'Coming and passing of day and nights pleases man,*
> *Whereas this passing heralds his own departure!'*

This is why Nabee ﷺ advised:

> *'Those people who remember death the most and prepare for Maut the most...these are the people who acquire sharāfat (nobility) of dunya and i'zāz (honour) of the Ākhirah.'*

Therefore, he who is most intelligent in the sight of Nabee ﷺ is also the most prudent in the Sight of Allah. He who not only remembers but also prepares for the stages to appear in the Ākhirah. Such preparation that when Angel of Death will appear...

> 'Verily, those who say: 'Our Lord is Allah (Alone)' and then they stand (firm), on them the angels will descend (at the time of their death) (saying): 'Fear not, nor grieve! But receive the glad tidings of Paradise, which you have been promised!
>
> We have been your friends in the life of this world and are (so) in the Hereafter. Therein you shall have (all) that your inner-self desires, and there you shall have (all) for which you ask. An entertainment from (Allah), the Oft-Forgiving, Most Merciful.' (41:30-2)

When is this possible? When the concern and worry of death is ever present whereby should any portion of the body incline towards evil this thought of the Ākhirah stops one. For example, the eyes wish to stare at a non-mahram, the ears wish to listen to evil, the tongue inclines towards falsehood, on all such occasions this concept of Maut prevents one from committing evil. This is what is meant by 'standing firm' upon the 'Straight Path,' when this is achieved,

> '...On them the angels will descend (at the time of their death) (saying): 'Fear not, nor grieve...!'

Upon approach of death, shaytān ascertains from signs the Mu'mins imminent departure from this world. Unable to bear somebody leaving with Imān and therefore entering

Jannah, Iblis summons a horde of shayāteen for an onslaught upon this Muslim in a final attempt to snatch away his Imān. The dying person is witnessing the arrival of *Malikul Maut* whilst numerous shayāteen try to tempt him towards *kufr*.

Shaykh Abul 'Abbās Ahmad Qartabi ؒ reports that he was present during the last moments of his brother, who when asked to recite the Kaleemah replied 'No.' When his brother regained consciousness he commented, "Two shayāteen were on my either side and conniving words like, 'O person! Just mumble quietly that, 'Muhammad was not the Prophet of Allah,' or 'There are two Allah,' or 'Islām is not a true religion, rather christianity and judaism are true.' This is why I replied 'No,' I was not negating the Kaleemah."

The Aid of Allah ﷻ

These shayāteen even appear in the form of the dying person's mother and plead, 'O my beloved! Look I passed away before you and became aware that Islām is not a true religion, but christianity and judaism are true, therefore quickly adopt one of these religions because Islām will only take you into Hell!' However, the person who had prepared for Maut and who was steadfast in Obedience of Allah ﷻ will find ~

> *'Verily, those who say: 'Our Lord is Allah (Alone)' and then they stand (firm), on them the angels will descend (at the time of their death) (saying): 'Fear not, nor grieve! But receive the glad tidings of Paradise which you have been promised!'*

Allah ﷻ witnessing His servant in anguish here Commands His Angels to quickly go and aid...whether this person be in a bedroom in Leicester or some remote hut in the outback of Africa. Upon arrival, these Angels open the doors of Jannah, whereby this dying person observes the rivers and streams of Paradise, 'Look Yonder!' beckon the Angels, 'Look at your Heavenly Mansions, Gardens and Maidens!' Witnessing these nemats, the Soul of the dying person forgets the whisperings of shaytaan and his friends and relatives who stand around crying. Now, the Mu'mins full attention is towards only Allah ﷻ as his *rûh* flutters to leave towards Jannah for meeting with its Creator. No sorrow of separation from dunya or associates hinder this person...as he hastens towards Allah ﷻ, 'He who hastens and looks forward to meeting with his Creator, Allah ﷻ too desires to meet him.'

> *'We have been your friends in the life of this world and are (so) in the Hereafter. Therein you shall have (all) that your inner-self desires, and there you shall have (all) for which you ask. An entertainment from (Allah), the Oft-Forgiving, Most Merciful.'*

Do not think you shall be alone in the grave or during accounting on the Day of Qiyāmah, or upon *Pûl Sirāt*, 'We have been your friends in the life of this world and are (so) in the Hereafter...' Because you had waged an offensive against the lowly dictates of nafs in this world for Our sake, ask here in the Ākhirah whatever you desire, We shall fulfil! This is why Nabee ﷺ commented:

> *'Those people who remember death the most and prepare for Maut the most...these are the people who acquire the nobility of dunya and i'zāz (honour) of the Ākhirah.'*

It is my humble appeal to everybody to save themselves from these schemes of shaytān and our nafs, which cling to us at all times. Remember, we shall reap what we sow,

> 'So whosoever does good equal to the weight of an atom shall see it. And whosoever does evil equal to the weight of an atom shall see it.' (99: 7-8)

Therefore, bring our nafs under control. Ensure our exterior is in accordance to the Sunnah of Allah's Rasool ﷺ. Ensure what we eat is halāl, make our *akhlāq* (character), *mua'asharat* (social life) those of Nabee ﷺ. Save yourselves from all such avenues and acts which displease Allah ﷻ and practice all those Fardh and Wājib acts which He has commanded. Then we shall achieve *Wilāyet* (friendship of Allah ﷻ) and success in both dunya and Ākhirah. Shaykh Sā'adi ؒ states,

> 'Paradise is very close, merely two steps; one step upon your nafsani (lowly bestial) desires, the other step straight into Jannah!'

May Allah ﷻ grant all of us, both young and old the Tawfeeq to remember and prepare for Maut.

Salāt and Salām upon Rasoolullah ﷺ and our final call and praise are to Allah ﷻ, the Creator of the Universe. Āmeen

Shaykh Muhammad Saleem Dhorat

dāmat barakātuhum

Shaykh Ihtishām-ul-Haqq Thānwi 🌸 relates, 'The great Scholar of Islām, 'Allāmah Ibn al-Jawzee 🌸 (508-597AH/c1200 CE) writes in 'The Seasons of Life,' there are many stations of life, with the desires, traits and longings of each season quite different from the others.

The famous poet Akbar had a son, who when seven years of age had requested his father to purchase for him a certain design of spinning-top. For some considerable period, Akbar had searched bazaars and toyshops, but to no avail. After some years, when his son had left for London to study, Akbar found this type of spinning-top and bought it.

His son returned after graduating, marrying and becoming a member of the upper echelons of society. A banquet was prepared in his honour, wherein the elite were all invited and sat down to eat. Akbar took out the spinning-top and presented it to his son in front of everybody. The guests began to whisper, 'Akbar has gone senile!' 'He's off his rocker presenting a spinning-top!' Undaunted, Akbar addressed his son:

> 'Dear son! I am not senile; I merely wish to relate a lesson to you. Remember, during every 'season' of man he cherishes a particular object...in one of these seasons (of play) you desired this type of spinning-top. However, you now observe how yesteryears' desire is today a source of embarrassment for you, something which you do not even wish to touch or know about. Therefore, I wish to teach you this lesson, that for the rest of your life, never perform any such deed which you will regret on the Day of Qiyāmah.'

(p 25, Lectures)

Chapter Nine

Episodes Related to Death & Punishment of the Grave

Based upon the Teachings

of

Shaykh-ul-Hadeeth Zakariyyā ؓ,

Shaykh Maseehullah Khān ؓ,

Shaykh Mufti 'Ashiq Ellahi Madanee ؓ,

Shaykh 'Abdul Mu'min Farooqee ؓ,

Shaykh Mufti 'Abdur Ra'oof Sakhrawee

The Fruit of Worldly Relationships

Shaykh Dr. 'Abdul 'Hai 'Ārifee ؒ whilst attending the funeral of Shaykh Zafar Ahmad 'Uthmāni ؒ recited the couplet ~

'The reward of a lifetime of friendship was thus,
My friends and associates came and threw dust.'

No matter how intimate the relationship, at the time of funeral, one's acquaintances will try to throw at least three handfuls of soil in the grave...as if this is the final *haqq* of a friend. By action, the living imply, 'henceforth, it is you and your deeds.' One should visit the graveyard to reflect upon these realities and the life to come in the Ākhirah.

Ā'ishah ؒ relates, 'Once a kāfir woman came to visit me. During conversation she mentioned *athāb-al-qabr* (punishment in the grave) and made du'aa of protection for me. Sometime after she left, Nabee ﷺ arrived home and I queried, 'O Rasoolullah! A kāfir lady came and mentioned athāb-al-qabr...is this true?' Nabee ﷺ replied, 'Yes! Athāb-al-qabr is a reality.' Ā'ishah ؒ relates, 'Henceforth, I used to hear Rasoolullah ﷺ make du'aa for protection from *athāb-al-qabr* after every Salāh.'

Herein is lesson for us, for we are to one day enter our graves, should this abode be comfortable, all forthcoming stages will become easy. Allah ﷻ forbid, should *athāb* appear in the grave, all subsequent stations will be too awful to comprehend.

Whenever 'Uthmān ؓ passed by the side of a grave, he wept so profusely that his beard became wet. Someone asked 'Why don't you weep when Paradise and Hell are described to you...for you weep so much standing next to a grave?' He replied 'I heard Rasoolullah ﷺ describing the grave as the first stage from the forthcoming world (Ākhirah). If one finds salvation therein...whatever is to come will be easy. However, should this stage be difficult...future stages will be unbearable.'

The Abode of Barzakh

This *athāb-al-qabr* takes place in *Barzakh*, an intermediary abode separate from this world. Athāb does not take place in the hole into which we lower the janāzah, however the *rûh* is transferred into *Barzakh* whilst still retaining a relationship with the body. Therefore, athāb, thawāb and comfort are experienced by the *rûh* in *Barzakh*. However, the body too is aware of whatever is transpiring in *Barzakh*.

This is easily understood by considering what happens in a dream...one is being attacked, assaulted, killed...all these are being experienced in a dream...and we may discern some of these fears by observing a person's body features (he may cry, sweat, physically move). Similarly, should a person be experiencing delights of Jannah (he maybe eating, drinking, strolling, etc., these too will be visible upon his face).

These are all examples to understand the relationship of how, in dunya, the mayyit experiences athāb and thawāb. However, sometimes in order to alert and correct us, Allah ﷻ displays some episode of *athāb-al-qabr* or a heavenly nemat.

Graves Advice to 'Umar bin 'Abdul-Azeez ؓ

Shaykh-ul-Hadeeth Zakariyyā ؓ relates, 'Once 'Umar bin 'Abdul-Azeez ؓ accompanied a Janāzāh and upon arriving at the graveyard, distanced himself, sitting down next to an old grave. Somebody enquired, 'O Ameerul Mu'mineen! You are the guardian of this funeral and you have gone and sat down separately?' He replied, 'Yes, a grave had summoned and addressed me by advising,

> 'O 'Umar bin 'Abdul-Azeez! Why do you not ask me how I deal with arrivals?
>
> I tear away their shroud and dismember their body to pieces; suck all their blood out, devour all their flesh...now shall I inform you of what I do with their joints?
>
> I separate the shoulders from the arms; the forearms from wrists; the waist from hips, the thighs from knees, the calves from ankles!'

Relating this, 'Umar bin 'Abdul-Azeez ؓ began to cry and commented, 'The stay in this world is very short yet its deceptions are many. Whomsoever is beloved therein is disgraced in the Ākhirah; whomsoever is wealthy therein is a pauper in the Ākhirah; its youth very quickly age; its living will shortly die. Be careful, lest its inclination towards you entraps you in deception, whereas you are observing how quickly it turns its face away. Foolish is he who succumbs to its tricks; for where are those affluent one's who inhabited large cities, built large canals and gardens...but passed away after a few days?'

Athāb-al-Qabr - A Reality & An Episode

Aboo Saeed Khudri ؓ relates that our Nabee ﷺ commented,

'Undoubtedly, 199 snakes are assigned to a kāfir in the grave...which continue to bite him until Qiyāmah. Their venom is so poisonous, that should even one (of these snakes throw its saliva) upon this world just once, the earth would stop growing any vegetation.'

(p 44, What Happens After Death)

Hāfez Ibn Rajab Hambalee ؒ relates in his kitāb *Ahwāl-al-Qaboor* the experience of a farmer who was returning from his field at twilight...

'I decided to pray Maghrib Salāh with two companions near a graveyard along the way. After performing Salāh, we were quietly completing our *mamoolaat* as darkness approached, when I heard the sound of wailing. I looked around, but no one was visible. After a short while, the same crying sound was audible... 'Oh! Oh!' Terrified, my hairs stood on-end as I realized the cry was coming from a grave. I walked over and placing my ear close to a nearby grave heard,

'Oh! Oh! For I used to pray Salāh and also kept Saum, therefore why am I being punished so?'

The voice was so frightening I moved away and summoned my companions to hear the cry. They too heard it and confirmed that it was not some imagination of mine. Quickly, we departed for home. Next day, we again prayed Maghrib Salāh at the very same place in expectation of hearing the same voice. After completing our *mamoolaat*, as darkness fell...the same cry was heard and I placed my ears to the grave. I was now convinced the inmate was being punished; as I arose, an intense fear overwhelmed me...which resulted in a fever that lasted for two months!

Regarding *athāb-al-qabr*, it appears in traditions of Bukhāree that the mayyit screams so loudly upon being punished, that except for humans and jinni, all other beings nearby are able to hear its crying and wailing. Muslims are aware that this *athāb* is due to sins and failure to make proper *Taubah* (repentance). A question arises at this point, why are humans and jinni unable to hear the noise and commotion that takes place in the grave?

Shaykh Mufti 'Ashiq Ellahi Madanee ؒ replies, 'All humans have a connection with the abode of Barzakh. Therefore, if they were to be shown the spectacle that takes place in the grave or the pleas and unbearable cries of those undergoing punishment, they would undoubtedly bring Imān...and practice good deeds. However, only Imān upon the Unseen, as related by our Nabee ﷺ is acceptable to Allah ﷻ:

> 'Blessed is He in Whose Hand is the dominion: and He is Able to do all things.
>
> Who has Created death and life that He may test you, which of you is best in deed. And He is the All-Mighty, the Oft-Forgiving...
>
> Verily, those who fear their Lord unseen (i.e. they are unable to observe Him, theirs will be forgiveness and a great reward (i.e. Paradise).' (67)

Athāb-al-Qabr - Lack of Purdah

Shaykh Maseehullah Khān ﷺ related, 'A young lady passed-away: after ghusl, kafn and Salāh, her brother descended into the grave to bury her and whilst doing so, some important documents dropped out of his pocket and became buried with his sister.

Upon arriving home, he realized the mishap and accompanied by a few relatives he returned to the cemetery to dig-up his sister's grave. As he reached the bottom, he saw the missing papers and as he stretched out to pluck them...he was astonished to observe the body of his sister 'arched' with the 'pony-tails' of hair tied to her feet...reminiscent of a bow!

Grieved and saddened he tried to untangle her hair from the feet...but as soon as he touched her hair...he screamed in pain and recoiled his burnt hand straight out of the grave! Hastily, the soil was replaced and they returned home with the brother clutching his hand in severe pain. He related the episode to his distraught mother who commented,

> 'Dear, your sister had a habit of exposing her hair in front of non-mahram men and I fear this is why she is being punished in the grave.'

No amount of medical treatment would relieve the pain. Eventually, they visited a Saint who recited some Qur'ānic ayahs and blew upon water. As long as the brother kept his fingers emerged in this water, he would find relief...but as soon as he extracted his hand, unbearable pain would return.' May Allah ﷻ protect all of us from such punishment.

Shroud Thief

In bygone day's, some thieves had the despicable habit of opening recently buried graves and stealing the shroud. In one locality, a Saint once asked his assistant to summon the local 'shroud-thief' and queried him...'Tell me, how much money do you get these days for a shroud?' The thief, after at first feigning innocence, replied, '10 dinnars.' The Saint commented, 'Look, I am giving you 20 dinnars, for heavens sake, do not steal my shroud!' The thief replied: 'What, steal your kafn? The kafn of a Saint? Preposterous! Impossible! Unthinkable! Incomprehensible!' The Saint commented, 'Now look here, bad habits die hard, I am giving you double what you would receive, promise you will not steal my kafn.' 'You have my word!' replied the thief.

After receiving money and exchanging greetings the thief departed. Some time later, the Shaykh passed away and was buried. At night, the thief appeared at the cemetery and dug-up the Saint's grave! Just as he was about to remove the shroud, the Shaykh grabbed his hand. Unable to tolerate this miracle, the thief had a heart attack and died immediately. That very night, the Saint appeared in a dream to one of his deputies and spoke...

> 'Brother, look we had even given him twice what he would have received, yet he still came to steal my shroud. I merely placed my hand on his hand...how was I to know he would die? Now you come here, remove his body: bathe, shroud, pray Salāh and bury him...whilst I will plea, 'O Allah! I have his hand in my hand; You out of Your Infinite Mercy Forgive him.'

One's Death and Grave is a Reflection of life

Allah ﷻ mentions in the Glorious Qur'ān:

'And your Lord has decreed that you worship none but Him. And that you be dutiful to your parents. If one of them or both of them attain old age in your life, say not to them a word of disrespect, nor shout at them but address them in terms of honour.

In addition, lower unto them the wing of your submission and humility through mercy, and say:.

'My Lord! Bestow on them Your Mercy as they did bring me up when I was young!' (17:23-24)

Nabee ﷺ commented:

'In whichever way you live your life, in this very state will arrive your death. Moreover, in whatever way your death appears, in this state will you be resurrected on (the Plain of) Hashr!'

Everyday events testify to this noble statement. You will observe the pious servants of Allah ﷻ, who devote their entire lives in the service and propagation of Deen and Muslims, their deaths too arrive very blessedly. Even after death, people continue to mention their names with respect and reverence. In complete contrast, those who spend their lifestyle differently: drinking alcohol; taking drugs; music; singing; watching TV; dealing in interest; gambling; adultery; disobedience to parents; stealing, etc., their deaths often appear in these very states.

A pious Muslim doctor comments, 'As a Muslim Physician practicing over forty years, I have witnessed the deaths of over one hundred Muslims and, I made a special point of noting and recording their final statements and 'state.' It pains me to inform you, that only three blessed souls departed with the *Kaleemah*, all the others mumbled or displayed worldly preoccupations!' A few of these eye-opening accounts are related.

Disrespect to Mother

A young man passed-away because of kidney failure. His final three days were so painful, I have never witnessed such a dreadful and evil death in forty years! His face turned blue, eyes popped-out and, a constant heinous gurgling voice could be heard as if somebody was choking him. This dreadful noise became so unbearable on the final day that other patients began to flee from the ward. We eventually had to seclude him. His father approached me and requested, 'Doctor, perform euthanasia, give him some medicine which will kill him quickly, we are no longer able to see him in this condition!'

The Professor asked him, 'Tell me, what sin did he commit to deserve such a death?' His father replied, 'What to say Doctor! To please his wife this son of mine used to assault his mother...I warned him many a times but he would not listen.'

Pious Lady who was Hāfiz of the Glorious Qur'ān

A noble lady was admitted to hospital with fever and somewhat recovered after treatment. One day, towards evening, I received a call from the nurse summoning me to the ward as this lady was loudly reciting the *Kaleemah*.

Quickly, I ran for the hospital...but before I arrived, she had become the Beloved of Allah ﷻ. I was later informed, this pious lady was very punctual with salāh, saum and was a Hāfiz of the Glorious Qur'ān.

Carelessness when Urinating

Abdullah ibn 'Umar ؓ relates, 'I was once on a journey when the need arose en-route to stay over at the cottage of an old lady. In the middle of the night, a frightening noise could be heard from outside...'Urine! O urine, what is urine? Water! O water, what is water?' Terrified, I asked the old lady who explained,

> 'That was my husband's voice, his grave is nearby. Whenever relieving himself, he had the careless habit of urinating just anyhow...without the slightest care for purity. When I used to remonstrate, pointing out that even animals adopt some form of caution and you as a human should adopt some care, he would ridicule and mock me. From the day he was buried, every night his voice is heard, 'Urine! O urine, what is urine?'
>
> The latter part of his cry regarding water, refers to an incident when a passing traveller arrived almost dying of thirst. He begged my tyrant husband for water...who pointed to an empty bucket some distance away and said, 'Over there is some ice-cold water, you may drink as much as you wish!' The poor soul staggered over, but when he beheld the empty container and sick joke he fell down and died. From the day he was buried, every night this voice is heard 'Water! O water, what is water?"

(p 78, Stories of Maut)

Abdullah ibn Abbas ؓ relates, 'Once Nabee ﷺ passed-by two unknown graves and commented,

> 'At present, the inmates of both these grave are experiencing the descent of punishment, and the castigation too is on account of really small misdeeds. One is guilty of failing to adopt caution from filth when urinating: whilst the other was in the habit of tale bearing (and backbiting).'

Thereafter, Nabee ﷺ broke a fresh twig and placed one upon each grave and related, 'As long as these sticks remain verdant, punishment will lessen.' (p26, Stories of Maut)

An Alcohol Drinker

Shaykh Hushab ؓ was once on a journey and stayed over at a village which had a cemetery nearby. At the time of 'Asr Salāh, suddenly a grave opened and a person with the head and voice resembling that of a donkey emerged and brayed before returning to the grave! Shocked, Shaykh Hushab ؓ asked his hosts, who replied,

> 'He is one of our youths who was also a habitual and heavy drinker of alcohol. His mother was an extremely chaste and pious lady who used to admonish him when he would recover from his drunken stupor, 'O fool! Islām has totally forbidden alcohol, then how are you, as a Muslim, able to do this?' He would retort, 'Get lost! Stop braying like a donkey!' Now from the day he died, everyday at the time of 'Asr, he emerges from his grave, brays three times and then disappears back into his grave!' (p 78, Stories of Maut)

The Mercy of Allah ﷻ

Shaykh Hasan Basree ؓ relates, 'Once a needy person came to a Masjid and pleaded for assistance. Nobody paid much attention to this poor soul who was completely famished and had not eaten for several days. When all his pleas failed, he retired to a corner of the Masjid and passed-away. Next morning, when the *Mu'azzin* arrived to perform the *Azān* for Fajr Salāh, he was shocked to notice a body lying on the floor. Inspection revealed it to be the needy person...alarmed, he summoned all the locals who arrived and started a collection to cover the costs of ghusl, shroud and burial. Suddenly, they noticed a ready-made kafn and piece of paper in the *Mihrāb* of the Masjid, wherein was written:

> *'You people are extremely stingy and misfortunate. We have no intention of accepting any kafn of yours for one of Our Friends. When he asked you for something to eat in the state of starvation, you people would not spare even a morsel! Remember, whomsoever becomes Ours, We too never accept or allow him to be indebted to others.'*

Shaykh Maseehullah Khān ؓ related, 'There was once an extrovert person, always joking and laughing with others and not very inclined towards good deeds. When the time of his death appeared, he requested his friends, 'When I die, for Allah's sake, cover my beard with flour so that it appears completely white.' His relatives remonstrated, 'You have spent your whole life laughing, why, are you going to depart joking as well?' 'No, for Allah's sake, cover my beard with flour, this is my last request.'

Accordingly, his beard was smeared with flour. When summoned, Allah ﷻ the All-Knowing asked him, 'What have you done, why have you coloured your beard white?' He replied, 'O Allah ﷻ! I have done this because of Your fear, for I have heard from the Ulamā that 'Allah ﷻ is ashamed of old people.' Now I do not have many good deeds, neither am I very old, so I thought maybe if I whiten my beard, You out of Your Infinite Mercy will forgive me?' Allah ﷻ replied, 'Go! I have forgiven you!'

Imām Al-Ghazāli ؒ relates that Nabee ﷺ narrated, 'On the Day of Qiyāmah, Allah Ta'ālā will bring out a writing from underneath His Throne wherein is written, 'My Mercy has defeated My Anger, I am the Most Merciful.'

'Allah has 100 Mercies, out of which he has distributed one mercy amongst men, jinni, beasts, birds and lower beings...with the remaining 99 Mercies left by Him. He will shower them on the Day of Qiyāmah upon His servants.'

A mother was frantically searching for her lost child on a battlefield. When she found him, they both ran and embraced each other with the mother crying, 'My child! My child!' Observing this scene, our Nabee ﷺ commented, 'Allah will display more kindness unto you than the mother showing affection to her child.' Hearing this, the Sahābāh ؓ departed in a state of joy. From these Ahadeeth, we may cherish hope of Forgiveness from Allah ﷻ even though we are not worthy of such favours.' (Vol 4, p535, Ihyā)

Chapter Ten

A View of Jannah (Paradise)

An
Abridged Lecture
from the Original **'Islaahi Khutabaat'**
of
Shaykh Mufti Taqee 'Uthmãni
dāmat barakātuhum
Delivered 1415 AH
(7th. November 1995)
at
Jāme Masjid, Karachi

Respected friends! Man has no way of finding out about the state after death; no avenues, no means are available to enable one to ascertain the condition after death. Whomsoever leaves this dunya is well aware of what has transpired; yet, those present are unaware of his condition.

An Amazing Episode

My late respected father, Mufti Muhammad Shafee' ﷺ often related the episode of a Saint, whose students once commented, 'Shaykh! Whichever person leaves this dunya does so in such a condition that he never relates where he has gone to, what has transpired or been observed, please show us some stratagem whereby we come to know of these things?' The Saint replied, 'Very well, when I pass-away, place a pen and piece of paper with my Janāzah, should the opportunity arise, I shall Inshā'Allah relate my experience to you the next day.' The students were overjoyed, 'At last we have somebody to show us.' Accordingly, when this Saint died his instructions were enacted.

Next day, some students arrived at his grave and saw a piece of paper. They became very happy, 'now we shall know of the Hereafter.' However, upon this paper was written the inscription ~

> *'This abode is one to be experienced and not one to be described.'*

Allah ﷻ has so hidden this state that nobody is able to ascertain it except from details revealed to us in the Glorious Qur'ān and Ahadeeth by Nabee ﷺ which we shall now briefly study.

The Lowest Ranking Person of Jannat

Mu'gheera Sh'ubah ؓ narrates that Prophet Moosā ؑ once requested Allah ﷻ, 'O Creator! Who will be the lowest ranking person in Jannat?' Allah ﷻ replied,

'When all people of Paradise will have entered Jannah, and the people of Hell will have entered Jahannam, one person, who would have failed to enter Jannah will be sitting thereabouts. Allah Ta'ālā will inquire, 'When you were in dunya, you must have heard of great kings. Pick any four such kings of your choice and tell me their names, thereafter describe what you remember of the limits and places of their kingdom. Accordingly, this person will describe four such kingdoms, their pomp, retinue and then request, 'O Allah! I too desire such kingdoms...' mentioning each by name.

Allah Ta'ālā will reply, 'Whilst you have mentioned four great kings and their kingdom, tell me what pleasures and comfort each was synonymous for and what similar luxuries you desire?' Consequently, this person will relate the grandeur of each kingdom desiring them for himself. Allah Ta'ālā will Comment, 'If I were to grant you such four kingdoms and their finery which you have described, will you be contented?' The servant will reply, 'O Allah! What greater nemat could I possibly receive, of a surety I would be satisfied.' Allah Ta'ālā will reply, 'Very well, I shall grant you ten times the size of these four kingdoms and those pleasures which you have selected.' Allah Ta'ālā then informed Moosā ؑ, 'This is the lowest ranking Jannatee.' Moosā ؑ thereafter requested, 'O Allah! When this be the state of the lowest ranking person, what will be the condition of your favourite and highest ranking servants?' Allah Ta'ālā replied, 'O Moosā! For my close and favourite servants I have prepared such items for their welcome with my Own Hands and thereafter stored and protected them under lock. They include such nemats, which until today nobody has ever witnessed, no ear has heard their description and which no human has even envisaged or thought of in his heart. Such nemats have I prepared.'

One More Hadeeth

In another Hadeeth, Nabee ﷺ has related the condition of a person who will be the last to enter Jannah. On account of his evil deeds, this person will have to spend time undergoing punishment in Hell...this principle applies to sinful Muslims; they will have to suffer for their evil. Now suffering and burning in Jahannam, this person will call-out, 'O Allah! The severity and fire of Jahannam have engulfed me, it would be a great favour of Yours, if You were to extricate me from here for a short while, so that I may be saved from burning for some time.'

Allah ﷻ will reply, 'If We were to remove and place you on the outskirts (of Hell), you will undoubtedly ask, 'Take me further away.' This servant will comment, 'O Allah! I promise, just move me away from here and I will not ask to be moved any further.' Allah ﷻ will reply, 'Very well, We shall accept your pledge.'

Accordingly, this person will be removed from Jahannam and placed outside. Sitting here for a while, his senses will somewhat return whereupon he will plead, 'O Allah! Indeed

You have extracted me from Hell, however the stench and glow of Jahannam is still perceivable, please take me away from here also so that I be saved from these vapours?'

Allah ﷻ will reply, 'Just now you had promised not to ask to be moved any further, and here you are already breaking your pledge!' 'O Allah! Let me go a bit further, I shall not ask for anything after this.' Accordingly, Allah ﷻ will move him further away from Jahannam. However, from this new place he will catch sight of Jannah. After some time he will begin to plead again, 'O Allah! Verily, you have removed me from Hell and now I am witnessing Paradise, please grant me permission to go up to its doors and have a small peep therein so that I may appreciate what Jannah is like.'

Allah ﷻ will reply, 'You are breaking your promise again! This person will beg, 'O Allah! When you have brought me here with Your Mercy, allow me just one look into Jannah?' Allah ﷻ will comment, 'If I allow you just one peep into Paradise, you will ask to be given permission to enter.' The servant will plead, 'O Allah! Never! Allow me one look, I shall not ask for anything after that.' Accordingly, Allah ﷻ will allow him a brief preview of Jannah as a result of which he will say, 'O Allah! You are *Arhamur Raahimeen*, when you have brought me here, please allow me through Your *Fadhl* (Excellence and Generosity) to go inside?' Allah ﷻ will reply, 'We told you from the beginning that you would not be able to keep your promise, nevertheless, now that We have brought you here with our *Rahmat* (Mercy), We shall enter you therein and grant you such space which is equal in size to the whole earth!' Shocked, this servant will mumble, 'O Allah! You as *Arhamur Raahimeen* are mocking with me? For, what am I and whither is such a large expanse of Jannah?' Allah ﷻ will reply, 'I am not joking, indeed you are being granted such a large tract of Paradise!'

The Hadeeth of 'Continuous Humour'

It is mentioned that Nabee ﷺ related this Hadeeth whilst smiling and whichever Sahābee ؓ narrated it to his student, he too was smiling. This mode of transmission has continued until it has reached us in this manner whereby both the speaker and listener smile. This is why it is known as Hadeeth *Musalsal bil dhihak* (Hadeeth of Continuous Humour). Accordingly, this will be the status of the lowest ranking Jannatee, that he will receive such a huge Paradise equal to the whole surface of the earth. Consequently, what will be the position of those much higher in rank? Since we are confined to the four walls of this world, it is not possible for us to perceive...moreover, the thought does arise as to what one person will really do with such large territory?

Comparatively speaking, our stay in dunya is similar to an unborn child's period of gestation in his mother's womb. Because the foetus is unaware of dunya, it regards the mothers stomach as everything, however the moment it appears in dunya it realizes that his mother's womb is nothing in comparison to the size of dunya. May Allah ﷻ grant all of us knowledge of the Ākhirah with His Pleasure, we would then have an inkling of the sheer magnitude of that everlasting abode which has been created for the Mu'min.

Shaykh Dr. Abdul 'Hai 'Arifee ؒ used to comment, *'Alhamdulillah! Jannah has been prepared for the Mu'min, a person of Imān. If you acknowledge Imān upon Allah ﷻ, then firmly believe that indeed it has been prepared for you. Yes, to reach Paradise and to avoid pitfalls along the way, you will have to make some effort... should you do so then Jannah is yours.'*

Attention of Aboo Hurayrah ؓ

It is related that Sa'eed bin Musayyeb ؓ, a high ranking Tābiee was walking with his teacher - the renown Aboo Hurayrah ؓ through a bazaar on *Jumu'ah* (Friday) to buy something. Upon returning, Aboo Hurayrah ؓ commented,

> 'O Sa'eed! It is my du'aa that Allah ﷻ gathers us both together in the bazaars of Jannah.'

Observe the attention of the Sahābah ؓ, even during mundane worldly chores they are contemplating upon the Ākhirah, thereby preventing dunya from submerging their hearts. They did not abandon dunya, here they are shopping, yet the mentor is teaching a du'aa whereupon Sa'eed bin Musayyeb ؓ asked, 'Why, will there be bazaars in Jannah? Because we have heard everything is available for free in Paradise; whilst only buying and selling takes place in bazaars.' Aboo Hurayrah ؓ replied,

> 'I have heard from Nabee ﷺ that upon every Jumu'ah in Paradise, bazaars will be organized for the Ahl-e-Jannah... and when these people have reached their respected stations in Paradise and will be enjoying such a luxurious existence

that the thought of going anywhere else will not even arise. Suddenly, an announcement will be made, 'All the Ahl-e-Jannah are hereby notified that they should depart from their residences and come towards a bazaar.' They will arrive at this bazaar and observe such astonishing spectacles and delights not witnessed before. It will be announced,

'Take whatever you desire from these shops.' Accordingly, all the Ahl-e-Jannah will roam through this bazaar and select whatever they wish.

The Bazaar of Allah ﷻ in Jannah

'When this selection will have finished, an announcement will take place on behalf of Allah ﷻ, 'Now all people should gather in the Court of Allah ﷻ for a congregation because today is the day of Jumu'ah, wherein in dunya you people used to leave your homes to gather for (salāh) in one place. Today, on Jumu'ah you are being granted an assembly as substitute, proceed towards the Court of Allah ﷻ.' Accordingly, all people of Jannah will arrive here where personalized seats will await each person...some made of diamonds and jewels, some of gold, some of pearls and silver...each in accordance with the individuals rank: the higher the status, more elaborate the chair. However, each person will consider his own chair to be so exquisite, the thought of desiring another will not arise...because in Jannah there is no vestige of sorrow or grief.

Even for the lowest ranking Jannatee, there will be mounds of musk and amber. After all the Ahl-e-Jannah will be seated, the Royal Court of Allah ﷻ will commence with

Angel Israafeel (who blew the Trumpet upon Qiyāmah) reciting the Glorious Qur'ān in such a sweet melodious tone as to totally denigrate all worldly music. Thereafter laden clouds will cover the horizon giving an impression of imminent rain. As the Jannatees will behold this sight, a shower of musk and saffron will cover every person thereby providing total fragrance throughout the Court, such pleasant smells which nobody had previously experienced or thought possible.

Greatest Nemat - Vision of Allah ﷻ

Then with the Command of Allah ﷻ, a delightful and invigorating breeze will blow causing every Jannatee's beauty to increase twofold. Thereafter, from Allah ﷻ a Mashrūb (drink) will be offered to every person, wherein will be such taste inexperienced in dunya.

Afterwards Allah ﷻ will ask, 'O people of Jannah! Have you received all the nemats We promised you in dunya in return for your Āmale Sālihaah and Imān or is there anything outstanding? All of Ahl-e-Jannah will reply with one voice, 'O Allah ﷻ! What greater nemat could there be which You have not blessed us, for You have fulfilled every promise and granted us everything. We no longer desire or know of any other wish?'

It appears in certain narration's that even here the Ulamā will be of assistance - for people will approach them and request, 'Inform us of any such nemat which we have still not received?' Accordingly, the Ulamā will advise, 'There is one remaining nemat which we have not received...ask for the Vision of Allah ﷻ.' Instantly, all of Ahl-e-Jannah will request with one voice, 'O Allah! One great nemat remains, that is Your Vision.' Allah ﷻ will reply, 'Yes, this nemat for you remains outstanding, now you will be granted this bounty.'

Thereafter, Allah ﷻ will display His Vision to Ahl-e-Jannah, who will feel that all previous and any future nemats are nothing in comparison. After this Vision, all people will return to their homes, whereupon their wives and hûrs will comment, 'What has happened today, for your beauty and appearance has increased so much from before?' Ahl-e-Jannah will reply, 'You too are much prettier than when we had left you!' It appears in Hadeeth, that Nabee ﷺ commented, this increase in beauty will be due to the breeze which Allah Ta'ālā caused to blow.'

This is a brief description of one event in Jannah which Allah Ta'ālā's pious servants will experience. May Allah ﷻ select all of us to be amongst them. Āmeen.

Impossibility of Comprehending Nemats

It is worth remembering that no amount of description, comparison or words may correctly describe the nemats of Jannah. Allah ﷻ relates in a Hadeeth-e-Qudsee,

> 'I have prepared for My pious servants such nemats, which until now no eyes have observed, no ears have heard and the thought of which has not crossed any heart!'
>
> (Islaahi Khutabat, Vol. 9, p 243)

This is why the Ulamā relate that whilst bounties of Jannah share the same names as items of this dunya, for example fruits: pomegranates; dates; etc., their reality are very different and inconceivable to us here in dunya today.

Similarly, it is reported there will be palaces in Jannah - this instantly conjures up a picture in our minds based upon what we have seen and heard, yet in reality, we are unable to comprehend these Heavenly palaces. It is also related there are streams of wine, milk and honey in Jannah. Because, we liken this to worldly milk and honey, their esteem and value does not arise in our hearts, hence we are unable to truly visualize the wine, milk and honey of Jannah.

No Sorrow or Worry in Jannah

Moreover, the biggest nemat of Jannah, which we are unable to fathom here, is the absence of any form of sorrow, regret or fear relating either to past, present or future events. This concept is impossible to achieve in dunya, because Allah ﷻ has created this worldly abode in such a manner where no happiness or pleasure is 'complete.' Here, some form of difficulty or worry is associated with every nemat. For example, you sit down to eat, the meal is indeed delicious and mouth-watering, yet the worry remains that should one overeat, indigestion or an unhealthy weight gain may follow. Similarly, should one commence drinking the most tastiest drink, the thought will appear (of constipation or having to rush to the toilet if too much is drunk). This awareness (no matter how remote) is present with all worldly pleasures, however, Allah ﷻ has created Jannah in such a manner wherein will be no regret of not being able to fulfil any desire or wish. Whatever you desire will be achieved!

A Brief Worldly Preview of Jannah

For example, it appears in Hadeeth, one will desire to drink the juice of a certain pomegranate. You will not have to undertake the trouble of harvesting and thereafter peeling or crushing the fruit. Immediately, the juice will present itself to you. This is not at all far-fetched as Allah ﷻ has displayed a few samples of this concept in dunya. Before when mention was made of this, people were prone to consider it as some magical tale, however, inventions and developments by the finite intelligence and experience of man has illustrated such wonders which would have been considered impossible or insane only 100 years ago. Take the Fax machine (e-mail, text & internet), place a piece of paper (or message) in Asia and within a minute it is reproduced exactly in detail by fax (e-mail or text) in America. Should you have forecast this invention only 20 years ago, one would have been considered insane, for it takes commercial jet travel the best part of a day to travel this distance.

When such has been achieved by the finite ability of man, entirely through Tawfeeq of Allah ﷻ, then why, is the Creator unable to achieve such nemats in Jannah for His servants through His Infinite Power and Rahmat (Mercy)? Here in the Jannatee's heart will arise a desire...and instantly this wish will be fulfilled!

In the final analysis, until realities are revealed to *Insaan* he is reluctant to firmly accept extraordinary occurrences. However, the Prophets ﷺ, who were bestowed such *Uloom* (knowledge) not granted to any other human, have foretold us of these nemats in Jannah with such surety that further details are not needed. Therefore, these glad tidings are undoubtedly true, Jannah and its nemats are all true, as Allah ﷻ reveals:

> *'And race one another towards Forgiveness from your Lord and towards a paradise the width of which spans the heavens and the earth. It has been prepared for the Muttaqeen (God-Fearing).' (3:133)*

However, to reach this Jannah, Nabee ﷺ commented,

> *'Jahannam is surrounded by desires and pleasures, (whilst) Jannah is encircled by hardships and difficulties.'*
>
> (Ma'āriful Hadeeth, p.284, Vol. 1)

Allah ﷻ has surrounded Jannah with such items which externally are unpalatable to one's nafs, just as some magnificent palace may be enclosed by fields of thorns and bushes. To enter this palace, one will have to overcome these obstructions, moreover until one does so, entry therein will remain barred. Similarly, Allah ﷻ has encircled this magnificent Jannah with *Farāidh* and *Wājibāt* (compulsory) Commands. These are annoying to one's nafs, for example, to withdraw from dunya and go to the Masjid and perform Salāt.

Similarly, the heart of man desires to commit many acts that have been labelled harām. For example, the eye has been prohibited from viewing some items; to view a non-mahram, to view TV, etc. All these restrictions are burdensome to man...who desires to indulge in these avenues, these are precisely the 'thorns' which encircle Jannah.

Another example is one's tongue; in company, the conversation veers towards the gheebat of someone. Now, the heart desires to 'slag-off' this person, however the Sharee'ah commands us to refrain from backbiting and control one's tongue...this too is burdensome and another 'thorn.' Therefore, if we wish to enter Jannah, of a surety we shall have to overcome these thistles otherwise Jannah will remain closed...this is the Sunnah of Allah ﷻ. The first part of this above Hadeeth states, 'Jahannam is surrounded by desires and pleasures...' Hell has been encircled by Allah ﷻ with desires and pleasing items; our hearts incline towards these, however they lead unto Fire.

Thorns Becoming Flowers - An Incident

Despite these 'thorns' encircling Jannah, Allah ﷻ has created them in such a way that should anybody make a firm intention to overcome them, He will transform these, for us, into flowers. They are thorns when viewed from afar and considered as obstacles impossible to be breached. The moment one makes a resolution to plough through them into Jannah, Allah ﷻ will open up a path whereby they became a bed of roses. A Sahābee ؓ was participating in *'Ella Kaleemataullah,* when the enemy in a mass assault tried to overcome and totally destroy the Muslims. Automatically, the following Kaleemah appeared upon his lips ~

> 'The time has arrived whereby tomorrow we shall meet with our friends and loved ones: Muhammad ﷺ and His Companions.'

Oblivious to the fray of swords and arrows, this Sahābee ؓ

happily launched himself into the enemy ranks to sacrifice his life. It appears in Ahadeeth, that whomsoever becomes a *shaheed* in the Path of Allah ﷻ, this person's death (despite any external injuries suffered) is as painless as the bite of some minute ant. In reality, this is what becomes of the 'thorn' between the Mu'min and Jannah when he firmly decides to sacrifice his life, which was from Allah ﷻ, for His Sake. Had he passed-away upon a bed, who knows what difficulties and death pangs would have to be experienced. Similarly, when we keep the views of others uppermost in our mind - that if we undertake a particular Deeni activity, people will belittle or mock us, call us with epithets of being *orthodox* and *backward*, understand well, the fear of such thoughts too is one thorn between us and Jannah.

Respect belongs only to those Practicing Deen

Happily accept such 'pin pricks' and become oblivious to worldly criticism. Thereafter, when you decide to firmly practice upon Deen and proclaim oneself to be so 'backward' as to look upon the Sunnah of Nabee ﷺ at every turn of life come what may...then understand these 'thorns' will become roses. Allah ﷻ is forever showing us here in dunya the plight of those who mock and belittle people who practice upon Deen. Even during the time of Nabee ﷺ, the *Munnafiqûn* (hypocrites) used to taunt the Muslims, whereupon Allah ﷻ revealed,

> 'Respect belongs to only Allah, His Rasool and the Mu'mineen, even though the Munnafiqûn know not, for they are unaware of reality.' (63:8)

Therefore, these 'thorns' which surround Jannah are only there for trial. As soon as you decide to confront them, Allah ﷻ will convert these into sweet smelling roses, whereby one will derive such joy in performing *ibaadaah,* which is unobtainable in any worldly act of pleasure. This is why Nabee ﷺ often used to state, 'Salāh is the coolness of my eyes.' Similarly, although giving up sins appear burdensome and heavy upon the heart, especially in the beginning, nevertheless repeated refusal to commit sins, solely in order to acquire the Pleasure of Allah ﷻ, produces such happiness, exhilaration and peace of mind unattainable elsewhere.

Ponder, why does the mother sacrifice her rest and comfort for her young baby? It is a wintry night, the child cuddled up to her has wet himself. Instantly, she will arise in middle of the cold night (without even the sleeping father's knowledge) remove, wash and redress the child. She returns cold and weary; soothes, feeds, comforts and lullabies the child back to sleep. Discomfort upon discomfort. However, because she regards the child as part of herself, her own flesh and blood, all discomfort is transformed into willingness. If anybody should be foolish enough to question her, 'Madam, you have to undertake so many hardships for this child, why let us take it away, you would then be rid of all these worries?' Immediately, the unselfish mother would reply, 'Difficulties a thousand times greater I am prepared to undertake than see my child being snatched away from me!' Why does she respond in this way? Because she has *muhhabat* for the child; such love and affection which makes any difficulty from the child appear more pleasurable than acts of desires.

Ponder Upon Jannah & the Ākhirah

Accordingly, the reason why Nabee ﷺ related the nemats of Jannah in so much detail and why the Glorious Qur'ān is so replete with mention is precisely to create its awareness and longing within us. This is why our elders recommend we regularly ponder over Jannah. Shaykh Ashraf 'Ali Thānwi ﷫ advises in his lectures,

'Every Muslim should daily spend some time reflecting upon the Ākhirah, especially the bounties of Jannah. Ponder in this manner: I am now leaving dunya; my janāzah is being placed in the grave; people have now buried me and departed...now I have reached Barzakh. Ākhirah has commenced; the Hisab-kitāb (reckoning) is being demanded, the Meezān (scales) are placed, Pûl Sirāt awaits, yonder is Jannah whilst below is Jahannam. Unimaginable delights await the fortunate in Jannah; whilst unbearable hardships and terror are the lot of those destined for Jahannam.'

Sit down for a few minutes and reflect upon these realities, because all day long we are ever so absorbed in dunya that we become totally neglectful of the Ākhirah. Although we, all of us, are certain of our departure from dunya towards Ākhirah, nevertheless, this belief is not sufficient, we need to vividly comprehend this reality. It is this *istihzaar* (comprehension) which convinces one to practice upon Deen and refrain from sins. May Allah ﷻ, through His infinite *Rahmat* and *Fadhl* grant all of us true awareness and appreciation of the nemats of Jannah.

Shaykh Mufti Muhammad Taqee 'Uthmāni

The father of Shaykh Ashraf 'Ali Thānwi ﷺ was a wealthy person whose income was halāl. However, upon his father's death, he had a doubt regarding certain aspects of his inheritance and therefore wrote and sought the advice of his patron Shaykh Rasheed Ahmad Gangohi ﷺ...
'I am hesitant with regards to accepting my share because of the doubtful nature of certain aspects of the estate and indecisive in refusing, lest I should regret it later on.'
His mentor replied, *'If you were to accept your share it is fatwā (a Sharee' ruling and therefore permissible), if you abstain then it is taqwā (Fear of Allah ﷻ)...as far as perplexities, Inshā'Allah, you will be free from them life-long!'*

Shaykh Ashraf 'Ali Thānwi ﷺ chose the path of taqwā and forfeited his share of inheritance, which was quite considerable, advising:
'A person should not act according to his opinion when pious elders are present, rather he should consult with them. When such people are not available, he should consult able and trustworthy contemporaries; if these too are not present, he should consult juniors. Moreover, the reason why I mention pious people is that only Allah ﷻ is truly aware of the piety and rank of people.' (p 113, Amazing Episodes)

Shaykh Maseehullah Khān ﷺ narrated,
'Nowadays people are willing to sell (and thereby destroy) their Ākhirah for the sake of acquiring one miserable extra penny in this world.'

Chapter Eleven

How Should Inheritance Be Distributed?

Abridged Lectures
(Audio-Tape Code U129)
of
Shaykh Muhammad Saleem Dhorat
dāmat barakātuhum
at
Masjid-An-Noor,
Leicester, UK,
before
Jumu'ah Salāh
on
18th. & 25th. June 1999

Respected Ulamā, brethren, elders, beloved young friends and my respected Mothers and Sisters (listening at home). Through Tawfeeq from Allah ﷻ, it has been a good fortune to recite in your presence one verse from Sûrah an-Nisā. Herein Allah ﷻ says,

> 'For men there is a share in what parents and the nearest of kin have left...'
>
> '...And for women there is a share in what the parents and the nearest of kin have left, be it small or large - a determined share.'

When parents and relatives pass-away, whatever wealth they leave behind (and which they had rightly owned), whether it is little or great, significant or insignificant, it will be distributed to both males and females within the family in accordance to the shares determined by Allah ﷻ.

When a father dies, Allah ﷻ has stipulated what shares will be given to his bereaved family: so much for sons, daughters, wife, etc. Similarly, when a son or daughter passes away, there is a share for parents, and in some cases for sisters, brothers, grandchildren, etc. The scenario, situation and circumstances of each deceased person will differ, therefore, one will need to contact the respected Muftiyan-e-Kiram to find out exactly what is due to whom, '...be it small or large - a determined share,' apportioned by Allah ﷻ. No Ālim, Mufti, even the deceased or his bereaved wife, eldest son or the elders of his family have any personal say in this distribution and shares fixed by Allah ﷻ,

'A determined share.'

When was this Glorious Ayah Revealed?

When the Call comes from Allah ﷻ every person has to depart from dunya at his appointed time. During the time of our beloved Nabee ﷺ, a Sahābee by the name of Aws ibn Thābit ؓ passed away. He left a widow, a minor son and two daughters.

Before the advent of our Nabee ﷺ and the subsequently revealed Sharee'ah, in Arabia, widows, girls and orphans had no rights in society. During this age of ignorance, only he was considered worthy of receiving inheritance who was capable of fighting on horseback in a battlefield against the enemy and, who would be able to bring home the 'spoils of war.' Obviously, neither ladies, nor immature boys or daughters posses this capacity. Therefore, in that era, whenever a man died, the thought of his wife receiving anything at all was not even considered. Rather, ignorance had stooped to such a low level that the widow was also considered part of the estate. Thus, if a son by another wife came to usurp his late father's estate, he was at will to do as he wished with his step-mother: to the extent he would even marry her without her consent; or marry her away to some other person!

Similar was the position of young boys and girls, because they were incapable of fighting in battle and bringing home 'war booty' or able to generate any sort of income by any other means. Accordingly, when Aws ibn Thābit ؓ passed away, his wife, son and daughters were thought of as unworthy of receiving any inheritance. His 'closest' relatives were two paternal cousins in the prime of their life.

Both young men arrived, and usurped the whole estate...and this was not even considered wrong, a perfectly normal thing to do, for it had become a custom. Whenever an incorrect practice becomes entrenched in society, this wrong is considered right in the minds of people. Consequently, when an attempt is made to reform this malpractice, any true voice is thought of as incorrect.

Reluctantly, the poor widow resigned herself to fate, however, the thought arose in her mind, 'I now have to fend for my self, my two daughters and one young son. If only these two would marry each of my daughters, at least the responsibility of fending for them would be removed from my head.'

Accordingly, the widow of Aws ibn Thābit ؓ proposed to the two young men, 'You have taken control of our entire estate because of prevailing custom. At least show some pity upon our condition, if you were to marry the daughters of your late cousin, I would be freed from the very real worry of their maintenance.' Both openly refused.

This poor widow approached and related the whole episode to our beloved Nabee ﷺ who had always disapproved of this vile practice and had been awaiting a Command from Allah ﷻ. Within a short time, the signs of *Wahee* became visible upon the noble Face of beloved Nabee ﷺ. Ā'ishah ؓ relates that on such occasions, when Jibra'eel ؑ arrived with Divine Command, the weight of *Wahee* would cause Nabee ﷺ to lower his head and beads of perspiration, like pearls, to stream from his forehead unto his beard. Even the camel upon which Nabee ﷺ rode would be forced to sit-down on such occasions.

The signs of *Wahee* appeared and the Glorious Ayah was revealed unto Allah's Rasool ﷺ, which once and for all annihilated this vulgar and cruel practice,

> 'For men there is a share in what the parents and the nearest of kin have left. And for women there is a share in what the parents and the nearest of kin have left, be it small or large - a determined share.' (4:7)

Equality in Inheritance

The 'right' to inherit is common to both men and women. So when the father passes away, just as the son has a right to inheritance so does the daughter (the only difference is the actual share or amounts). Similarly, when the son dies, just as the father has a share so does the mother and wife. And should he leave behind only brothers and sisters, then they too will inherit.

People who have an understanding of Arabic will have realised that Allah ﷻ could have easily revealed that both men and women have a right in inheritance, but no,

> 'For men there is a share in what the parents and the nearest of kin have left. And for women there is a share...'

This separate mention of women is to emphasise and make people realise the fact that females too enjoy the same right to inherit. Upon arrival of these ayahs, Nabee ﷺ divided the estate in accordance to the Commands of Allah ﷻ...which in this case resulted in both cousins receiving nothing. Why? Because upon the death of someone, the principle of *'Al akrab fal akrab'* (closest before the close) is applied; i.e. should children of the deceased be living, the question of cousins receiving anything just does not arise.

Divine Portions for Women

Accordingly, the greatest Mufti of all time, the Messenger of Allah ﷺ apportioned one-eight of the estate to the widow, because when a man dies and leaves behind a wife and children, she receives one-eight (12.5%). And, should he be survived by only his wife and no children, then she receives one-quarter (25%).

Of the remaining estate (87.5%), Nabee ﷺ divided it into four equal parts (21.875%); and granted one portion to each daughter and two shares (43.75%) for the son. These were the circumstances of this Ayah, which resulted in the cousins receiving nothing!

> 'For men there is a share in what the parents and the nearest of kin have left. And for women there is a share in what the parents and the nearest of kin have left, be it small or large - a determined share.'

Therefore, irrespective of whatever amount the deceased leaves behind; be it only £500, an apparently trivial sum which becomes extremely small when divided up, all the inheritors will receive their Divinely determined share. This is why our *Fuqaha* (Jurists) have stated - through which the sensitivity and gravity of this Command will be understood: whatever set of clothing the deceased passed-away in; which is removed prior to *ghusl*, even this forms part of the estate. No inheritor has the right to distribute or dispose of these clothes without the prior willing consent of *every* inheritor, irrespective of wherever they be present at home or abroad in another continent. This applies to everything of the deceases: *it'r, tasbeeh, topi,* spectacles, pen, blanket, bedding...any possession, whether it be significant or insignificant.

Minor's 'Consent' & Wrong Customs

Sometimes, the deceased leaves behind minor inheritors. Even if they be present, their consent is not acceptable to the Sharee'ah. Why, because their intelligence is not perfect yet. Should elders try to convince and obtain their consent, 'we wish to do so-and-so with this estate, do you approve?' these children often willingly approve; however their consent is not valid.

Nowadays, immediately upon death, relatives, friends and associates descend to the bereaved home. Without the consent of inheritors, people from Batley, Blackburn and London, from far away places come to a *Janāzah* in Leicester and all are dined at an expense of some hundred pounds! After some time (when the 'dust' has somewhat settled), the inheritors will sit down to finalize accounts. First, they will tally the cost of *tajheez & takhfeen* (shroud and burial). One should remember this only incorporates the expenses of bathing; kafn; soaps and perfume; plot in the cemetery; transportation. However, nowadays people also include therein the expense of hosting and feeding all those people who had arrived from distant places. This cost has no relationship with the bereaved, yet people deduct it from the estate as part of *tajheez & takhfeen*.

Accordingly, when *non-baaligh* children are also amongst the inheritors, then all these unnecessary expenses (of hosting and feeding) is in actual fact usurpation of wealth which belongs to orphans! All those who consume this food are also eating from the wealth of these orphans. Remember, Allah ﷻ relates,

> 'Surely, those who eat up the property of the orphans unjustly, they only eat fire into their bellies, and soon they shall enter a blazing Hell.' (4:10)

Seek Advice & Guidance from the 'Ulamā

Reflect upon this verse and with surety hasten towards changing these incorrect customs which are rampant in our society. Within your towns, cities and community are present such 'Ulamā, who are willing to guide and help you; turn towards them and inquire the correct method for distributing inheritance.

Allah's Rasool ﷺ commented, those who unjustly eat the wealth of orphans, tomorrow on the Day of Qiyāmah when they arise from their graves, embers of fire will be in their stomach and flames will belch out from their ears, mouths, eyes and nose!

Once a Saint went to visit an ill person (iyaadah) at night... when a lamp was burning. As fate had destined, this ill person passed away during this visit. Immediately, the Saint extinguished the lantern, and ordered an accomplice to go and buy a lantern and some oil from somewhere. These were purchased and lit, someone present enquired, 'Shaykh, what need was there for this trouble...especially at this hour of night?' The Saint replied, 'As long as this person was alive, the oil and lantern belonged to him and was halāl for us to benefit from. However, the moment his *ruh* departed, all his belongings, including this lantern and its oil became the property of his inheritors. Now, it is not possible to make use of anything without the willing consent of all of them...and all of them are not presently here. Therefore, I did not consider it appropriate to make use of this property.'

Allah Ta'ala's Choice of Distribution

We, all of us should remember, that it is Allah ﷻ who has determined who receives what and how much. Herein, not even the decease has any choice, he cannot claim, 'so-and-so was a great friend who assisted me a lot, therefore when I die, he should receive half of my estate.' Similarly, 'of my two sons, this one was more loyal and devoted, therefore, he should receive the greater share.' Likewise, the elders of a clan or community have no right to decide who should receive what. Remember, *'And Allah is All-Knower, All-Wise.'* Allah ﷻ is fully aware of which child has been more devoted and who is weak or strong. The *Ilm* of Allah ﷻ is infinitely greater than ours, however as well as being *'Aleem*, He is also *Hakeem* (the All-Wise) and it is with these great qualities have shares of inheritance been determined: so-much for the widow, husband, son, daughter, parents, etc. Herein, none of us have any say or opinion, after death everything of the decease belongs to the inheritors and will be shared in accordance to the Rules of Sharee'ah. The Guardians of this Sharee'ah, in this era, are none other than the Ulamā-e-Haqq and Muftiyan-e-Kiram. Therefore, we will need to consult them and present all the facts: the estate and number of inheritors and, seek their explanation of how much to distribute and to whom.

The purpose for this explanation is to emphasize the fact that everything the decease leaves behind and, which was his/her property, is the *tarakah* (estate), which becomes now the property of every inheritor. It is therefore not permissible, for example say for five beneficiaries, to decide on this estate without the consent of the sixth inheritor.

Order of Distribution

Why? Because, upon every penny, each of the six (in this case) have some form of claim and right until it be divided in accordance with the Sharee'ah. Also, this Sharee'ah has outlined a detailed order of how the estate is to be distributed:

1) Tajheez & Takhfeen (Bathing, Shroud & Burial)

On account of the estate having belonged to the deceased, the first Haqq is that of *tajheez & takhfeen* (the cost of bathing, shroud & burial). It is of course, quite another matter, if out of love and affection one or more of the inheritors decide to personally bear this expense.

The basic principle to remember here is that neither should one adopt *fuzul kharchee* (extravagance) nor *bukhl* (stinginess). The deceased has now left dunya, therefore what benefit is there in buying very expensive cloth? Aboo Bakr Siddeeq ؓ made a *Waseeyat* at time of his death, 'Bury me in the same clothes which I am wearing, because new cloth is more befitting a living person.' Nowadays, expensive lined coffins, polished and lacquered are purchased. Whilst not advocating *bukhl*, neither should there be such extravagance.

2) Qardh (Debt)

After *Tajheez & Takhfeen,* one will need to ascertain whether the deceased has left any unpaid *Qardh* (debt). Scrutinize his diaries, record books and statements, also people will themselves come and claim 'he owed us such and such!' Therefore, the second priority will be to pay-off all unpaid debts. Should a person have passed-away leaving behind a house valued at £50,000 and he has debts of £50,000, then the house will have to be sold in order to pay the debt. The inheritors will receive nothing. In this circumstance, should the inheritors refuse to clear the debt and unjustly claim the £50,000 for themselves, remember this money will be *ghasab* (akin to stealing) and harām. Why? Because this money did not belong to the deceased, it was a loan from others, therefore it must be returned to its rightful owners.

We, all of us, are drowned in *Ifrāt-ō-tafreet* (excesses and shortcomings). We fully remember what is owed to us, because the deceased had written it down, however we conveniently overlook that somewhere this person will have also noted what he owes to others. Accordingly, when a debtor arrives to claim back his money, which the deceased had written down...the reply will be, 'Our late father never mentioned anything about this £5,000 to us, present your proof!' Do not glee upon having deprived this person of his rightful £5,000; ponder as to who is responsible for the punishment which will befall father in his grave because of our greed for £5,000!

Loyalty demands that children acknowledge and endeavour to clear any genuine debts their father had left behind... 'Although our father did not leave sufficient monies to clear the debt immediately, please adopt sabr whilst we strive to pay you. Do not worry, from today his debt is our responsibility.' This is the demand of affection for one's father: the person who nourished and nurtured us from childhood, today Allah ﷻ has granted us an opportunity to assist him. Yet, nowadays our actions and selfish behaviour becomes a means for his suffering in the grave. Allah ﷻ says,

'...after (settling) the will you might have made, or debt.'

(Glorious Qur'ān 12:4)

Therefore, should a person leave behind an estate valued at £50,000 with debts of £45,000, then this *qardh* will be cleared first. The remaining £5,000 will be distributed amongst the inheritors in accordance to their determined share after seeking guidance from an Alim.

3) Waseeyat (Bequest in 33% of Estate)

A person has the *haqq* (right) to make a *Waseeyat* (bequest) whereby he states that, 'Upon my death, from my estate, *x* amount should be given to the following person/s...for example, £5,000 should be donated to this Masjid.' However, even in a *Waseeyat* rules apply. Firstly, the decease may not make a *Waseeyat* for any of his inheritors. Whilst his wife will receive her determined share, he cannot also say, 'She should be the beneficiary of an extra £1,000.' Why, because Nabee ﷺ stated, *'There is no Waseeyat for an inheritor.'*

Therefore, only those who will not inherit may be nominated

to receive *Waseeyat*. For example, sometimes one's brother will not receive anything. A person may be leaving a wife, sons, daughters and parents. Obviously, here circumstances are such that the brother will not be an inheritor, a Mufti should be consulted, and thereafter one may appoint the brother to be the recipient of *Waseeyat*.

The second point to remember is that *Waseeyat* only operates in one-third (33.33%) of the estate. For example, a person makes a *Waseeyat*, 'after my death, £5,000 should be donated to Masjid-An-Noor.' Because the Masjid is not an inheritor, it is possible for it to receive *Waseeyat*. However, upon death, the cost of *Tajheez & Takhfeen* and debts will be deducted from the estate. Now, if it is found that only £9,000 remain, Masjid-An-Noor will not receive £5,000 as proposed in the *Waseeyat*, the Masjid will receive only £3,000 because any *Waseeyat* operates in one-third of the estate *after* deduction of *Tajheez, Takhfeen* and debts. For clarity,

Waseeyat (to Masjid) £5,000

Estate (after *Tajheez, Takhfeen* and debts) £9,000

Two-Thirds for Inheritors £6,000

Amount *actually* donated to Masjid £3,000

Causes of Incorrect Wills

Therefore, fully appreciate these two rules. Firstly, the decease may only make a *Waseeyat* in one-third of the estate, two-thirds will be distributed in accordance to the Sharee'ah. Secondly, it is not permissible to make *Waseeyat* for any inheritor.

When these *ahkāms* are understood, one automatically

realizes the mistake people make in Wills nowadays. Modern-day Wills operate in 100% of the estate... 'Whatever I leave behind, 10% should go to so-and-so, 15% to so-and-so, 20% to so-and-so, etc.' No cognizant is taken of the fact that *Waseeyat* only operates in one-third of the estate or that, in general, Wills are made specifically for the benefit of inheritors. The amount for one's wife is already determined, therefore, what right do you have to specify 50% for her? The Sharee'ah forbids this, she is already an inheritor, for whom the Sharee'ah has specified a share. After your death, you have no right and your Will (to the contrary) is of no significance, she will receive only that amount (no more, no less) which the Glorious Qur'ān and Sharee'ah have allocated.

The purpose here is not to confuse anybody with *masa'eel* (rules), merely to bring to attention the big mistakes prevalent in our society, thereby encouraging our readers to behave correctly when somebody passes-away by consulting the Ulamā.

The wife should never take unfair advantage of *kufr* legal rights and court proceedings to enforce she be the recipient of 100% of the estate thereby preventing her children from receiving their dues until her own death. Such a *baatil* Will is of no consequence in the Sharee'ah, it is akin to stealing or breaking into someone's house and robbing them at gunpoint. Just as a thief fills his pockets with *harām* money, so does the person who employs *kāfir* laws to gobble up the estate. Should orphans be amongst the deprived inheritors, then:

'Surely, those who eat up the property of orphans unjustly, they only eat fire into their bellies, and soon they shall enter a blazing Hell.' (4:10)

The 3 Criteria's for a Waseeyat

Accordingly, when a person dies, first deduct the cost of *Tajheez & Takhfeen* and debts from the estate. Thereafter examine the Will to see whether it is incorrectly in favour of any inheritor. Secondly, ensure all *Waseeyats* are within one-third of the estate. Thirdly, scrutinize, whether the *Waseeyat* is for any harām or sin.

For example, a person 70 years of age is so intoxicated with *maal* (wealth), that despite suffering a couple of heart attacks, he still fails to reform. His character has so deteriorated, he wishes to deprive those children who failed to fulfil his every whim and tantrum. He consults with his cronies and lawyers to draw-up such a Will wherein the local Masjids will receive the lion-share of his estate. The reason for such apparent generosity to a good cause? Nothing other than to spitefully deprive his children from their rightful due! This is a sinful *Waseeyat*.

Ikhlaas (sincerity) in Waseeyats

Similarly, although some people do specify *Waseeyat* in only one-third of their estate, as is their *haqq*, nevertheless their *niyyat* here again is to deprive their children, for whatever reason. Thus, a person has £30,000, of which he makes a *Waseeyat* of £10,000 for the local Masjid. It appears to everybody that this generous act will take him into Jannah, but in reality, because his motive is lacking in *ikhlaas* (sincerity), the moment the Masjid receives this £10,000, he will enter Jahannam! May Allah ﷻ grant all of us correct understanding and, Tawfeeq to undertake actions which earn His Pleasure.

Consult and seek guidance from the Ulamā thereby reforming all your actions. Of course, there are also such pious people who make correct Sharee' *Waseeyat*, for example, upon my death I shall be leaving my wife, 4 boys, 2 daughters and parents.' Therefore, my final *Waseeyat* is that after death, my estate should be distributed in accordance to the Sharee'ah amongst my inheritors, and in this regard whatever the Islāmic Da'wah Academy or Darul Uloom Bury, or a certain institute, ālim, mufti decides is to be upheld and enacted.

Such *Waseeyats* are a means of acquiring *thawāb* and the Pleasure of Allah ﷻ, why, because not only has this person saved himself from sin, he has also ensured all his inheritors behave within limits of the Sharee'ah. Even if his children; sons and daughters should squabble amongst themselves and take their arguments to a court of law, the ruling will still be what the Muftiyan-e-Kiram decides: for this *Waseeyat* was stipulated in the Will. Let us reiterate and ponder upon what Allah ﷻ says in the Glorious Qur'ān:

Depriving Sisters - An Ill within our Muaasharat

> 'For men there is a share in what the parents and the nearest of kin have left. And for women there is a share in what the parents and the nearest of kin have left, be it small or large - a determined share.'

Another point to remember, which is quite prevalent amongst Gujarati Muaasharat (society) is the false notion that father had given all he wanted to his daughters during his lifetime.

O really? What is the Arabic meaning of *meerāth*? What is the English meaning of inheritance? What is the Urdu meaning of *wirāsat*? In addition, what is the Gujarati meaning of *warsaah/wejhree*? Each means the same thing, the distribution of a person's estate *after* his death! Obviously, anything, which a father gives to his children during his lifetime, is called a gift. After death, no account is taken of these gifts, no matter what their size or nature for now a new system of accounting comes into order, inheritance!

Many males who label themselves as *'deendar'* (pious) very cunningly phone or meet their sisters to inquire, 'Sister, as I intend to behave within the Sharee'ah, what shall we do with your part of the inheritance which our beloved father has left?' Observe how sisters are pressurized and embarrassed in a *muaasharat* wherein ladies are expected to waive and not accept their share of inheritance. These poor souls will be constrained to reply, 'Yes, brother, I am very happy in my home, you do as you wish with the inheritance.' Ponder, when we owe somebody some money, do we go up to them and ask, 'I owe you £50, what shall I do with it?' Of course not, we physically hand the money over, then why do we ask our womenfolk whether they wish to receive inheritance?

This is deception, fraud and stealing; it is a surreptitious ploy to deprive ladies from their rightful due. What we should do is neither ask nor deceive, but physically hand over a cheque (cash or whatever) to her. Should she state, 'Brother, you do as you wish with it.' One may reply, 'Sister, Allah ﷻ has granted you intelligence also, accept it now and do whatever you wish with it. If after 2 or 3 months you are still unsure of how to use it, then seek my guidance.' It is the responsibility of males to hand-over the share of womenfolk, not ask silly stupid questions in a bid to gobble up their share.

The supposed financial well being of (married) daughters and any poverty of sons are irrelevant as far as distribution of the fathers estate is considered. Should brothers refuse to hand-over their share, remember this will be harām wealth in his possession, which will be transformed into embers of Hell in his stomach! Moreover, this will continue as long as this harām wealth remains in his lineage right unto Qiyāmah.

Final Word

Now we have realized the compulsion of distributing inheritance we should consult with the Ulamā & Muftiyan-e-Kiram to ensure correct behaviour in this regard, to succeed in the Ākhirah. Remember these Scholars fully understand and appreciate the need to maintain in secret and confidence whatever you mention...in order to safeguard their Ākhirah! They will not go-around advertising your matters and dilemmas, try it, consult them. If you feel hesitant ask them about a supposed third person, for example, 'A certain person has a wife, 2 sons, 4 daughters and so much wealth. However, his sons are complete rogues, is there anything that could be done to protect the interest of the womenfolk? Are there any avenues available within the Sharee'ah to ensure the womenfolk receive their fair share, guide us.' Present your problems and predicaments to them and accept whatever they advise in accordance to the Ordinances of Allah ﷻ: no matter how bitter their suggestion. Inshā'Allah, in this way you will succeed in both dunya and Ākhirah.

Separate Ownership

Another point, quite often overlooked, is the need during one's lifetime to maintain correct records of everything owned by separate members of a family. We find joint bank accounts in the name of husband and wife, both deposit their monies herein...what will happen when one of them dies, who will know how much belongs to whom?

The wife passes-away, there is £25,000 in the account and the husband comes along to Mufti and asks, 'My wife has died, we wish to distribute inheritance, however we have no records of how much belonged to her.' Under such circumstances, how may anybody ascertain what and how much to distribute? The same problem often arises in business partnerships and joint accounts between father and children. The son hands over his weekly wage to his father, under the assumption of safekeeping. Now when father dies, the son will, quite rightly, wish to reclaim his earnings whilst other family members will maintain, 'this was father's own wealth!' Beginning of problems.

Similarly, there might be a car in the household, jointly owned by father and child. One person paid £1,200, the other £300, what will happen upon death? Therefore, keep a written record, one person (in this case) owns 80% whilst the other owns 20%.

It is well-documented about the Grand Mufti of Pakistan, Mufti Muhammad Shafee' ﷺ, that at the time of his death, it was possible to know each item he owned, right down to every pen and pencil in his office. How? Because he only allowed that item to be kept in the room he was staying in, which belonged to him.

If this appears pedantic, just ponder how humans react. The wife purchases a fridge with her own money, the whole family will be using and deriving benefit from it. However, because no written records are kept, upon death or divorce, arguments start, both parties claim possession. Had separate records been maintained, such disputes would not arise. Reflect upon how husband and wife keep their clothes and wardrobe separately, does anybody have the audacity to suggest, 'all this because they do not have love for one another.' Of course not, household affairs are maintained in this way to ensure comfort: consequently, why is it improper to maintain separate bank accounts and a record of ownership for each item owned? Mutual love is not reduced nor diminishes by an iota, quite the contrary, because correct distribution of inheritance is a Command of Allah ﷻ, maintaining a record of ownership greatly assists in this Deeni matter.

Summary & Du'aa

Beloved reader, from these lectures we should heed and endeavour to act upon what has been related. Firstly, maintain a record of ownership at home: this does not imply nobody else may make use of our items. This pillow belongs to so-and-so, yet every member of the family may use it. Secondly, whenever somebody passes-away at home, all his estate will be isolated and thereafter we shall consult with a Mufti to decide how and to whom this is to be distributed. Thirdly, remember, this age is one of depravity, therefore, sit down with an Ālim and draw-up an Islāmic Will (such a document has been prepared and is attached as an Appendix, in this book, alternatively you may write to the Islāmic Da'wah Academy for a copy). Thereafter, consult with a lawyer and Ālim thereby avoiding any disputes amongst inheritors.

Finally, honestly reflect upon our mistakes to-date. Whatever inheritance we have failed to hand-over to our womenfolk... everybody is full aware of this and the amounts involved. Therefore, irrespective of any financial hardships involved, this harām wealth (for us) should be returned to them thereby saving ourselves from the horrendous hardships of the Ākhirah.

May Allah ﷻ give us all the true understanding of the Sharee'ah and tawfeeq to practise upon it fully. Āmeen.

Shaykh Muhammad Saleem Dhorat

dāmat barakātuhum

Shaykh Mufti Muhammad Shafee' ﷺ commented, 'By not distributing inheritance correctly, one commits 3 forms of *zulm* (tyranny). Firstly, understand that inheritance is a gift from Allah ﷻ, which the bereave receive without any effort. Accordingly it is a Divine present, therefore it is incumbent on the inheritors to distribute it correctly to all (Sharee') inheritors. Now, when anybody interferes in this inheritance, they are guilty of misappropriating this Divine Gift. This is the first *zulm*.

The second *zulm* is to withhold the rightful due of one's sibling. Whenever the father passes-away, all brother's and sister's inherit in his estate...together with his wife. Now, when we usurp this estate, obviously we are pillaging somebody else's due and to 'steal' another's share is also *zulm*. It is the same as stealing another person's money or property.

The third *zulm* is to deprive (all successive) inheritors from their *haqq* (right). When the practise of inheritance is abandoned, whereby sons' and thereafter grandsons' fail to distribute *meerath*, one is actually depriving forthcoming generations of their due. The sin of all those who successively sin, falls upon that person who committed this *zulm* by failing to distribute his fathers wealth in accordance to the Sharee'ah. Therefore, immediately after burial, payment of (any) debts and fulfilment of *waseeyat* (in one-third of the estate), it is incumbent to divide the whole inheritance as quickly as possible. This will bring relief; for the longer one delays: the greater the worries, problems and in-fighting!'

(p166, Islāhi Lectures)

Chapter Twelve

Esãl-al-Thawãb
(Virtuous Acts which Benefit the Deceased)

&

Customary Qur'ãnic Recitation Ceremonies

An Abridged Lecture

of

Shaykh Mufti 'Abdur Ra'oof Sakhrawee
dãmat barakãtuhum

With Notes from the Teachings of

Shaykh-ul-Hadeeth Zakariyyã 🌷
Shaykh Mufti Ashiq 'Ellahi Madanee 🌷
Shaykh Ahmad Sadeeq Desai
dãmat barakãtuhum

Rasoolullah ﷺ commented, 'When a Mu'min passes away, his *amal* (deeds) come to an end, however it is possible to receive the reward of seven deeds:

1) Whomsoever had taught another person Deeni 'Ilm (Knowledge), its reward is perpetually received as long as this 'Ilm remains in the world.
2) His pious children; whom pray on his behalf.
3) A copy of the Glorious Qur'ān (which people read).
4) Construction of a Masjid.
5) A Rest house for the benefit of travellers.
6) Construction of a well or (source of water for public usage).
7) Donation of *Sadaqāh* during his lifetime.

As long as these items remain, this person will continue to receive their rewards.' (Ahqāme Mayyat, p 263)

Shaykh-ul-Hadeeth Zakariyyā ﷺ relates, 'We should be extra-vigilant in performing acts of *Esāl-al-Thawāb* for our deceased parents, husband, wife, brothers & sisters, children, other relatives; especially those from whom we may have derived either spiritual or worldly benefit, such as one's Ustaadh & Mashā-ikh. Nabee ﷺ commented, 'When a person passes-away, the rewards of his āmal finish. However, there are three such actions the thawāb of which accrue even after death:

1) Sadaqāh-e-Jaariyah.
2) Such 'Ilm (of Deen) from which people benefit.
3) Pious children who pray for him after his death.'

(Fadhāeel Sadaqāt)

Allah ﷻ states in the Glorious Qur'ān:

'And whatsoever the Messenger (Muhammad ﷺ) gives you, take it; and whatsoever He forbids you, abstain (from it)...' (59:7)

Respected friends! The Glorious Qur'ān was revealed for the benefit of our guidance unto Nabee ﷺ who himself was a living example thereof. Whatever our beloved Nabee ﷺ stated or enacted, all formed a practical expression of the Glorious Qur'ān, thereby providing us with an example to follow.

Consequently, whatever is contained in Ahadeeth is a commentary and elucidation of the Glorious Qur'ān. We should therefore judge all our actions within the *Light* of these principles. Whatsoever we do not find in the *Sunnah* of our beloved Nabee ﷺ is to be shunned, because only those deeds are acceptable to Allah ﷻ which comply with the Sunnah. Accordingly, any deed contrary to the Sunnah, no matter how beneficial it may appear to us, is rejected, because it does not strictly follow the Way of Nabee ﷺ.

Customary Collective Recitation

I wish to draw attention towards a practice so widespread in our *Muaasharat* (society) but which has no basis in the Sunnah. This is the custom of announcing and arranging collective recitation of the Glorious Qur'ān immediately after burial of the deceased. Sometimes, even posters and newspaper notices, with mention of time and location are placed to advertise these events. People (including non-mahram women) thereafter travel from afar to these venues. In any locality wherein a death takes place, people will congregate at specific intervals for a period up to the fortieth day with great gusto, invitations, meals, etc.

What we have to discern and understand is whether our beloved Nabee ﷺ or His Sahābah ؓ carried out this practice? Remember, genuine Sunnahs were those carried out by Rasoolullah ﷺ, His Khaleefh's and Ashāb's ؓ, their students the Tābi'een, Tabe Tābi'een ؓ and successive generations of Ulamā and Sulahā.

Every single Sunnah has reached us in its pristine form in this manner, nothing altered or hidden. When these criteria's are matched to the current vogue of collective recitation of the Qur'ān after the death of someone, we realize this practice just did not exist during the time of Nabee ﷺ, His Khaleefh's, Ashāb's, the Tābi'een and Tabe Tābi'een ؓ. Obviously, if this custom was acceptable, Nabee ﷺ himself would have ordered it: for many beloved Companions, Daughters, Sons and Mothers of the Believers ؓ, died during His lifetime. However, one will not find a single occasion wherein Rasoolullah ﷺ announced or gathered His Companions together at Masjid-An-Nabawee for completing recitation of the Glorious Qur'ān. No such method of Esāl-al-Thawāb is recorded during either the time of Nabee ﷺ or His Deputies. It is therefore obvious that later people initiated this practice and, because this custom has no Sunnah basis, many of its features undoubtedly will conflict with the Sharee'ah.

Some Foul Features

Neither is this form of collective recitation Fardh, Wājib or Sunnah, at most, it may be termed naf'l. Moreover, it is not permissible to pressurize (including emotional forms), boycott, oppose or harbour ill-will against anybody who fails to attend. Such stress upon non essential deeds is discouraged by the Sharee'ah, because when Allah ﷻ and His Rasool ﷺ have not classified this practice as either Fardh, Wājib or Sunnah, who are we to accord such importance to these acts? Another vulgarity of this practice is, generally, people attend in order to please others, the sole purpose now is not the Pleasure of Allah ﷻ.

Three Conditions of Qur'ānic Recital

An episode of Shaykh Ashraf 'Ali Thānwi ؒ is related by one of his students. One day, when the respected Shaykh was teaching at Kanpoor, his students entered the classroom for a lecture, when they beheld him sitting very sadly...signs of sorrow and melancholy were clearly visible upon his face. After a brief pause, the students asked respectfully, 'Shaykh, what is the matter? Why are you sitting so sadly?' He replied, 'A message has arrived from home...my eldest sister has passed-away, this is why I am sad.' The students responded, 'We shall not recite our lesson today!' Shaykh Ashraf 'Ali Thānwi ؒ replied, 'I have come to teach.' Ponder for a few moments, his eldest sister has passed-away, even though he is sad there is no large gathering, he is prepared to carryout his daily routine of teaching. When the students insisted on cancelling the class for the day, Shaykh Ashraf 'Ali Thānwi ؒ accorded to their wish. The students now suggested, 'In this hour, we wish to recite some Qur'ān and transfer its reward to the deceased?' Shaykh Ashraf 'Ali Thānwi ۞ replied, 'If you are able to accept the following conditions, you have my permission:

1) Firstly, you should not recite the Qur'ān together, rather recite it separately and privately.
2) Secondly, everybody should recite only as much as he wishes with ease: a quarter, half or whatever...even if it be recitation of Surah Ikhlaas only three times. It is not at all necessary to finish the entire Glorious Qur'ān.
3) Thirdly, when you have finished recitation, no Taalib-ul-Ilm should come to inform me of how much he has recited for my late sisters' benefit...what need is there to inform me?

The reason for this final condition is to ensure *ikhlaas*, because if you recite in order to inform me, you will be placing a load upon yourselves to recite more, 'What will Shaykh think if I say I have only recited half a Juz? Is this your concern and affection for me?' Sincerity will be absent, and when there is no *ikhlaas*, what *thawāb* is there to transfer? Now, when you are free to recite as much as you wish, it is better to recite Surah Ikhlaas only three times with sincerity than recite the whole Qur'ān with pretence.'

Accordingly, we too should adopt these three conditions: each of us should privately recite as much as easily possible thereby acquiring *thawāb*. This form of private *esāl-al-thawāb* is so easy that it may be enacted daily throughout one's life.

Problems of Collective Esâl-al-Thawāb

In reality, only anxieties are created by congregating: travelling from afar; changing one's daily schedule...all in order to arrive and participate at one specific time and venue. On the contrary, there is nothing but ease in private recitation which is totally in keeping with the Teachings of the Sharee'ah, because to complete the whole Glorious Qur'ān in one sitting is not easy. Somebody may be occupied, ill, in a rush to return, etc., all now become tied down...the 30 Juz need to be completed as quickly as possible with no regard for *tajweed* (correct recitation). The result of self-imposing these rituals is not only hardship but also sin, because incorrect recitation of the Glorious Qur'ān acquires a curse for oneself. It appears in many narration's that many are those who recite the Glorious Qur'ān but only achieve its curse. Our Ulamā have explained that should recitation of *huroofs* (letters) be inaccurate, the Qur'ān curses its reader. Now when the Glorious Qur'ān itself is cursing, what chance is there of acquiring or transferring *thawāb*. Remember, it is *wājib* (compulsory) to recite the Glorious Qur'ān correctly, and to oppose any *wājib* act is sinful.

Finger Khatams & Sajda Tilaawat

Another misfortune of organizing and pressurizing people to attend such *khatams* is the participation by such people who are unable to read the Glorious Qur'ān. Unwilling to admit their inability, they too collect a Juz from the mimbar and pass their index finger over the text and, or recite *Bismillah* over each word...as if they too are reciting!

Other harms of these events include the vile habit of publicizing the numbers of people who attended; names of important dignitaries; number of *khatams* completed; type of food, drink and snacks served, etc. In reality, all these are acts of *riya* (ostentation) which totally destroy the possibility of acquiring *thawāb*. Our Ulamā have stated that this custom of feasting (meals, snacks, drinks) after these *khatams* is akin to receiving a payment in return for having read the Glorious Qur'ān.

A further mischance, is the failure by many of those who attend, to perform *Sajdatut Tilaawat* (those 14 places in the Glorious Qur'ān after the recitation or hearing of which Sujood becomes compulsory). You will observe many reciting in the congregation...yet not a single person is viewed performing *Sajdatut Tilaawat*. Why? Because most people are either unaware, careless or indifferent. Many are now burdened with the responsibility of discharging this Wājib...a burden they carry unto Qiyāmah. It is even reported that in certain quarters the organizers themselves wrongly perform all 14 Sujoods on behalf of the whole gathering!

Quack Leaders

These leaders and organizers are like the half-baked quacks described by Shaykh Ashraf 'Ali Thānwi ﷺ in one of his lectures. A certain quack arrived to meet his followers in a distant far-flung village. Observing his lean, haggard and despondent physique, the villagers asked, 'Shaykh, why have you become so weak?'

The quack replied, 'Ah! What to say? Why should I not

become weak? I have to pray and fast on behalf of everybody...furthermore, I have the back-breaking worry and concern of taking you all along with me upon *Pûl Sirāt* (the bridge over Hell, which is sharper than a sword and thinner then a strand of hair). Moreover, because you all are my followers, I have the additional responsibility of ensuring I enter all of you, into Jannah! This grief is with me all the time...this is why I am becoming weaker!'

A landowner, who was also present, upon hearing this woeful tale was touched. In a spate of emotion, he announced, 'Shaykh! You are undergoing such hardship on our account? The very least I can do is to gift you one of my paddy-fields... I insist you accept!' This quack was no fool... 'It is not enough to just promise, show me where it is so I may physically accept and take over.' Undaunted, the landowner proceeded to take the quack through the rice fields...which were flooded with water held back by retaining terraces. As they walked along these slippery mud-walls, the quacks feet kept slithering (for he was unused to such country toil) until eventually, he slipped and plunged headfirst into the flooded paddy field. Immediately, the landowner kicked him from behind and said, 'Liar! When you cannot even tread upon a broad terrace, what chance have you got of walking over *Pûl-Sirāt*? It appears even there you will drop us into Hell! Be-off rascal, I am not giving you my field!'

Ease & Comfort in Following the Sunnah

Understand well, there is nothing but ease and comfort in following the Sunnah. One may recite as much of the Glorious Qur'ān as easily possible, in fact this is not the only form of *Esāl-ë-Thawāb,* others include making Zikr or donating money on the deceases behalf, or the very least to make du'aa with attention...

> 'O Allah! Forgive him, have Mercy upon him, save him from Punishment of the grave and the Fire of Hell. Grant him the highest Station in Jannah!'

It appears in Hadeeth, that when a living person makes such du'aa's for the deceased, Allah ﷻ blesses and grants *thawāb* equal to the size of a mountain. Every person is able to perform this Sunnah with the utmost of ease.

Virtues of Sûrah Ikhlaas & Kaleemah Tayyibah

However, should one insist on reciting the Glorious Qur'ān as *Esāl-al-Thawāb,* in Ahadeeth many virtues and blessings are mentioned of Sûrah Ikhlaas:

> 'Reciting Sûrah Ikhlaas 3 times earns the reward of completing one whole Glorious Qur'ān.' (Bukhāree)

> 'Whomsoever recites Sûrah Ikhlaas 12 times after Fajr Salāh, Allah Ta'ālā bestows the reader with the reward of (having completed) 4 Glorious Qur'ān!' (Kanzul Ā'amāl)

> 'Whomsoever recites Sûrah Ikhlaas 200 times, Allah Ta'ālā will forgive (his minor sins) of 200 years.' (ibid.)

> 'Whomsoever recites Sûrah Ikhlaas 10 times, Allah Ta'ālā creates a Palace for (the reader) in Jannah.'

> Hearing this 'Umar ؓ commented, 'O Rasoolullah ﷺ! In that case we shall have built numerous Palaces in Jannah!' Nabee ﷺ replied, 'Allah Ta'ālā is able to grant more!'

> 'Whomsoever recites the Kaleemah Tayyibah 70,000

times and thereafter blesses its reward to some Marhoom, then such a person is saved from Athāb of the grave.'

(p 69 & 74, Vol 1, Islāhi Lectures)

Gifting Esāl-al-Thawāb does not Lessen Thawāb

Now if all associates of a deceased were to make a habit of reciting Sûrah Ikhlaas 12 times after Fajr Salāh daily, just ponder how much reward and benefit will the decease gain and how happy they will become? All these blessings and ease from practicing within the limits of the Sharee'ah.

This is why Shaykh Ashraf 'Ali Thānwi ﷺ had the routine of transferring the *thawāb* of all Naf'l acts performed daily to all Muslim deceased: all the Prophets ﷺ, Sahābāh, Tābi'een, Tabe-Tābi'een ﷺ and successive generations of Ulamā, Sulahā and all members of the Ummah.

One should remember, our Ulamā have stated that it is not permissible to transfer the reward of any Fardh and Wājib acts, however, by transferring the reward of Naf'l ibaadahs, one does not lose out...Shaykh Ashraf 'Ali Thānwi ﷺ has illustrated this concept by means of two examples. Firstly, consider how it is possible to alight 100 candles from just one candle, without the light of the first candle diminishing in the least.

Secondly, ponder how one Ālim (qualified scholar) spends his entire lifetime imparting Uloom to others...without his Ilm diminishing in the least. If an Ālim teaches a kitāb today, he does not forget it tomorrow, quite the contrary, his own uloom increases as well as that of his students. Ilm is a spiritual *Nûr*...and just as alighting umpteen candles from one candle does not diminish the light of the original candle, similar is the case with Deeni Uloom and *thawāb*. This is precisely why Shaykh Ashraf 'Ali Thānwi ﷺ routinely transferred the *thawāb* from his nafl acts...and this is something which we too should practice daily.

An Easy Daily Routine of Esāl-al-Thawāb

One should make a habit when leaving and returning home from the Masjid for the five daily Salāhs of reciting Sūrah Ikhlaas 10 or 20 times along the way. In this manner, one will easily recite Sūrah Ikhlaas 200 times and acquire the *thawāb* of having completed the Glorious Qur'ān almost 70 times! In addition, one will acquire 20 Palaces in Jannah, now should this staggering reward be transferred to all *marhumeen* (deceased Muslims), just ponder how happy they will become! Why such happiness? Because this world is the abode of *amal* (practice) wherein through the Fadh'l of Allah ﷻ, we are able to gain and transfer reward for the Ākhirah. This is why our *marhumeen*, the People of Barzakh await our du'aa's of *maghfirat* (forgiveness). We should therefore make our own preparations whilst the opportunity is available and not await gifts from others. Nobody sits around in this world and expects others to come and feed him, we all work and strive in order to survive and prosper, similarly, we should not await help from others. Strive and practice good deeds whilst the chance is here. This world and our existence therein will finish quite soon, relates Allah ﷻ:

> 'Whatever is with you, will be exhausted, and whatever is with Allah (good deeds) will remain...' (16:96)

Advise from the Dead - Episodes

Once a Saint was passing a graveyard, when the condition of one inmate was miraculously revealed unto him. He observed a person lying in tranquillity...whose grave he approached and after exchanging Salāms enquired, 'What have you experienced?' The deceased replied,

'I am perfectly well and wish to relate something to you. Whatever we had heard in the world about Barzakh, i.e. reward in the grave for good and punishment for evil deeds I have observed and is quite true. However, now I am unable to do anything unlike you, who although not having witnessed Barzakh are still able to practice good deeds...but do not do so.'

Another Saint whilst passing a graveyard also had a similar experience. He observed a *mayyit* sitting in the grave and reciting the Glorious Qur'ān. Surprised, he inquired, 'We have heard there is either reward for good or punishment for evil deeds in the grave. I was unaware that one could engage in recitation, zikr, salāh in the grave...then why are you reciting the Glorious Qur'ān?'

The mayyit replied, 'Whenever a person arrives in *barzakh* from dunya, immediately he is asked 3 questions. Thereafter, he is informed that he is to spend his time in this grave until Qiyāmah. However (if he was pious), he is allowed to choose his most beloved good deed in dunya. As recitation of the Glorious Qur'ān was my dearest act, I chose and was granted permission to recite the Qur'ān until Qiyāmah. Sitting here alone I have completed 70,000 khatams, nevertheless I am prepared to gift this to you in return for the reward of you reciting just one *Subhān'Allah.*' Astonished, the Saint commented, 'But this would be a unbelievable bargain, why?' The mayyit replied, 'The reality is that from where you are speaking, one *Subhān'Allah* earns great reward...infinitely more than completing 70,000 khatams of the Glorious Qur'ān here (in Barzakh).'

Prepare now for the Ākhirah - An Example

Understand well, we are at present able to perform good deeds in dunya, wherein recitation of just one *Subhān'Allah* will earn a tremendous 'Tree' in Jannah. Similarly, reciting Surah Ikhlaas 10 times will earn a 'Palace' of Jannah. However, when we enter our graves, reciting many *Subhān'Allah's* or khatams will not earn any *thawāb*. May Allah ﷻ grant us *tawfeeq* to perform good deeds whilst the opportunity is available.

Shaykh Mufti 'Ashiq Ellahi Madanee ﷺ relates the final moments of 'Allamāh Juzree ﷺ. His sister was sitting at the bedside and crying upon the imminent departure of her beloved brother...when suddenly, 'Allamāh Juzree ﷺ opened his eyes and inquired, 'Why are you crying?' His sister replied, 'Brother, this is the time of your departure and our separation!' 'Allamāh Juzree ﷺ advised, 'Dear sister, do not cry upon my death...' (thereafter, pointing towards one corner of the room, he spoke), 'Your brother has completed 18,000 khatams of the Glorious Qur'ān in that corner. I have great hopes from Allah ﷻ, through whose tawfeeq, Rahmat and Fadh'l all these khatams were completed, that He will Forgive me.'

These 18,000 khatams were those completed in one corner of the house...just ponder how many others he must have read at other places!' Allahu Akbar!' How is this humanly possible? Allah ﷻ grants great barakah in the time of His Friends...the Awliyaa. Whilst time is one and the same, the amplitude and breadth therein is different for these pious souls. Neither is there any loss of *tajweed* in their recitation.

A Reward of Twenty Thousand

Finally, I wish to draw attention towards a simple deed which will earn a reward of 20,000 virtues in a matter of seconds! Recite this easy Kaleemah,

لَآ اِلٰهَ اِلَّا اللّٰهُ وَحْدَهُ لَاشَرِيْكَ لَهُ اَحَدًا صَمَدًا لَمْ يَلِدْ وَ لَمْ يُوْلَدْ وَ لَمْ يَكُنْ لَهُ كُفُوًا اَحَدٌ

The first portion is a Kaleemah whilst the second part is a portion of *Surah Ikhlaas*. Such a simple *amal* which earns tremendous reward. One should make a habit of reciting this kaleemah, say 5 times, before and after every Salāh: a daily income of 10 x 5 x 20,000 = 1 million virtues. Now gift this daily to our Nabee ﷺ, parents, children, family members, ustaadh, mashā-ikh and all marhumeen. It is not necessary that all these be those who have died...even the living have a right over us.

May Allah ﷻ grant all of us correct Tawfeeq.

Shaykh Mufti 'Abdur Ra'oof Sakhrawee

Visiting the Graveyard

Prophet Muhammad ﷺ commented,

'Visit the quboor (graves), for verily, it reminds you of death.'
(p38, Kitabul Janā-iz)

The main purpose of visiting Muslim graves in a cemetery is to remember one's own death and make *esāl-al-thawāb* for the dead. Along the way make *thikr* and abstain from useless talk. When approaching the graves, recite:

اَلسَّلَامُ عَلَيْكُمْ اَهْلَ الدِّيَارِ مِنَ الْمُؤْمِنِيْنَ وَ الْمُسْلِمِيْنَ وَ اِنَّا اِنْ شَآءَ اللهُ بِكُمْ لَلَاحِقُوْنَ، نَسْأَلُ اللهَ لَنَا وَ لَكُمُ الْعَافِيَةَ، اَنْتُمْ لَنَا فَرَطٌ وَّ نَحْنُ لَكُمْ تَبَعٌ

'Peace be upon you, O dwellers of this place among Believers and Muslims! Surely, when Allah wills, we are sure to join you. We beg Allah for ours and your safety. You are forerunners to us and we are to follow you.'
(p233, Al-Hisnul Haseen)

Be extremely careful not to step or walk upon the graves and approach the graves from the feet side and stand facing the grave with your back towards the *qiblah*. Again make Salām... our Ulamā have stated that the etiquette of visiting the dead is similar to visiting them whilst they were living. Recite a portion of the Glorious Qur'ān silently. It is preferable to recite Surah Yāseen, Surah Mulk and the Surahs from *Surah Takaathur* to the end of the Qur'ān. It is best after completing Tilāwat, to turn towards the *qiblāh* and make du'aa without raising your hands.

Chapter Thirteen

Fikr
(Meditation)
Upon Death

from
Arba'een
of
Imām Al-Ghazāli

& the Teachings

of

Shaykh Ashraf 'Ali Thānwi,
Shaykh 'Ashiq Ellahi Meerathi,
Khwajah 'Azeez-ul-Hasan Majzoob,
Shaykh Dr. 'Abdul 'Hai 'Ārifee,
Shaykh Hāfiz Dr. Sulayman Kaflethwi

Fikr (Meditation) of Death

Imām Al-Ghazāli ﷺ relates in his epic *Arbaeen* (Tableegh Deen), 'Allah ﷻ states in the Glorious Qur'ān:

'Say (to them): Indeed the death from which you flee will of a surely meet you...' (62:8)

Prophet Muhammad ﷺ commented:

'Increasingly remember the destroyer of all desires (death).'

Ā'ishah ؓ narrates she once asked Nabee ﷺ, 'O Rasoolullah ﷺ! On the Day of Hash'r (Reckoning), will anybody arise with the Shuhadāh (martyrs)?'

Nabee ﷺ replied,

'Yes, he who remembers death 20 times during the night and day.'

Rasoolullah ﷺ also commented:

'There is no greater lecture (for admonition) than death.'

'If animals had as much knowledge of death as Bani Adam (humans) possess, you would not find one plump animal to eat.'

'I leave behind two Wa'aiz for you: one a silent lecture; that is death; and the other lecture which is audible: the Glorious Qur'ān.' (p 320, Tableegh Deen)

How to Meditate upon Death

Understand well, death is frightening and the events which transpire thereafter are even more terrifying. Remembering death often, creates indifference towards dunya and removes its esteem and love from one's heart. It is this *muhabbat* for dunya which is the root of all evil and sins, therefore when this love is removed from the heart, one has achieved everything. Detestation for dunya will be possible only when awareness and concern for death ingrains itself... that quite soon a dreadful event is to transpire! The best way to make *fikr* of death is to sit alone for a few minutes everyday (and because nowadays the moment we lie down upon our beds to make *zikr* we doze-off to sleep: it is best to fix a certain Salāh, say after Fajr or 'Esha). At this time, empty and remove all thoughts from your heart, now with firm intention and full attention reflect upon death.

Firstly, ponder upon all those relatives and associates who have left this dunya, think about where each of them has disappeared to? What hopes and aspirations they have taken with them? What greed and actions did they display? O how they craved for fame, glory and wealth...yet today all these ambitions are scattered in dust as they lie underneath; with none to remember or mention them.

Secondly, reflect upon the bodies of these people, how delicate and beautiful they were, yet now they are dismembered, putrefied and food for insects, worms and maggots. Thereafter, ponder upon every feature of the body, think of that tongue which never knew how to maintain silence! What has happened to those hands which were always in motion? Have those enchanting eyes and prominent features not become food for snails!

Nabee ﷺ commented~

'As-Sa'eedûh (fortunate) is he who derives lessons from others.' (p 321, Tableegh Deen)

Meditating daily on death in the above manner will Inshā'Allah transform one into *As-Sa'eedûh* (fortunate), because it is indeed heartbreaking to observe how unmindful we are of such a catastrophic event as death. Upon this very earth which we are treading today, thousands have walked and passed before...yet we blissfully assume we will live forever. The traumatic journey of death lies in front of us but we are uncaring. This is because *tûlul amal* (useless long hopes) have drowned us. Should this ignorance be cured; an awareness of death would dawn upon us. This is why Nabee ﷺ advised 'Abdullah ibn 'Umar ؓ,

> *'When evening approaches do not await the morning; when the morning approaches do not wait for evening. Moreover as you have arrived in dunya, make preparations for death whilst alive, and worry about maut in good health, because O 'Abdullah! What knowledge is there regarding what is to happen to your personality tomorrow, whether you be dead or alive? Whichever event has no fixed time as to its appearance...one should worry about it all the time.'* (Bukhāri quoted on p 322, Tableegh Deen)

Usāmah ؓ once bought a servant for 100 dinars upon credit for two months. Hearing of this Nabee ﷺ commented,

'Be amazed upon Usāmāh's condition: when life cannot be relied for even one day; he has brought a servant on credit for two months! This is precisely tûlul amal. By Oath of Allah! Whenever I place a morsel in my mouth, I do not have any certainty whether it will be swallowed... for it is possible, before it descends, I may choke and die. O people! If you have any intelligence, count yourself amongst the dead. By Oath of that Being in Whose Control is the life of Muhammad (ﷺ), whatever has been promised is to transpire, and what is to appear is very near. If you harbour a desire to enter into Jannah, then reduce futile concepts of dunya and always keep the thought of death in front of you. Moreover be ashamed of Allah Ta'ālā as is His Haqq to be ashamed, Inshā'Allah (then) you will enter Jannah.' (p 322, Tableegh Deen)

Shaykh Ashraf 'Ali Thānwi ﷺ commented, 'The reality of death is severer than the simultaneous strikes of 600 swords. Just grasp and uproot one hair and then observe what pain and discomfort is experienced by the whole body! Now ponder, what happens when the soul is extracted from the entire body...even if there be no other punishment, this difficulty itself is enough to sour all comforts of the world.' 'Fix a free-time wherein you ponder about your standing before Allah ﷻ with the Scale of Deeds nearby and Reckoning taking place. Pûl-Siraat is in front and you are commanded to proceed across it. Now observe how fear is created and how your heart disinclines towards sins; henceforth it will become easy to live in accordance to the Sharee'ah...'

When a Mu'min Passes-Away

Baraa' bin Aathib ؓ relates, 'One day we accompanied Rasoolullah ﷺ for the funeral of an Ansāree ؓ to the graveyard. Upon reaching the grave (which was still being dug), Nabee ﷺ sat-down and awaited. We too sat down out of respect: ever-so silently as if birds were sitting upon our heads. Nabee ﷺ had a stick in his *mubarak* hand with which he was stroking lines (as if in deep remorseful thought). Thereafter, he raised his *mubarak* head and spoke,

'Seek protection from athāb (punishment) of the grave (he repeated this statement 2 or 3 times). Undoubtedly, when the Mu'min is about to depart for the Hereafter, Malaa'ikah (angels) with glittering faces come to him from Heaven. They bring with them kafan and fragrances from Jannah. There are so many of them...as far as the eye may see. Malikul Maut thereafter arrives and sits by his head and speaks, 'O pure soul! Come towards the Maghfirat (forgiveness) and Ridhā (Pleasure) of Allah Ta'ālā.'

Accordingly, (the Mu'min's) soul leaves with such ease as a water droplet emerging from a container of water...the Malaa'ikah take possession of his soul and wrap it in the heavenly kafn and fragrances...(which are more beautiful than the most fragrant musk available on earth)...The Malaa'ikah proceed with the (pure) soul upwards. Every group of angels living on earth, whom they pass, enquire: 'Whose pure soul is this?' The accompanying Malaa'ikah reply by addressing the soul with various honourable names...child of so-and-so. In this way they reach the first heavens and request the doors to be *opened; they proceed in this way with the angels of each Heaven accompanying this retinue to the next Heaven until the Seventh Heaven. Herein Allah Ta'ālā Comments, 'Place the Record of Deeds of My servant in 'Illeeyeen and return him to earth, for I have created man from soil and unto it will he be returned and from it he will be resurrected a second time.'*

Accordingly, his rûh is returned to his (earthly) body. Thereafter, two Angels arrive, make him sit up and ask the following questions: 'Who is your Creator?' The (Mu'min) replies, 'My Creator is Allah!' 'What is your religion?' 'My religion is Islām!' 'Who is this Gentleman who was sent unto you?' 'He is Allah's Rasool (ﷺ)!' 'How were your deeds?' 'I read the Kitāb of Allah, brought Imān upon it and accepted it.'

Thereafter, an announcer from Heaven (upon Allah's Command) proclaims...'My Servant has spoken the truth, therefore spread the bedding of Jannah for him, clothe him with garments of Jannah and, open unto him the doors of Jannah.' Accordingly, the gates of Jannah are opened for him...through which arrive the comfort and smells of Jannah. His grave is expanded unto the limits of eyesight. Now a person with an extremely handsome face, clothing and fragrance appears to proclaim, 'Listen to glad tidings, for you this is that day which you were promised.' The Mu'min queries, 'Who are you, for indeed your face is worthy of being called a countenance and relating good news?' 'I am your good deeds!' (Out of sheer joy and ecstasy) the Mu'min says, 'O my Creator! Let Qiyāmah commence so that I may reach my (Heavenly) family, children and wealth!'

When a Non-muslim Passes-Away

Nabee ﷺ (continuing with the same hadeeth) commented,

'Undoubtedly, when a kāfir servant is about to leave this dunya for the Ākhirah, black-faced Angels arrive with a sack and surround him as far as the eye may see. Thereafter, Malikul Maut appears and sitting by his head scowls, 'O hideous soul! Come towards the Displeasure of Allah.' Hearing this announcement of Malikul Maut, the soul runs hither-thither in the body. Accordingly, the Angel of Death extracts his soul in the same way a meat-skewer is dragged through wet cotton (i.e. with extreme severity, pain and harshness)...

The soul is then handed over to the other Angels who enwrap it in the sack containing such foul putrefied smell akin to a bloated decomposing body. These Angels proceed towards the Heavens and, whichever group of Malaa'ikah they pass enquire, 'Whose revolting soul is this?' They address it by the most offensive and disgraceful names, 'son of so-and-so.' When they reach the First Heaven, a request for the doors to be opened is refused:

> 'Verily, those who belie Our Ayāt and treat them with arrogance, for them the Gates of Heaven will not be opened and they will not enter Paradise until the camel passes through the eye of the needle (which is impossible). Thus do We recompense the Mujrimun.' (Glorious Qur'ān, 7:40)

Thereafter, Allah ﷻ Commands, 'Place his kitāb in Sijjiyeen which is the deepest expand of earth.' Consequently his soul is *thrown from Heaven: Nabee ﷺ recited the Ayah:*

'...And whoever assigns partners to Allah, it is as if he had fallen from the sky, and the birds had snatched him, or the wind had thrown him to a far off place.' (31:22)

Thereafter, his ruh is returned to the body and two Angels appear, who command him to sit up as they ask: 'Who is your Creator?' He stutters, 'O, I do not know.'

'What is your religion?' He stutters, 'O, I do not know.'

'Who is this person who was sent unto you?' He stutters, 'O, I do not know.'

Upon this questioning and replies, an announcer from Heaven proclaims, 'He has lied, spread fire underneath him and open the doors of Hell unto him!'

(Accordingly the doors of Hell are opened for him) whereby the heat and vapours of Hell reach him. His grave becomes so narrow that both sides of his rib-cage press into each other. A hideously ugly person dressed in revolting clothes appears, from whose body emerges foul smell to announce, 'Receive news of difficulties, this is the day which you were promised would come!' The deceased ask, 'Who are you, for your ugly face heralds misfortune?' 'I am your evil deeds.' (For fear of receiving even greater punishment the deceased cries out), 'O Creator! Do not establish Qiyāmah.' (p32, What Happens After Death)

Allah ﷻ mentions in the Glorious Qur'ān:

'Verily, We have warned you of a near torment - the Day (of Qiyāmah) when man will see (the deeds) which his hands have sent forth, and the disbeliever will say: 'Woe to me! Would that I were dust!' (40:79)

The Deception of Life

Shaykh Ashraf 'Ali Thānwi ﷺ relates, 'When death arrives...that states transpires which Allah ﷻ addresses in the Glorious Qur'ān:

> '...My Lord! If only You would give me respite for a little while (i.e. return me to the worldly life), then I shall give sadaqāh of my wealth and be amongst the righteous (performing good deeds).' (63:10)

Those of us who consider ourselves intelligent, labour under the notion that upon completion of a certain task we shall free ourselves from everything and engage in the obedience of Allah ﷻ ~

> 'Every night, we say tomorrow we shall abstain from this act and engross in the (obedience) of Allah ﷻ. When the morrow arrives, we repeat that tomorrow we shall abstain. In this manner life is wasted away.'

Whether one be a Prophet or Saint, there will be no extension to life. At such a time one will desire, 'had I possessed the whole kingdom of the world, I would exchange it for just one more day.' However, this is not possible as Allah ﷻ mentions:

> 'And Allah grants respite to none when his appointed time comes. And Allah is All-Aware of what you do.' (63:11)

Who possessed a greater kingdom than Prophet Sulaymān ؑ? He was supervising the construction of Masjid-Al-Aqsa (Palestine) when message of his imminent death arrived. He supplicated, 'O Allah ﷻ! Grant me such a respite whereby this Masjid be completed, otherwise it will remain unfinished?' The Divine Reply was, 'There can be no extension of time, however the Masjid *will* be completed. Stand supporting yourself upon your *asaa* (staff)!'

Accordingly, Sulaymān ﷺ stood-up leaning upon his *asaa*... in this manner was his noble soul extracted, but his body remained upright. The jinni, witnessing him present and standing continued constructing. In this way the Masjid was completed. After some time, ants ate away the staff and the body of Sulaymān ﷺ fell down. Close inspection revealed that he had died some time before.

Ponder, a prophet such as Sulaymān ﷺ and a work of the magnitude of Al-Aqsa, but no respite! Now, if we persist with the thought that upon completion of our (numerous) objectives (in life) we shall incline towards Allah ﷻ (and the Ākhirah), then remember such an opportunity will never arise. The only way this is possible is to trample upon this notion and understand that whilst the time of our death may appear afar, in reality it is quite near. For this *dunya* is nothing but thoughts and excessive ambitions...'

When our Prophet Muhammad ﷺ passed-away, Sayyidina Khidr ﷺ consoled the Sahābāh ﷺ,

'There is peace from the Personality of Allah ﷻ in all hardships and a reward for each bereavement. Therefore, place trust and hope in only Allah ﷻ, because completely loss is only he who is dispossessed of all thawāb and a Muslim is never deprived of thawāb.'

Meditation upon Death

Based upon the epic Muraqabah Maut

by

Khwajah 'Azeez-ul-Hasan Majzoob ❀

Y ou were created for worship, remember,
To bow humbly unto Allah, remember,
    Otherwise, there will be disgrace, remember,
      For life is but a few days, remember,
  One day we have to die, Death is ultimate,
  Do whatever you wish, Maut is ultimate.
Were you to acquire status & rank, so what?
Vaults of gold and riches be in your hands, so what?
    Lavish mansions you were to erect, so what?
      Display your pomp and vanity, so what?
  One day we have to die, Death is ultimate,
  Do whatever you wish, Maut is ultimate.
Caesar, Alexandra & Kisra have all departed,
Napoleon & Rustam have all departed,
    What great brave leaders have all departed,
      Displaying their worth have all departed!
  One day we have to die, Death is ultimate,
  Do whatever you wish, Maut is ultimate.
How many houses has death annihilated,
The play of many has maut annihilated,

Many of gigantic build has death annihilated,
Huge statures has maut annihilated,
One day we have to die, Death is ultimate,
Do whatever you wish, Maut is ultimate.
Yes, O ignoramus, departure is whence?
Arise from negligence, break of dawn will commence,
Pack your provisions, the journey is hence,
Annihilation of every man will commence,
One day we have to die, Death is ultimate,
Do whatever you wish, Maut is ultimate.
Nafs & Shaytān to your bosom are snare,
The attack is imminent, O negligent beware,
Lest weakness arises in your Deen and good fare,
Halt! Stop your evil deeds which scare,
One day we have to die, Death is ultimate,
Do whatever you wish, Maut is ultimate.
Suddenly, death will arrive upon your skull,
then whither you and where Darul Amal?
Will perish this golden opportunity,
never again to arise for eternity,
One day we have to die, Death is ultimate,
Do whatever you wish, Maut is ultimate.
Concern for the Akhirah, to you O negligent is nothing,
Do not blunder, worldly comfort in reality is nothing,
Life is but a few days and naught else,
To rely upon it is folly, naught else!

One day we have to die, Death is ultimate,
Do whatever you wish, Maut is ultimate.
You have to depart from here one day,
Will be laid out in your grave one day,
Will show unto Allah ﷻ your face, one day,
Now no longer waste in folly even one day!
One day we have to die, Death is ultimate,
Do whatever you wish, Maut is ultimate.
All and sundry travel towards an ending,
Advance viciously towards this ending,
Flows from everywhere this smell of ending,
Emerges from everywhere this smell of ending,
One day we have to die, Death is ultimate,
Do whatever you wish, Maut is ultimate.
Worldly delights are but for a few days,
O ignorant, do not be enamoured by its ways,
One lives in this finite world but for a few days,
Now, perform deeds of the Ākhirah for the remaining days,
One day we have to die, Death is ultimate,
Do whatever you wish, Maut is ultimate.

❧❦❧

Our Opportunity to Reform

Shaykh Naseeruddin 🌸 relates a beautiful episode of justice by Shāh Alap-ar-Salān 🌸 (d. 420 AH/1072 CE). Once the Shāh was on a journey and encamped in a village en-route. Nearby was a field belonging to a old-lady whose sole income came from a cow grazing therein.

A few of the Shāh's soldiers (without permission) slaughtered and feasted upon this cow. When the old-lady became aware of this, she asked some of the locals to escort her to the bridge on the far side of the village over which the Shāh would pass on his departure. Early next morning, as the Shāh's entourage came to cross this bridge, the old-lady started to cry and complained loudly,

> 'O Shāh! Repay me for my loss on this bridge now, otherwise tomorrow when Allah 🌸 will ensure Justice, I shall grab you by the neck on the Pûl (Bridge) of Sirāt and demand reckoning!'

Hearing this woeful plea, Shāh Alap-ar-Salān 🌸 alighted from his horse and came over and sat down on the bridge at the feet of the old-lady and spoke humbly,

> 'Tell me, what oppression has been done so that I may redress it?'

The old-lady related how the Shāh's soldiers had slaughtered her only means of livelihood. Immediately, Shāh Alap-ar-Salān 🌸 ordered his whole retinue to camp upon this bridge and sent his minister to ascertain the facts behind this incident. The Wazir returned and confirmed the old-lady's complaint. Shāh Alap-ar-Salān ؓ ordered the guilty soldiers be severely punished. Thereafter, he purchased eighty (80) expensive high-yield milk cows and addressed the old-lady,

> 'One cow is being returned to you to ensure justice, the other 79 is my gratitude to you for having informed me. Now, tell me how many relatives do you have, so that I may fix a monthly allowance for all of them. Even now, if you have any other complaint or grievance, tell me upon this bridge for I will have no reply to give you tomorrow on the Pûl of Sirāt.'

Amazed and overwhelmed, the old-lady departed from the bridge giving her du'aa's. Some years after this incident Shāh Alap-ar-Salān ؓ passed-away. When the old-lady heard this sad news, she immediately prostrated and cried,

> 'O Allah ﷻ! You are the Lord of Shāh Alap-ar-Salān ؓ. Out of Your Fear he had showed justice and magnanimity to us in dunya. You are Raheem and Kareem, shower Your Fadhl upon him.'

That very night, numerous Mashā-ikh and Ulamā observed Shāh Alap-ar-Salān ؓ in a dream wherein he was strolling through *Jannah* dressed in Heavenly garments and commented, 'Because Allah ﷻ had accepted my justice to the old-lady, here Allah ﷻ has showered me with His Favour!'

(p. 135, Why, are you ready for death?)

Therefore, dear reader we should constantly take stock of our lives and strive with all our resources and faculties to redress any wrong, injustice or shortcoming with any fellow creation: be he a Muslim or non-muslim.

Chapter Thirteen

Death of an 'Ãlim (Scholar) is Death of the Ãlam (world)

Abridged & Edited Final Inspirational Lecture
of the Renown Scholar of Bukhãri
Shaykh-ul-Hadeeth
Mufti Sahbãn Mahmood
Delivered One Day before His Death at
Jãme Masjid, Karachi, Pakistan
on Friday, 28th. Zull Hijjah 1419 AH
(17th. April 1999 CE)
Translated from the Original Urdu article written by
Shaykh Al Hasan Mahmood
in
'Al Balã'gh'

Respected friends! I had planned on speaking about something else but immediately upon arising, this sudden thought has arisen in the heart from Allah ﷻ: that life is passing very quickly whilst we slumber in negligence without ever thinking of how much time we have wasted! Who knows when death will appear and remove us from this world? This is why it appears in the Glorious Qur'ān:

> 'Draws near for mankind their reckoning, while they turn away in heedlessness.' (Ayah 1, Sûrah Al-Ambiyā)

We snugly while-away our time carefree in the thought that come old age we shall make *taubah*. It appears from Hadeeth that people slumber in ignorance, oblivious to reality, only when death arrives upon our head will eyes truly awaken! Both the Glorious Qur'ān and Hadeeth are replete with the remedy to curb ignorance and negligence. In brief, one should ponder upon the events that transpire after death in the Ākhirah, the *hisāb-kitāb* (reckoning), visualize these events in front of you, they are very near, one more step and I shall enter the grave, etc. When this mode of reflection becomes a regular practice, these events will become a reality, negligence will disappear and a tremendous revolution will be perceived in one's life. The heart will soften and the most effective method of achieving this is to daily set aside a few minutes from your hectic lifestyle and sit in seclusion.

Now reflect, I am about to die, *Malikul Maut* has arrived, I am lying on my death bed: my wife, children and relatives are standing nearby; the doctor is trying his utmost to save me; an injection; the drip; the ubiquitous oxygen mask; however, the Command of Allah ﷻ cannot be overridden. I am leaving, my wife, children and relatives are crying, but their tears are of no avail as the Angels drag forth my soul towards the Heavens. Nobody was able to help me, I depart all alone.

Beloved! This moment is to transpire, think upon it, it is incumbent to do so for the sake of curing negligence. If you do so with consistency, love of the world will diminish, enthusiasm and desire to meet Allah ﷻ will increase.

Worldly relationships are of no avail

To make this meditation even more effective, reflect how relatives and friends will gather to prepare, bathe and shroud me. Lying motionless and unable to communicate, they turn me hither thither, rub and scrub my face. Why? Is this event not going to occur? Undoubtedly so, every one of us will experience these events...nobody will be able to prevent it, the sole relationship which will avail will be the *ta'allûq* (bond) with Allah ﷻ. One's wife, parents and children will prepare us for our departure and arrange for Janāzah Salāh, transportation to the cemetery and lowering into the darkness and forlornness of the grave. It appears from Hadeeth, when the mayyit is placed upon a bier for taking to the graveyard, if the person was pious, he calls out (although we are unable to hear him), 'Take me quickly towards my *manzil* (station), do not delay!' This is because at the time of his death, he is informed of his final abode in *Jannah*, and he knows what bounties await.

If Allah ﷻ forbid, the *mayyit* is a disbeliever, he wails and screams, 'Woe unto you! Where are you taking me?' Imagine these events as we proceed...when we reach the cemetery, with haste people bury us as quickly as possible. Now, one's beloved children, relatives and associate are placing planks and thereafter rush and clamour to throw soil. Sealed forever, no sound may come in or go out...a tomb 2 meters long by 1.5 meters deep!

Honour of the person who is regular with Salāh

It appears in Ahadeeth, when *Munkar* and *Nakir* arrive in the grave to question a person who was punctual with salāh, this pious soul experiences a scene in the grave reminiscent of when the sun is about to set. Quickly, this person calls out, 'For Allah's Sake, leave me alone otherwise my 'Asr Salāh will become *qadhā*...allow me time to pray my 'Asr Salāh!' Who will make such a statement? A person punctual with Salāh or somebody like us? The Angels will reply, 'You have been transformed from the world, here there is no Salāh, it is time for questioning now.'

Our answers will reflect our life on earth. 'Who is your Creator?' 'What is your religion?' 'What is the name of your Nabee?' The *Mu'min* will reply, 'My Creator is Allah ﷻ, my religion is Islām and my Nabee is Muhammad ﷺ.' The angels will comment, 'You have spoken the truth, we had expected you to do so.' Thereafter, they will expand every side of the grave and ask him to look up towards *Jannah*, 'O Friend of Allah ﷻ! This is your abode forever, for you had obeyed Allah ﷻ.' Our Nabee ﷺ commented, 'By Oath of that Being in Whose Control is my life, this person will experience such happiness on this occasion which will never return.' Seventy doors of *Jannah* will then be opened, from where cool breezes and fragrances will flow. An announcer from the Heavens will proclaim,

'My servant has spoken the truth, therefore spread the bedding of Jannah for him in the grave, clothe him with silken apparel, open unto his right side the windows of Jannah.'

Rebuke & Punishment for the kãfir

Accordingly, the Mu'min rests in peace and comfort until Qiyāmah. In complete contrast, the person who is unable to reply...he who lived a worldly life in accordance to his desires, in conflict to the Sunnah of Nabee ﷺ and the Glorious Qur'ān, he will only be able to mutter, 'I do not know,' to every question. 'Whatever people said in the world, I too believed it.' Hearing this response, *Munkar and Nakir* will strike him with such a scorching axe whereby sparks will abound in the grave as this person is reduced to smithereens. May Allah ﷻ save us from such a calamity!

Thereafter, an announcer form the Heavens will proclaim, 'He has lied, spread a blanket of Hell-Fire in his grave and clothe him with the apparel of *Jahannam*.' Ninety-nine snakes will be let loose upon him, with the poison of one so toxic, that if even one drop were to fall on earth, the whole planet would become bereft of any vegetation.

Enemies are Reshaping our Muaasharat

My intention is merely to advocate such daily remembrance and meditation whereby, Inshā'Allah, all negligence and apathy will disappear. Consequently, *Nûr* will be created in one's heart and soul thereby facilitating the performance of good deeds and enthusiasm to love and follow the Sunnah of our beloved Nabee ﷺ. The foundation of our negligence and deterioration is aping of the alien ways introduced with great cunning and ploy into our *Muaasharat* by the enemies of Islām. Our younger generation are drowned in sport & play with our homes furnished with the shaytānic scourge of TV, video, cable and satellite programmes. We feel happy with our lives, little knowing that both our deeni & worldly life is being destroyed.

Friends! Remember, life will pass very quickly, and when arrives death...our eyes will truly open. Death comes very quickly, Heaven forbid if we are then compelled to say:

> '*Alas, my grief! How I was undutiful to Allah...*'
> (Glorious Qur'ān 56:39)

Hence, we should daily reflect upon death and our stay in the grave. Whatever sins we have committed, we should make *Taubah* and strive to make ourselves amongst the pious servants of Allah ﷻ and a complete and loyal follower of the Sunnah of Nabee ﷺ. Inshā'Allah, success in this world and the Hereafter will then be automatic. May Allah ﷻ dispel our negligence and grant us Tawfeeq to prepare and worry about death and the everlasting life to come in the Hereafter. Āmeen

Shaykh-ul-Hadeeth Mufti Sahbān Mahmood ﷺ

Chapter Fifteen

Shar'ee Legalities

Delaying Janāzah

*Courtesy of Shaykh Mufti Taqee Uthmaani,
Editor-in-Chief, AlBalagh,
Darul 'Uloom Korangi of Karachi, Pakistan*

&

Overseas Burials

*Courtesy of Shaykh Mufti Isma'eel Kacholvi,
Institute of Islāmic Jurisprudence, Bradford, UK
(The English Translation was kindly edited & verified by
Shaykh 'Abdul Hafeez of the Islāmic Da'wah Academy of Leicester in 2000)*

Darul 'Uloom Karachi's Ruling on Delaying Janāzāh Salāh & Burial

What do our Respected Ulamā advise regarding the modern-day trend of delaying the Janāzāh Salāh and burial for famous personalities? Sometimes, considerable time lapses in expectation of leading figures (such as ministers) attending the Janāzāh Salāh. No doubt, some people attribute the visit of these people as acts of respect towards the dead and bereaved, however those people who have been awaiting are considerably inconvenienced.

Furthermore, this practice is giving greater impetus to the notion amongst lay people, 'who are already victims of non-Sharee customs with regards to Janāzāh Salāh and burial,' that it is permissible to delay Janāzāh Salāh.

Therefore, in the Light of the Sharee'ah, would you kindly advise us of the limits regarding delaying of Janāzāh Salāh. How many hours delay is permissible? What reasons justify a delay?

Does the Sharee'ah allow a delay for any personality, because we read in 'Aap Beti,' that Shaykh Yahya ﷺ died at 8 o'clock and was buried by 9 o'clock. Similarly, upon the death of Shaykh Ashraf 'Ali Thānwi ﷺ, no delay was made to even allow Ulamā or students to attend from the nearby Darul Uloom in Saharanpur.

Is it makruh to delay Janāzāh Salāh?

(p433, Al Balagh, Rajab 1421/October 2000)

Reply with Tawfeeq from Allah ﷻ, Praise, Salāt & Salāms

1) It appears in Ahadeeth, that whenever a person passes away, one should make haste with the *Tajheez* and *Takhfeen* (shrouding and burial). Nabee ﷺ advised,

'Whenever a person dies from amongst you, then do not keep him by you rather, hasten him towards the grave.'
(Baihaqee)

'Three acts are such in which there should be no delay: (performance of) Salāh, when its time arrives; Janāzāh, when (the mayyit) is present; and the marriage of a lady, when her match is found.'

'Make haste with the Janāzāh, for if it is pious, the grave, wherein you are quickly taking him to is good for him. However, if he is not pious, then there is a evil burden upon your shoulders, which by walking quickly you will be discharging from your shoulders.' (Bukhāree, Muslim)

2) In accordance with these Ahadeeth, our *Fuqaha'* (Respected Jurists) have proclaimed it *Mustahab* to make haste when undertaking Janāzāh and burial.

Whilst no specific quantified time for delaying Janāzāh Salāh, in terms of hours or minutes has been specified, the principles observed from the Teachings of our *Fuqaha'* are:

a) To delay until *tajheez* and *takhfeen* is performed in accordance with the Sunnah is permissible.

b) If there is fear of the body undergoing transformation (i.e decomposing), then to make haste is *Wājib* (compulsory) and to delay is Harām!

c) Should the *Walee* (guardian) of the mayyit be at a nearby location to the Janāzāh, then some *Fuqaha'* have granted permission to wait (the short time) for him to arrive as long as there is no danger of any transformation occurring to the mayyit's body.

d) Without a valid reason (Tajheez, Takhfeen and awaiting arrival of the nearby Walee), it is *makruh* (impermissible) to delay (the burial) by more than half-a-day. A classic example, is to await performance of Jumu'ah Salāh (in expectation of greater participants) which is *makruh*, however, where there is danger of missing the Jumu'ah Khutbah (in Arabic) or the Salāh, then in such cases it is permissible to delay until performance of Jumuah and its Sunnah Salāh.

Obviously, by *makruh* is implied *makruh tahreemee* (highly reprehensible)...hence, to await the arrival of ministers, leading dignitaries, relatives or friends in order to allow them to view or pay their 'respects' or to achieve a larger gathering is impermissible.

This impermissibility is all the more severe when others are also inconvenienced. However, whilst a small delay is permissible, without a real cause this too is not *mustahab*.

Shaykh Mufti Taqee 'Uthmāni *et al*

Religious Ruling Regarding Overseas Burial

Shaykh Mufti Ismā'eel Kachholvi
dāmat barakātuhum

Question: Respected & venerable Shaykh, Assalamualikum Warahmatullahi Wabarakātuhu. In our community, when a person passes-away, there is the custom of bathing, shrouding and thereafter praying Janāzāh Salāh before transporting the deceased back to our 'ancestral land' for burial. In this regard, committees have been established and this practice has existed for some time. Recently, some newly qualified Ālims (Scholars) have raised objections to this custom. What is the correct Mas'alah (ruling)? Kindly reply, with proofs, thereby assisting us in correct practice.

Reply with Tawfeeq from Allah ﷻ, Praise, Salāt & Salāms

The Sharee'ah's ruling is that whenever any Muslim male or female passes-away, then as expediently as possible, the *mayyit* should be bathed, shrouded and buried in the Masnûn way. It appears in *Marāqiyul Falāh* (p 371):

'When death is certain, then make haste in kafn and burial. Therein, is correct respect for the mayyit, as it appears in Ahadeeth to make haste with burial. It is highly inappropriate to delay the body of a Muslim.'

In whichever locality the death takes place, it is Masnûn and Mustahab to bury herein. Without any valid Sharee' reason, it is *Makrûh Tahreemee* (severely reprehensible) to transport (the mayyit) to another town or country.

*'If there are no local Muslim cemeteries or there exists a (genuinely) similar handicap, then (under such dire circumstances and necessity) it will be permissible to transport (the mayyit) to the **nearest** place (of Muslim burial).'* (ibid.)

Here in the UK, there exists a sizeable Muslim population, with many Muslim organizations present to facilitate and organize burials. Furthermore, the authorities have allocated Muslims separate burial grounds wherein we are able to bury, with ease, our dead in accordance with the Sharee'ah. Therefore, the *mayyit* should be buried (in the nearest) Muslim cemetery. Should there be a post-mortem or other legal delay in receiving permission to bury, then under such compelling circumstances there is no sin.

A principle of the Sharee'ah is that in adopting a permissible or doubtful act, should the need arise for any sin or *Makrûh Tahreemee*, then the permissible act will be forbidden. Bearing this principle in mind, in transporting the *mayyit* to another town or country, many prohibited acts, hereunder listed, are undertaken. Therefore (this practice) will be labelled illicit and forbidden.

1) Sometimes there is a delay of 2 to 3 days or even greater in burying the mayyit, whilst the Sharee'ah's command is to make haste in burial. Therefore, this foul practice is in conflict with this command.
2) Sometimes the body begins to transform, smell and decompose.
3) In the Hanafi (School of Jurisprudence), it is permissible to pray Janāzāh Salāh only once. It is forbidden to pray it

2, 3 or more times as is (generally) the case with overseas burials.

4) It is necessary to follow the environmental laws of both countries, this involves pumping chemicals into the mayyit's body thereby contradicting the sanctity and respect due: which should be comparable to that shown to a living person.

5) According to some reliable reports, internal body organs are removed (during embalming), if these reports are true then grave disrespect and sacrilege is committed in discarding these organs.

6) After placing in a coffin, the mayyit is transported like a piece of luggage...this is gross disrespect of the body.

7) Without any Sharee' or real worldly need, great expense and effort are expended; this too is forbidden.

8) Upon death of the husband, the *'iddat* (period of waiting) of his wife commences, however usually the widow too accompanies the mayyit overseas, which is harām.

The above are obvious foul features associated with this practice, there are others also, therefore it is incumbent to reform this corrupt custom. Those Ulamā who object, are only discharging their duty in stating the correct Sharee' ruling: we should listen to them. For a detailed Ruling, also consult *Ahsanul Fatāwā* (Vol. 4), wherein reply is given to those who advocate this practice.

Moreover, Allah Knows Best.

Shaykh Mufti Ismā'eel Kachholvi *et al*

4 Rabi'ul Awwal 1421 AH, (6th July 2000 CE)

Shaykh Tāreeq Jameel *damat barakātuhum* related, 'Once Caliph Haroon Rasheed ﷺ and Shaykh Muhammad bin Simāk ﷺ were sitting together. As the Caliph was about to drink a glass of water...

Shaykh: *'Wait...tell me, if you were dying of thirst and somebody arrives and offers you this glass of water for a price, what would you be prepared to pay him?'*

Caliph: *'Why I would save my life...I would offer him half my kingdom!'*

Shaykh: *'Okay, drink the water...now tell me, Allah Forbid, should the water become blocked in your body and you are desperate to empty your bladder but cannot do so, and a person arrives and offers to cure you at a price, what would you be prepared to offer him?'*

Caliph: *'Again, I would save my life...I would offer him the other half of my kingdom!'*

Shaykh: *'O Ameerul Mu'mineen! That Empire, the value of half of which is equal to a glass of water with the other half equal in value to only a few drops of urine...why is it worthy of being traded in lieu of the Ākhirah (Hereafter)?'*

Whilst Caliph Haroon Rasheed ﷺ was the Leader of a vast Empire, comparatively speaking, what do I or you posses whereby we go and lose the Ākhirah for a few items and fleeting glory of this world?'

Chapter Sixteen

The Importance of Wills in Islām

Contents

* The Importance of Wills in Islam
* Copy of Health Care Proxy & Living Will
* Copy of Last Will & Testament
* What is Probate?
* What is Inheritance Tax?
* How to Legally Avoid Inheritance Tax?
* The Four Stages in Acquiring a Probate

The Importance of Wills in Islām & Guidance Notes

The law of England states that if a person dies without making a Will, then such a person's wealth is distributed in accordance with the laws of *Intestacy* i.e. the law of the land. In such cases, Islāmic Law will have no bearing on how the deceased's Estate is distributed. This form of distribution is not in accordance with the Words of Allah ﷻ mentioned in the Glorious Qur'ān:

> 'For men there is a share in what the parents and the nearest of kin have left. And for women there is a share in what parents and the nearest of kin have left.' (4:7)

We see from the Verses of the Glorious Qur'ān that the only certainty in life is death:

> 'Every soul will taste death.' (3:185)

> 'Wherever you are, death will overtake you.' (4:78)

'Abdullāh ibn 'Umar ﷺ, the eminent Scholar and Companion of the Prophet ﷺ narrates that the Messenger of Allāh ﷺ said:

> 'It is not permissible for any Muslim who has something to will to stay for two nights without having his will and testament written and kept ready with him.' (Bukhāri)

Hence it is extremely important one makes a Will, so that the Estate can be distributed in accordance with the Sharee'ah (Islāmic Law of Jurisprudence), especially if one fears the inheritors will not act according to the Sharee'ah.

In order towards securing your Hereafter, Inshā'Allah, and to avoid a major sin, ensure that your wealth, however small, is distributed in accordance with the Commands of Allah ﷻ.

Islamic Guidance Related to Making a Will

Islām has laid down specific rules with regards to inheritance and Wills. In Islām, if no Will is made, the Shar'ee inheritors automatically inherit according to the laws of Sharee'ah from the whole of the Estate. If one wishes to bequeath anything to his friends and/or relatives or fulfil his religious obligations (e.g. unfulfilled Salāh, Sawm, Hajj, etc.) then this can be only done if a Will has been prepared. However, such a bequest, which is known as *'wasiyyat'*, is only permissible provided it is in accordance with the Sharee'ah.

Firstly, one should understand that a person during his lifetime, being in sound health and mind, has complete authority and power over his rightful possessions. He is free to spend (within the boundaries of Sharee'ah) or gift to whomsoever he wishes. If one wishes to give something during his lifetime he may do so, and such gifts will be valid provided the conditions of 'gift' are met. One must remember that merely naming something to someone's name in accordance with the country's law does not validate it to be the named persons asset according to the Sharee'ah if the other conditions of gift are neglected.

Secondly, one must understand that after one's death the deceased has very limited authority with regards to the way his Estate will be distributed. In making a *Wasiyyat* (Will) the following points should be upheld:

1) The *Wasiyyat* can only be made up to one third (1/3) of the Estate that remains after discharge of the funeral expenses and any unpaid debts. Funeral expenses and financial debts must be paid back even though there may be nothing left for the relatives.

2) That he/she only bequeaths to friends and those relatives who are **not** entitled to any share in the inheritance. Such a bequest cannot include Islāmic heirs as such heirs inherit automatically from the Estate of the deceased according to Sharee'ah.

3) Unpaid debt as mentioned in item (1) above does not include religious liabilities and obligations e.g. unpaid Zakāt, unaccomplished Hajj, unkept Fast, unperformed Salāh and undischarged Qurbāni etc.

4) The discharge of religious debts can only be fulfilled if a *Wasiyyat* is made. It is *wājib* (compulsory) to make a *Wasiyyat* for such debts. Such debts can only be discharged to one third (1/3) limit of the *Wasiyyat*, i.e. this discharge can only be a constituent of *Wasiyyat*. If no money remains after the payment of funeral expenses and financial debts then these obligations should not be discharged.

5) Similarly, if after the discharge of funeral expenses and any financial debts, the religious debts exceed one third of the remaining Estate, then only up to one third of the Estate could be used to discharge such religious obligations.

6) The remainder shall be left to the discretion of the inheritors. If the inheritors wish to give more then the one third to discharge religious debts then all the inheritor's must be mature (*bāligh*) and give with their own free will i.e. without any pressure or persuasion.

7) *Wasiyyat* for any harmful activity or innovation (bid'ah) etc. shall not be carried out.

8) Since a large number of people are overcome by innovation (bid'ah) in Deen, particularly with regard to funerals, a Muslim should also order in his/her Will that he/she should be prepared for burial and buried upon the Sunnah method and forbid innovative practices.

9) It is forbidden to make a Will in order to cause harm and oppression, for example a person makes a Will so that the inheritors get a third less than what they would have or he makes a Will contrary to the distribution of Sharee'ah.

10) He/she should have as witnesses at least two just Muslims who are not beneficiaries/inheritors.

11) The witnesses should witness the signing and declaration only by the testator (i.e. one who makes the Will) at the end of the Will and must sign in the presence of the testator and of each other.

12) *A person who fears his spouse may later object to the Shar'ee distribution of his Islāmic Will and take recourse to the Courts to demand a greater harām share of his estate should request her to sign an affidavit accepting his Islāmic Will in the presence of her solicitor & witnesses.*

General Guidance for Completing a Will

In order for any Will that we make to be valid and legal under English Law certain formalities have to be fulfilled.

1) Please carefully read your Will and only sign it if you are sure that it is correct. All pages should be bound or stapled together.

2) All signatures should be made in ink or by ballpoint pen, as should any amendments if these are necessary.

3) The testator (one who makes the Will) must sign the Will in the presence of the two witnesses who in turn must sign in the presence of the testator and of each other.

4) The Will must be signed in the presence of two Independent witnesses aged over 18 years.

5) These two Independent witnesses should not be, Beneficiaries in your Will or Husbands or Wives of Beneficiaries.

6) For the purpose of signing Wills, beneficiaries include executors, administrators and guardians.

7) All three of you must remain present at the same time until the following procedure has been completed:

   a) You date the Will in the appropriate place.

   b) The testator and witnesses sign (with full signatures) any deletion, amendment or alteration.

   c) You sign your name with your usual signature at the end of the Will.

   d) Each witness should then sign his or her name where

indicated and print their full names, addresses and occupations where provided.

8) Witnesses do not need to know the contents of your Will.

9) Please ensure that you do not attach anything to the Will by means of paper clip or otherwise.

10) Ensure that your Will is stored in a sealed envelope at a safe place preferably known to your Executor/s

11) If your Estate is of reasonable value and/or includes properties other then your main residence then consult a financial advisor or accountant as Inheritance tax and/or Capital gains tax may have to be paid.

12) In consultation with your accountant and an Islamic Judicial body or an Ālim, some of your tax liabilities could be minimised if part of your Estate is distributed during ones lifetime. This should never be done so as to deprive the rightful heirs of their inheritance.

13) The Will should be regularly updated to reflect any changes in ones circumstances.

14) Make your Will as simple as possible because complicated wills incur undue expense and management.

ADVANCED DIRECTIVE & LIVING WILL

If a time comes when I am incapacitated to the point where I can no longer actively take part in decisions for my own life and am unable to direct my physician as to my own medical care, I wish this statement to stand as a testament of my wishes.

I, the undersigned:

....

Residing at:

....

....

....

hereby appoint the following individual as my advanced directive and living will agent:

....

....

This advanced directive and living will shall take effect if and when I become unable to make my own health care decisions.

In respect of each decision made for me by my agent, it is my wish and direction that my agent be guided solely by my agent's Islamic faith as to what my own decision would have been in the same circumstances. Without limiting the unrestricted scope of my agent's authority hereunder, I expressly authorize my agent to direct that no treatment be conducted or withheld from me if to do so is against the teachings of Islām, to the best of understanding of my agent.

I direct that medication be judiciously administered to me to alleviate pain. I do not intend any direct taking of my life. I also direct that 'life support systems' may be used in a judicious manner and its use discontinued, just like any other medicine, if it becomes reasonably apparent that it has no therapeutic value. The 'life support systems' include but are not limited to artificial respiration, cardiopulmonary resuscitation, artificial means of providing nutrition and hydration, and any pharmaceutical drugs.

I request that when I am close to death the best of people with the most faith and Muslim scholars be called to encourage me to say the words of *Shahādah*: *'La ilāha ill-Allah, Muhammadur Rasoolullah.'* This is in accordance with the saying of Prophet ﷺ,

> *'Anyone whose last words were "La ilāha ill-Allah" will enter Paradise.'* (Ahmad, Aboo Dawood & Hākim)

BURIAL ARRANGEMENTS

1) When my soul departs then let them close my eyes and supplicate good for me and hasten to prepare me for the burial and to bury me according to the Sunnah of the Prophet ﷺ.

2) That encouraging me to say the *Shahādah* after I have died to be totally prevented.

3) My body should be prepared for burial in keeping with Islamic Law as soon as possible.

4) Under no circumstances should my body be voluntarily turned over for an autopsy or embalming or for organ donation. However, if a post mortem is necessary due to statutory requirements then the first course of action should be to carry out a MRI Scan if recognised and approved by the Coroner in the locality of my death.

5) Before and after my body is prepared for burial there is to be no viewing of my remains by any non-mahram.

6) I hereby direct that average expenses be incurred on my shroud, coffin and other burial expenses. No extravagance should take place in this regard.

7) I hereby direct that my body be buried within the town/country that I die and must not be moved to another country.

8) It is my express wish that should I die in the locality of my normal residence then I be buried at:

....

10) My grave be dug in complete accordance with Islamic Law and should face the direction of the Qiblah.

11) My body is buried without a coffin or any other encasement that separates the shroud from the surrounding soil unless it is due to statutory requirements.

12) In the event that the local laws require coffin burial, I command that such coffin is simple, modest and of the

least expensive type possible and I furthermore command that the casket be left open during burial and filled with soil unless prohibited by law.

13) My grave is covered by soil only. The marking, if necessary, should be a simple rock, headstone or plaque. There should be no embellishing inscriptions, symbols or verses.

14) My burial should take place as soon as possible. Under no circumstances should the burial be unduly delayed.

15) Absolutely no non-Islamic religious service or observance shall be conducted upon my death, or on my body or at the gravesite. No pictures, crescents, statues, decorations, crosses, flags, flowers, plants, burning of incense any symbols or music be involved at any stage of my burial.

16) No one is permitted to cry, moan or wail at the burial site. Only what comes from the eye, naturally is acceptable (tears). Muslims are requested to make du'ā for me and that my questioning is made easy and my grave is made spacious and comfortable.

17) Refrain from acts such as wailing, beating your cheeks, or tearing your clothes, as the Prophet ﷺ has prohibited these acts.

18) That those things which have become common, compulsory reciting the Glorious Qur'ān over the dead during the funeral preparations, or on the day of Jumu'ah or after forty days, and other innovations are to be prevented. Also, no compulsory complete recitation

of the Glorious Qur'ān or Azān is permitted over my grave.

19) No food preparation is made for guests attending the funeral and no announcements made after the burial at the graveyard of such preparations.

20) That henna should not be sprinkled in the grave, nor should any pillow or the like be placed beneath my head.

21) That condolence should only be given upon the first meeting with the family of the deceased. Islām permits relatives to mourn for no more than three days.

CUSTODIANS: EXECUTOR AND ADMINISTRATOR

1. I hereby nominate and appoint

to act jointly and severally, to be the Executor(s) of my Will and Administrator(s) of my Estate, granting to them all such powers allowed in law, especially the Power of Assumption.

	Full Name & Address	Date of Birth
1		
2		
3		
4		
5		

I hereby give all my Estate: cash, bank accounts, real property, shares in any business, and any other property not mentioned in this will, to the person named above, who shall act also as an Executor to serve without bond, to distribute it according to Islamic Law as practised by Ahlus Sunnah Wal Jamāʿah according to the _____ School of Thought.

I direct that the Executor/s take all actions legally permissible to have the probate of my estate done as simply and as expeditiously as possible.

I give my Executor/s power to settle any just claim for or against my Estate.

In the event of any one or more of my said Executor(s)/Administrator(s) predeceasing me, or dying during his term of Office or declining to act, then the remaining or surviving Executor(s)/Administrator(s) shall be authorised to act alone. Furthermore in the event of all such Executor(s)/Administrator(s) predeceasing me or dying during his/their term of Office or declining to act, then I declare that any Islamic Judicial body (of the Ahlus Sunnah Wal Jamāʿah who rule according to the _____ fiqh) shall be authorised to appoint one or more Executor(s)/Administrator(s).

My said Executor(s)/Administrator(s) shall not be obliged to furnish any security to the Master of the Supreme Court for the due and proper administration of my estate as laid down by the provisions of Act 66 of 1965 or any law governing the administration of estates.

I direct that my family, all physicians, hospitals and other health care providers and any court or judge honour the decision of my agent/alternate agent. This request is made, after careful reflection, while I am of sound mind. Signed and declared by the said,

_____

on _____this day of_____ 20 _____ CE, corresponding with the Islamic _____ day of _____ 14_____AH

We, the undersigned witnesses declare that the person who signed this document is personally known to us and appears to be at least eighteen years of age, of sound mind and able to understand the nature and consequences of health care decisions at the time this document was signed, and acted willingly and free from duress. The person signed this document in our presence. We are not the persons appointed as agent/s or alternate agent/s by this document and we sign this document as witnesses at this person's request.

	Full Name & Address	Signature	Occupation
1			
2			
3			

Salāt and Salāms upon the Messenger ﷺ

LAST WILL & TESTAMENT

of _____

ARTICLE 1: PREAMBLE

All praises are due to Allah ﷻ in Whom we believe and from Who we seek Forgiveness and Guidance. We seek refuge in Allah ﷻ from our evil doings and our bad deeds. Whomsoever Allah ﷻ guides, no one can lead astray; and whomsoever Allah ﷻ leads astray; no one can guide.

According to the order of Prophet Muhammad ﷺ to Muslims to have their wills written; I hereby bequeath the following while being in full mental capacity and good health. I, the undersigned,

_____

hereby revoke and cancel all former wills and testamentary dispositions of whatsoever nature hereto formed by me, and declare this to be my last Will (wasiyyat) and Testament.

I bear witness that there is no deity except Allah ﷻ, having no partner, and that Muhammad ﷺ is His slave and Messenger and that the hour will come, no doubt, when Allah ﷻ will resurrect all who are in their graves.

I ask of those who survive me from among my relatives to fear Allah ﷻ and correct the relationships between themselves and to obey Allah ﷻ and His Messenger ﷺ, as Allah ﷻ orders in the Glorious Qur'ān.

I also enjoin upon those of my family who survive me with the advice directed by Prophets Ibrāheem & Ya'qoob ﷺ to their sons:

> 'O my sons, Allah has chosen for you the religion (of Islām), so do not die except as Muslims (in a state of submission to Allah).' (2:132)

I enjoin upon you the fear of Allah and patience, especially at the occurrence of my death, and that your speech be good. Ask of Allah ﷻ His Forgiveness and Mercy for me. Ask Allah ﷻ to allow me to enter Paradise and to save me from Hell Fire. I request that all who are present upon my death repeat the following:

> 'La ilāha ill-Allah. Inna lillāhi wa inna ilayhi rāji'oon. Allahumma' jurnee fee museebatee wakhluf lee khayrun minha.'

> 'There is no deity except Allah. Indeed, to Allah we belong, and indeed, to Him we will return. O Allah, reward me in this affliction and replace it with something better for me.'

I declare that I have forgiven everyone who has backbitten me and forgive whoever has mistakenly taken anything belonging to me.

I ask all my relatives, friends, and all others - whether they choose to believe as I believed or not - to honour my Constitutional right to these beliefs. I ask them to honour this document, which I have made, and not to try to obstruct it or change it in any way. Rather, let them see that I am buried as I have asked to be buried and let my properties be divided as I wanted them to be divided.

ARTICLE 2: ISLAMIC LAW

Wherever in this document reference is made to Islamic Law it will be deemed to refer to Islāmic Law as practised by Ahlus Sunnah Wal Jamā'ah according to the _____ School of Thought.

Wherever in this document reference is made to Islamic Judicial body or Alim/Mufti it will be deemed to refer to such a body or person who are in accordance to Ahlus Sunnah Wal Jamā'ah and rule according to the _____ School of Fiqh.

I direct that if you differ in anything among yourselves that you refer the decision to Allah and His Messenger ﷺ for Allah ﷻ said:

> 'And no, by your Lord, they will not believe until they make you, (O Muhammad), judge in what they dispute among themselves and then find within themselves no discomfort from what you have judged and submit in full, (willing) submission.' (4:65)

ARTICLE 3: MY IMMEDIATE FAMILY

I, a Muslim man, am married according to the law of England to:

_____

Furthermore, according to the Islamic Sharee'ah, the following Muslim ladies are in my nikāh:

1) _____

2) _____

3) _____

4) _____

Accordingly, the Islamic haqq (right) of these *zawjain* should be respected and fulfilled.

I, a Muslim lady am married to _____ and all reference in this will to my husband is to him.

I am the father/mother of the following children whose details are given below:

	Full Name & Address	Date of Birth
1		
2		
3		
4		
5		
6		
7		

ARTICLE 4: EXECUTOR AND ADMINISTRATOR

1. I hereby nominate and appoint

	Full Name & Address	Date of Birth
1		
2		
3		
4		
5		
6		
7		

to act jointly and severally, to be the Executor(s) of my Will and Administrator(s) of my Estate, granting to them all such powers allowed in law, especially the Power of Assumption.

I hereby give all my Estate: cash, bank accounts, real property, shares in any business, and any other property not mentioned in this will, to the person named above, who shall act also as an Executor to serve without bond, to distribute it according to Islamic Law as practised by Ahlus Sunnah Wal Jamāʿah according to the _____ School of Thought.

I direct that the Executor/s take all actions legally permissible to have the probate of my estate done as simply and as expeditiously as possible.

I give my Executor/s power to settle any just claim for or against my Estate.

In the event of any one or more of my said Executor(s)/Administrator(s) predeceasing me, or dying during his term of Office or declining to act, then the remaining or surviving Executor(s)/Administrator(s) shall be authorised to act alone. Furthermore in the event of all such Executor(s)/Administrator(s) predeceasing me or dying during his/their term of Office or declining to act, then I declare that any Islamic Judicial body (of the Ahlus Sunnah Wal Jamāʿah who rule according to the _____ fiqh) shall be authorised to appoint one or more Executor(s)/Administrator(s).

My said Executor(s)/Administrator(s) shall not be obliged to furnish any security to the Master of the Supreme Court for the due and proper administration of my estate as laid down by the provisions of Act 66 of 1965 or any law governing the administration of estates.

ARTICLE 5: BURIAL ARRANGEMENTS

1) When my soul departs then let them close my eyes and supplicate good for me and hasten to prepare me for the burial and to bury me according to the Sunnah of the Prophet ﷺ.

2) That encouraging me to say the *Shahādah* after I have died to be totally prevented.

3) My body should be prepared for burial in keeping with Islamic Law as soon as possible.

4) Under no circumstances should my body be voluntarily turned over for an autopsy or embalming or for organ donation. However, if a post mortem is necessary due to statutory requirements then the first course of action should be to carry out a MRI Scan if recognised and approved by the Coroner in the locality of my death.

5) Before and after my body is prepared for burial there is to be no viewing of my remains by any non-mahram.

6) I hereby direct that the least possible expenses be incurred on my shroud, coffin and other burial expenses.

7) I hereby direct that my body be buried within the town/country that I die and must not be moved to another country.

8) It is my express wish that should I die in the locality of my normal residence then I be buried at:

....

9) My grave be dug in complete accordance with Islamic Law and should face the direction of the Qiblah.

10) My body is buried without a coffin or any other encasement that separates the shroud from the surrounding soil unless it is due to statutory requirements.

11) In the event that the local laws require coffin burial, I command that such coffin is simple, modest and of the least expensive type possible and I furthermore command that the casket be left open during burial and filled with dirt unless prohibited by law.

12) My grave is covered by dirt only. The marking, if necessary, should be a simple rock, headstone or plaque. There should be no embellishing inscriptions, symbols or verses.

13) My burial should take place as soon as possible, preferably before sunset of the day of my death or the following day. Under no circumstances should the burial be unduly delayed.

14) Absolutely no non-Islamic religious service or observance shall be conducted upon my death, or on my body or at the gravesite. No pictures, crescents, statues, decorations, crosses, flags, flowers, plants, burning of incense any symbols or music be involved at any stage of my burial.

15) No one is permitted to cry, moan or wail at the burial site. Only what comes from the eye, naturally is acceptable (tears). Muslims are requested to make du'ā

for me and that my questioning is made easy and my grave is made spacious and comfortable.

16) Refrain from acts such as wailing, beating your cheeks, or tearing your clothes, as the Prophet ﷺ has prohibited these acts.

17) That those things which have become common, compulsory recitation of the Glorious Qur'ān over the dead during the funeral preparations, or on the day of Jumu'ah or after forty days, and other innovations (bid'ah) are to be prevented. Also, no compulsory complete recitation of the Glorious Qur'ān or Azān is permitted over my grave.

18) No food preparation is made for guests attending the funeral and no announcements made after the burial at the graveyard of such preparations.

19) That henna should not be sprinkled in the grave, nor should any pillow or the like be placed beneath my head.

20) That condolence should only be given upon the first meeting with the family of the deceased. Islām permits relatives to mourn for no more than three days.

ARTICLE 6: ASSETS & BUSINESS COMMITMENTS

For the guidance of my Executor(s)/Administrator(s), I list below my assets and business commitments:

	Full Details & Address	
1		
2		
3		
4		
5		
6		
7		
8		

ARTICLE 7: DEBTS and TRUSTS

My debts are:

	Full Name & Address	Amount/Item
1		
2		
3		
4		
5		

What is <u>Due</u> to <u>me</u> may be collected from:

	Full Name & Address	Amount/Item
1		
2		
3		
4		
5		

Of the trusts kept in my custody, please return the following to:

	Full Name & Address	Amount/Item
1		
2		
3		
4		

I hereby direct that my said Executor(s)/Administrator(s) proceed with the distribution of my Estate in the following order of priority as commanded by Islamic Law:

1	Payment for my funeral expenses (bathing, shroud and burial)	
2	Payment of all my debts as set out in clause 1 above including such expenses incurred by my last illness.	
3	Payment of the Wasiyyat (Bequest not exceeding 33.33% of my Estate) as set out in Article 8 below	
4	Distribution of the residue of my Estate to my Islāmic heirs in accordance with Islamic Law.	

My said Executor(s)/Administrator(s) shall endeavour to ascertain what amount, if any, is due by me in respect of my religious liabilities and obligations in accordance with the tenets of the Islamic faith until the date of my death. For the guidance of my Executor(s) and Administrators, I hereby declare that at present my liabilities in this respect are as follows:-

	Complete & Amend As Appropriate	Amount/Details
1	Unperformed Salāh	
2	Unpaid Zakāt	
3	Un-kept Saum (Fasts)	
4	Unperformed Hajj	
5	Unfulfilled Compensation (Kaffaarah	
6	Un-discharged Vow (Nazar/Mannat etc)	
7	Un-discharged Sacrifice of animal (Adh'hiyah/Qurbāni) or other Wājib (Lawful obligation)	
8		
9		

I hereby direct and make Wasiyyat that such amounts shall be paid as a first charge to such persons or institutions/ establishments as my Executor(s)/Administrator(s) shall determine to be entitled thereto according to the laws of Islām. The total amount payable under this clause shall not, in any case, exceed thirty-three and one-third per cent (33.33 %) of the net value of my estate after the payment of my entire lawful obligation, and all debts contracted by me during my lifetime. This includes funeral expenses and expenses connected with the administration of my Estate.

ARTICLE 8: BEQUESTS

In the event of any balance remaining out of the thirty three and one-third per cent of the net value of my estate as mentioned in Article 7 above, then I hereby make Wasiyyat according to the laws of Islām and bequeath in sadaqah as scheduled in the table below.

List in the schedule details of the charitable institution/ establishment, friends and relatives (excluding those relatives who will automatically inherit).

	Full Name & Address	Amount/Item
1	Islāmic Da'wah Academy 120 Melbourne Rd, Leicester, LE2 0DS	
2	Ashraf's Amānat PO Box 12, Dewsbury, W. Yorkshire, UK, WF12 9YX	
3		
4		

Or Alternatively;

The amount of £_____ (_____)
from my wealth is to be spent upon works for admonishment and guidance, and for the establishment of the rites and practices of the Sharee'ah, and I have left the decision as to when and where it is to be spent with my Executor(s) and Administrator(s).

ARTICLE 9: ADMINISTRATION INSTRUCTIONS

It shall be the duty of my Executor(s)/Administrator(s) to determine who my rightful heirs are in accordance with Islamic Law. They shall also determine what share each is entitled to receive. I do hereby nominate such persons in the shares determined, to be the heirs of the whole of the residue of my Estate, wherever situate, in the UK, or elsewhere.

A Certificate stating the rightful heirs in my Estate, showing their respective shares therein in accordance with the Islamic Law issued by the Mufti of any recognised Islamic theological body, or by any certified Ãlim (qualified scholar of Islamic Law), shall be accepted for all purposes as a lawful document, determining my rightful heirs.

In determining my heirs, my Executor(s)/Administrator(s) or any Muslim Judicial Council/ Body or any certified Ãlim of the Islamic religion shall take full cognisance of any marriages lawfully contracted by me anywhere in the world according to the tenets of the Islamic faith.

I hereby direct that any share under this Will hereto falling to a female shall be paid to and belong to her as her sole, absolute and exclusive property, and be excluded from the community of property that may now or hereafter exist between her and any husband she has married or may marry and shall be from the *jus mariti* and right of administration ordinarily to him accruing whether by virtue of the law of community of property or otherwise. The receipt alone by any female inheritor in my Estate, without the assistance of her husband, shall be a good and sufficient discharge to my Executor(s)/Administrator(s) therefore.

It is my express desire that my Executor(s)/Administrator(s) shall wind up my Estate as promptly as possible. Any business carried on in my name at the time of my death, or any other assets belonging to my Estate, by arrangements between the heirs, be taken over by any or all of them.

Any inheritance accruing to a minor child in terms hereof shall be retained by my Executor(s)/Administrator(s) in trust for the benefit of such a minor until that minor attains the age of majority as determined by Islamic Law, in which event my said Executor(s)/Administrator(s) shall pay over to the said minor his/her share of the inheritance

In pursuance to the foregoing, my Executor(s)/Administrator(s) are authorised in their discretion to apply any income or a portion of the capital of the Trust assets for the maintenance, education and general welfare of the beneficiary of the Trust.

No minor heir shall be entitled to participate in any discussion or matters affecting my Estate, without the approval of my Executor(s)/Administrator(s). If no agreement is reached between my heirs within a reasonable time, all Estate assets shall be realised and the proceeds distributed in the manner aforementioned. My Executor(s)/Administrator(s) shall have the right to carry on and continue any business carried on in my name in partnership or otherwise, at the time of my death, so long as they may consider it desirable for the benefit of my heirs in their absolute discretion.

My said Executor(s)/Administrator(s) shall not be required to pay any minor's inheritance into the Guardian's fund, nor shall they be required to furnish any security to the Master of the Supreme Court for the due administration of the inheritances due to such minors.

My said Executor(s)/Administrator(s) shall be entitled to make reasonable periodical payments for the proper maintenance, education and support of such heir, and to deduct such payment from the inheritance of such heir.

I hereby direct that a certificate issued by a competent Islamic Judicial body or by any qualified Ālim/Mufti in Islamic Law shall be binding and conclusive as to the aforesaid Islamic Law and the distribution of my Estate.

I hereby direct that this Will be examined by an Islamic Judicial body or by any qualified Ālim as described in Article 2 above, and a certificate as to the validity of it in Islamic Law be obtained from the said person or body.

I hereby direct that if the Will is in conflict with Islamic Law, the Islamic Judicial body concerned in examining this Will have the right to annul the whole of it, if the whole be in conflict with Islamic Law or annul that portion of it which contradicts with Islamic Law.

ARTICLE 10: WITNESSES

I direct that if any part of my last Will and Testament is determined invalid by a court of competent jurisdiction, the other part shall remain valid and enforceable.

I declare that this is my last will last Will and Testament, and I am free before Allah ﷻ from saying or doing anything that contradicts the guidance of Allah's Messenger ﷺ.

Signature: _____

Signed and declared by the said,

_____

the TESTATOR, as and for his/her last Will in the presence of us both at the same time, who at his/her request, in his/her presence, and in the presence of each other, have hereunto subscribed our names as witnesses by the following:

THUS DONE and EXECUTED on this _____ day of _____ 20____ CE corresponding with the Islamic date of _____ 14_____ AH, in the presence of the subscribing witnesses, who signed in each other's presence, all being present at the same time.

WITNESSES:

Name Address	Signature	Occupation

My Will ~ Amendments

Page(s)	Amendment(s)

THUS DONE and EXECUTED on this_____day of _____20 CE corresponding with the Islamic date of _____ 14_____ AH, in the presence of the subscribing witnesses, who signed in each other's presence, all being present at the same time.
WITNESSES:

Name Address	Signature	Occupation

What is Probate?

Irrespective of whether a will has been made or not and, in the UK it is estimated that 68% of the population do not have a will, when a person dies, UK Law insists that somebody deals with their estate (all their worldly property, money and possessions left) by accounting and collecting in all the money, paying any inheritance tax first, thereafter debts and distributing what is left to those people entitled to it. Muslims are also governed by a Divine Shar'ee System, which specifies to whom, in what quantity and manner the estate is to be distributed.

To obtain legal authority in the UK to access and distribute the estate, the deceased's *Personal Representative* (either the *executor* named in a Will or an *administrator*) has to obtain a legal document known as **Grant of Representation** from the **Probate Registry** ~ a section of the Court Service. If the estate meets certain conditions, a grant is obtainable by providing only basic information. Such an estate is known as an *excepted estate*.

Islāmically, all **Grants of Representation** need to be shown to an Alim/Mufti for further guidance and to avoid the common but grave mistake of incorrect Shar'ee apportion.

The three types of Grant (of Representation)

1) *Probate*

Issued to one or more Executor(s) named in the deceased's Will.

2) **Letters of Administration (With Will)**

Issued when there is a Will but there is no executor named or when the executors are unable or unwilling to apply for the grant.

3) **Letters of Administration**

Issued when the estate is *intestate* (i.e. when the deceased did not made a Will, or any Will made is not valid).

Is a Grant always necessary?

Institutions (such as banks, building societies, employers, pension funds, insurance companies, etc.) holding money in the deceased's name need to know to whom that money should be paid and the grant is legal proof that the person named in it is authorised to 'collect' (but not necessarily keep) the money. According to UK Law, when a person dies the estate left behind passes to the people named in his or her Will and if no such document is present than it passes to his or her next of kin. The distribution of the estate is the responsibility of the person named in the grant.

Small Estates & Estates in Joint Names

If the estate is small, a grant may not be required and one could ask anyone, including institutions holding the deceased's money whether they will release it without seeing a grant. They may insist on a signed, witnessed document to act as receipt and proof.

A grant may also not be required if the entire estate is held in joint names because according to UK Law it passes automatically to the surviving joint owner, nevertheless a Muslim still needs to consult a Mufti/Alim to find out the

Shar'ee ruling. Many Muslim widows take unfair advantage of this automatic transfer to deprive the other inheritors, especially their late husband's parents and children with whom they may not be on the best of terms.

Grants & Selling or Transferring Property

A grant is always required to sell or transfer a property held in the deceased's sole name. Therefore, it is not wise to advertise any property for sale too soon after the owner's demise because it is not possible to complete conveyance until a grant has been obtained and there is no guarantee that a grant will be issued to coincide with the final stages of any sale or transfer.

Who is entitled to a Grant?

The Probate Service has produced a leaflet, 'How to Obtain a Probate' wherein is related,

> 'There are rules which govern who may be given a grant. The following points are a brief guide for you:
>
> • If there is a Will with named executors they are the first people entitled to a grant.
>
> • If there are no executors or the executors are unable or unwilling to apply, the next person entitled to a grant is any person named in the Will to whom the estate or remainder of it, after gifts have been paid, has been given.
>
> • If the deceased has not made a Will, application for a grant should normally be made by his or her next of kin in the following order of priority:
>
> 1) Lawful husband or wife (Note: Common-law partners

have no entitlement to a grant)

2) *Sons or daughters (excluding step-children)**
3) *Parents*
4) *Brothers or sisters**
5) *Grandparents*
6) *Uncles or aunts*.*

* Or if any have died in the lifetime of the deceased then their children may apply Note: A grant cannot be issued to any person under the age of 18.

If you are not sure whether you are entitled to apply you should still complete and return the forms and the Probate Registry will let you know. If you are a distant relative please supply a brief family tree showing your relationship to the deceased.

When more than one person is entitled to a grant they may all obtain a grant together. However, a maximum of four applicants is allowed and all applicants will have to attend an interview.

In most cases only one person needs to obtain the grant but there are circumstances when it may be necessary for two people to do this, e.g. if anyone entitled to the estate is under the age of 18. If this is the case the Probate Registry will let you know as soon as possible after they have received your application.

Although the Probate Registry needs to account for all the executors named in a Will they do not all have to apply for probate. The other executor(s) may either renounce all their rights to probate or they may reserve the right to apply for probate should it become necessary in the future (power reserved). The power reserved option is the most common one and is used, for example, when the executors live in different parts of the country or it is not convenient for one of them to attend the interview due to work commitments. Only the executor(s) who attend the interview will be named on the grant and then only their signature will be required to release the assets.

Please ask any executors who do not wish to apply which option they prefer and complete their details on form PA1. The Probate Registry will send you the relevant form for them to sign once they have checked your application

If the person who is entitled to the grant does not wish to apply, they may appoint someone else to be their attorney to obtain the grant on their behalf. If this is the case you should complete their details on form PA1 (Section C). The Probate Registry will send you a form for them to sign after they receive your application.

If it is not possible to issue a grant to you, the Probate Registry will explain the reasons.'

(© Crown Copyright ~ How to Obtain a Probate, PA2 –w3)

The granting of probate is linked to Inheritance Tax. It is therefore prudent to be aware of its existence and workings.

Inheritance Tax (IHT)

The tax on the estate of a person who has died is called **Inheritance Tax (IHT)** and is often referred to as a tax on death. Inheritance Tax is dealt with by Inland Revenue (Capital Taxes). IHT only applied to a very small percentage of estates, however with the recent huge rises in property values, it applies to many more estates, an estimated 2.4m extra homes. More and more 'ordinary' Muslims in the UK are now faced with the likely possibility that their heirs will be faced with Inheritance Tax upon their death. May Allah forbid, but if IHT does become due, the beneficiaries of the estate will normally have to pay at least some of the tax before the Probate Registry will issue the grant. The government prioritises its own interest first...

> 'The issue of the grant does not mean that Inland Revenue...have agreed the final Inheritance Tax liability. They will usually contact you again after you have received the grant. Subject to the requirement to pay some of the tax before obtaining the grant, IHT is due six months after the end of the month in which the person died. Inland Revenue will charge interest on unpaid tax from this due date whatever the reason for late payment.'
>
> *(© Crown Copyright, ibid.)*

IHT Tax has been described as a 'voluntary tax' because it is perfectly legal and reasonable to avoid or at the least minimise it by prudent planning and forethought. However, because Muslims have drifted far from Deen and abhor the mention or thought of death, they fail to act intelligently,

'The son of Adam ages whilst two things of his grow younger: greed for wealth and greed for (longer) life.' (Tirmizee)

Many Muslims having failed to realise that the wealth in their possession was an *amānah* from Allah ﷻ act so unwisely that many a times inheritors end up having to pay a huge tax bill before they may even access the estate.

How to Legally Minimise Inheritance Tax?

In the UK, the threshold for Inheritance Tax is £263,000 and the average cost of a house in summer 2004 was £175,401 and rising. In order to avoid IHT a Muslim (especially if he dreads the probability of his inheritors disputing and wrangling) may distribute his assets during his lifetime. Islām has taught us a beautiful moral code and etiquettes even when gifting, therefore one should remember two fundamental points:

1) The motive must not be to deprive any of the heirs whose shares have been ordained by Allah ﷻ ~ however, if one of the heirs is grossly disobedient and given to evil ways, it may be justified to withhold a gift from him (or even hold it in trust until, when and if he rectifies his ways).

2) Both daughters and sons should happily be given equal amounts during one's lifetime, the difference in inheritance only applies after death. It is not permissible and below the dignity of a Mu'min to discriminate between daughters and sons when making gifts merely on the basis of gender. However, if one is distributing the whole estate and would like to gift it on the principles of inheritance, he may do so although equality is more preferable.

How To Legally Avoid Inheritance Tax?

These are some of the legal ways in which one could avoid IHT:

- **The Nil Rate Band** ~ You only pay IHT on cumulative transfers of assets **over** £263,000 (as of 6 April 2004). Below this figure it is a 'Nil Rate Band.' £263,000 may sound like a lot, but remember it is absolutely everything that you own - including your house.

- **Transfers Between Spouses** ~ No IHT is paid on any transfer of assets on death from husband to wife (if both have the same domicile), or vice versa. Whilst this appears very generous it often merely delays the IHT liability until the other spouse dies.

- **Annual gift of £3,000** ~ You can give away up to £3,000 worth of gifts every year to whoever you like, and if you can afford to do so, you should try and use this exemption every year.

- **Gifts out of Income** ~ regular gifts out of surplus income, as opposed to capital, are exempt from IHT. <u>This is a little used, but quite useful exemption, but gifts do need to be regular.</u>

- **Gifts on Marriage** ~ You can give £5,000 to your own child (including step-child or adopted child) on their getting married, £2,500 to your grandchild and £1,000 to anyone else. Only applies to one marriage per person. (Nevertheless, to a child in the year they marry, you could give £5,000 as a wedding gift plus £3,000 as another gift, and these would be exempt).

- **Small gifts of up to £250** ~ This is £250 per person, but it cannot be the same person you gave the £3,000 annual gift to. Useful if you have plenty of cash and several grandchildren.

_(www.lawontheweb.co.uk ~ reproduced with permission of LAW on the WEB UK Ltd, the copyright holder)

- **Gifts to Charities** ~ Gifts to charities are not only exempt from IHT but UK income tax payers can make their donations go further during their lifetime, without any cost to them, simply by completing a Gift Aid Declaration (Write to the Islamic Da'wah Academy for a copy).

- **Discretionary Will Trusts** ~ the majority of homes in the UK are held under 'joint tenancy' which implies that when one of the couple dies, the property (according to UK law but not necessarily to the Shareeah) passes to the surviving spouse. In order to avoid IHT, by consulting with a Mufti and Solicitor a discretionary will trust may be established wherein it is possible to change the 'joint tenancy' to a 'common tenancy,' whereby surviving children inherit each of the parents' share and property up to the value of £526,000 thereby avoiding a potential tax bill of £126,000.

- **Potentially Exempt Transfers (PETs)** ~ Many gifts that a person makes during his lifetime, apart from those mentioned above, are excluded from IHT, except those made seven years prior to one's death. Those under seven years and totalling more than £250,000 are liable to IHT.

The Four Stages in Applying for a Probate Grant

1) Ascertain Value of Estate

Firstly, the Personal Representative will need to produce a schedule of all the assets of the deceased. Islāmically, immediately after burial of the *mayyit*, the inheritors should leave their emotions aside and courageously take stock and make a written inventory and costing of all the items which belonged to the deceased. This will include property, bank and building society accounts and savings, cash, jewellery, all household furniture and goods, vehicle(s), clothing, money owed, business, stocks and shares, etc., etc. Estimated market values of these should be marked as 'estimates,' however one should remember that Islāmically the value of any property is the actual sale price at the time of sale.

2) Complete Grant & Inheritance Tax Forms

Secondly, in order to obtain a grant the following forms will need to be completed:

- *The Probate Application form (PA1) and PA1a*

    Forms PA1 and PA1a are available from your nearest Probate Registry or may be downloaded from the Probate Registry website (www.courtservice.gov.uk).

- *Account of the estate (IHT205 & booklet IHT206)*

    IHT205 and 206 are available from the local Inland Revenue (Capital Taxes) Office or may be downloaded from the website (www.inlandrevenue.gov.uk/cto).

3) Returning Forms/Documents

You need to send to the controlling Probate Registry (by registered post and after keeping copies of original) the completed forms (i.e. PA1, IHT205 or D18), a cheque for the fee payable and supporting documents:

    a) An **official** copy (not photocopies) of the Death Certificate or a Coroner's certificate.

    b) The **original** Will/codicils or any document in which the deceased stated any wishes about distribution of his estate.

    c) Any other documents requested in form PA1.

4) Attending Interview At the Probate Registry

Upon receipt the Probate Registry examines the application and may contact the applicant if there are any complications. For straightforward cases, an appointment is sent out within two weeks for a date within one month of the application. The purpose of the short fifteen-minute interview is to confirm the details submitted on the forms and to answer any queries either party may have. Each applicant (who will need to show some form of identification) is requested to sign a form of oath and Muslims have the right to affirm (rather than swear an oath) in the presence of an interviewing officer that the information submitted is true and to the best of their knowledge.

After the interview, the Probate Registry prepares and sends the grant by post. It is best to request a number of copies, because some institutions will only accept sealed official copies and not photocopies.

Prescription for Immediate Entry into Jannah

Prophet Muhammad ﷺ commented:

'In whichever way you live your life, in this very state will arrive your death. Moreover, in whatever way your death appears, in this very state will you be resurrected!'

(p49, Preparations for Death)

Shaykh Mufti Muhammad Taqee 'Uthmāni *hafizahullah* relates, 'Dr. 'Abdul 'Hai 'Ārifee ؒ often advised, 'At night before sleeping, carry out these few simple acts:

* Make *taubah* (repentance) for all sins committed during that day and throughout one's life.
* Sleep in the state of *wudhu* (ablution).
* Recite the sunnah du'aa's and this du'aa also:

$$\text{آمَنْتُ بِكِتَابِكَ الَّذِىْ أَنْزَلْتَ وَ نَبِيِّكَ الَّذِىْ أَرْسَلْتَ}$$

'I bring Imān (faith) upon Your (Allah's) Kitābs (Heavenly Books) which You have sent and upon Your Nabee whom You have sent, i.e. Muhammad ﷺ.'

* Thereafter sleep upon your right-hand side.

Through the blessings of these few simple deeds your whole sleep will be transformed into *Ibaadah* (worship) and should death arrive in this state, Inshā'Allah, one will go straight into Jannah. If Allah ﷻ Wills, there will be no obstructions.'

Other Ashraf's Amānat Titles

Set A: *Ashraf's Beloved* *(Ideal for Early years)*
1. Ashraf's Colouring Book 1
2. Ashraf's Nursery 1
3. Ashraf's Nursery 2
4. Ashraf's Alphabet
5. Ashraf's First Words
6. Ashraf's First Sentences

Set B: *Ashraf's Juniors* *(Series for ages 5-13 yrs)*
- *Classics 1:* A Town Named Injusticebury
- *Classics 2:* Beautiful Reward of Patience
- *Classics 3:* Moosaa ﷺ
- Ashraf's First Maktab
- Ashraf's Beautiful Muaasharat

Set C: *Nabee's Roses* *(Graded Series for ages 6-18 yrs)*
1. Allah Ta'ālā's Rasool ﷺ
2. Khadeejah ؓ
3. 'Ā'ishah ؓ
4. Daughters of Prophet Muhammad ﷺ
5. Mothers' of the Believers ؓ
6. Sahābeeyat ؓ

Set D: *Ashraf's Roses* *(Graded Series for ages 6-18 yrs)*
1. Aboo Bakr ؓ
2. 'Umar ؓ
3. 'Uthmān ؓ
4. 'Ali ؓ
5. Guiding Stars (Senior Sahābāh) ؓ

Set E: *Ashraf's Readers* *(For the whole family)*
- Ashraf's Blessings of Marriage
- Great Imām's of Fiqh ؒ
- Ashraf's Advice upon the Death of a Muslim
- Ashraf's Advice upon Tazkiyah (Due Soon Insha'Allah)
- Ashraf's Orchard
- Ashraf's Blessings of Ramadhān

Ashraf's Amānat©
PO Box 12, Dewsbury, West Yorkshire, UK, WF12 9YX
Tel: +44 (0)1924 488929 ~ email:info@ashrafsamanat.org